Peter Aughton is a visiting lecturer at the University of The West of England, specialising in engineering and the mathematical aspects of computing. In the 1970s he worked on the Concorde supersonic airliner. He has written several highly acclaimed local histories, including one on Bristol where he has lived for more than thirty years. Peter's latest book is *Newton's Apple*, and he is currently preparing a book on Cook's second voyage.

BY PETER AUGHTON

North Meols and Southport
Liverpool: a People's History
Bristol: a People's History
Endeavour: The story of Captain Cook's First Great Epic Voyage
Newton's Apple
Resolution

Acknowledgements

THE AUTHOR would like to thank Dilys Aughton, Victoria Huxley, Susan Haynes, Caroline Brooke, Ken Wilson, Peter Brooks and the staff of the University of The West of England for their help with this project.

THE PUBLISHERS would like to thank the staff of the British Library, National Library of Australia, National Maritime Museum, Natural History Museum, Public Records Office and the State Library of New South Wales for their help.

ENDEAVOUR

*The Story of Captain Cook's
First Great Epic Voyage*

••

PETER AUGHTON

PHOENIX

A Windrush Press Book

Dedicated to Emily

A PHOENIX PAPERBACK

First published in Great Britain in 1999
by The Windrush Press

Illustrated edition published in 2002
by Cassell & Co in association with
The Windrush Press

This paperback edition published in 2003
by Phoenix,
an imprint of Orion Books Ltd,
Orion House, 5 Upper St Martin's Lane,
London WC2H 9EA

The Windrush Press
Windrush House
12 Adlestrop
Moreton-in-Marsh
Gloucestershire
GL56 OYN

A CIP catalogue record for this book
is available from the British Library.

ISBN 0 75381 732 2

Printed and bound in Great Britain by
Clays Ltd, St Ives plc

CONTENTS

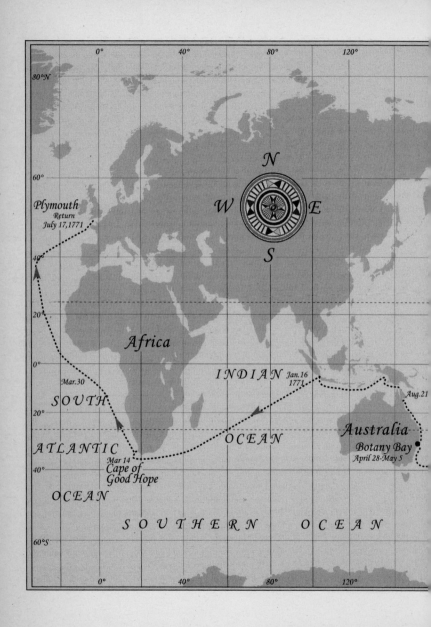

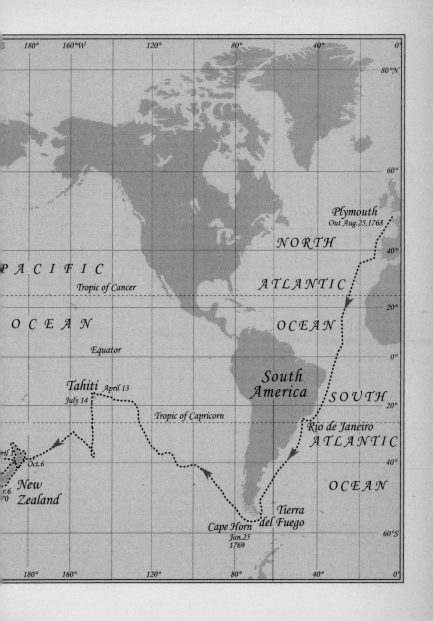

180°   160°W   120°   80°   40°   0°

80°N

60°

Plymouth
Out Aug.25,1768

N O R T H   40°

P A C I F I C   *A T L A N T I C*   20°

Tropic of Cancer

O C E A N   *O C E A N*   0°

Equator

*South
America*   *S O U T H*   20°

Tahiti April 13
July 14   Tropic of Capricorn

Rio de Janeiro
A T L A N T I C

rif I.   40°

Oct.6

r.6
70   *New
Zealand*   *O C E A N*

*Tierra
del Fuego*

Cape Horn
Jan.25
1769   60°S

180°   160°   120°   80°   40°   0°

....

CHAPTER I

PREPARATIONS

To 26 August, 1768

N O SANE PERSON, argued Alexander Dalrymple, could seriously doubt the existence of the great southern continent. It could be scientifically demonstrated that a great landmass in the Southern Hemisphere was necessary simply to maintain the equilibrium of the spherical Earth as it revolved about its axis. All the great cartographers showed the existence of the continent on the map of the world. Had not parts of the continent already been discovered? As long ago as 1642 Tasman had made a landfall in a latitude of about forty degrees at a place he called 'New Zeland'. The sailors of His Majesty's Ship the *Dolphin*, recently returned from their circumnavigation of the world, were convinced that they had glimpsed the snow-capped mountain peaks of the unknown continent on their southern horizon as they crossed the vast Pacific Ocean. The map-makers gave it the name of *Terra Australis Incognita* – meaning 'the unknown southern land'. Alexander Dalrymple had no problem at all in tracing the outline of *Terra Australis* – his system was the same as that of the sixteenth-century cartographers: simply to plot all the known routes of the navigators across the Pacific Ocean, then to fill in all the uncovered area with land.

The Spanish, the Portuguese and the Dutch had all opened up profitable trade routes to remote parts of the globe. The *Terra Australis* was guaranteed to be rich in silks and spices, precious metals, pearls, and other exotic luxuries as yet unknown to an unsuspecting western world. Mariners of old brought back strange stories of a pagan people who tipped their arrows with points of silver. All that was needed was a modern Marco Polo to venture into the South Seas and to open up the trade routes. A ship must be provisioned and despatched post haste to the Southern Hemisphere to discover this continent and to claim it for the British Crown. If the expedition were not despatched immediately then the French, the Spanish or the Dutch would certainly discover the continent first and claim it for themselves. He, Alexander Dalrymple, scientist, geographer, explorer, gentleman – a man of great talent, knowledge and enthusiasm – was, he admitted modestly, the ideal man to lead the expedition to the South Seas.

Dalrymple was persuasive. It was quite true that, ever since Magellan had discovered the tortuous passage into the Pacific Ocean, ships had always navigated across it by sailing northwards to warmer climes and sticking slavishly to the trade winds which blew in the neighbourhood of the tropics. Very few had ventured south of the trodden path and returned to tell the tale. Two British expeditions had recently returned from the South Seas but both had sailed only in the latitudes of the tropics and like others before them they had missed their opportunity of discovering the *Terra Australis*.

The Admiralty slowly warmed to the idea of sending another vessel to explore southwards off the beaten track – but there was a minor problem. Other nations would soon hear of the expedition, they would look on it with jealousy and suspicion. The French in particular had already organised an expedition of their own and, although the war with the French was at an end, they were still smarting after their losses in Canada and they could be relied upon to do all in their power to hinder the British expedition. The Dutch looked with suspicion on any vessel which entered the waters of their East Indian territories and they guarded their Spice Islands jealously. The Spanish had a deep distrust of any vessel of any nation which entered the Pacific Ocean where they still considered any new discoveries to be their preserve. These factors were not in themselves sufficient to make the expedition a nonstarter but they reduced the chances of success and presented the Admiralty with additional headaches.

Then, by a stroke of good fortune, a perfect solution to the problem presented itself at exactly the right moment. The Royal Society wanted to send a ship to the South Seas to observe the passage of the planet Venus across the face of the sun, a phenomenon known to the astronomers as the transit of Venus. Such an expedition would be purely scientific and designed to add to man's knowledge of the universe. The French loved science, the laws of nature did not acknowledge political boundaries, all nations would be allowed to benefit equally from the results of the observation. Other nationalities would look on such an expedition with favour and leave the ship unmolested. A scientific expedition to observe the transit of Venus, but with secret orders to explore the Pacific Ocean and to search for new lands which could be annexed to the Crown. It was a brilliant conception or a low-cunning deception, depending on how you looked at it.

The transit of Venus would enable the astronomers to obtain a more accurate figure for what they called the solar parallax. The Royal Society claimed confidently that this would have great benefits to navigation. In fact they knew perfectly well that, apart from a more accurate estimate of the longitude of the observation point, such benefits to navigation were virtually nil. But what they also knew was that the only way to obtain money for scientific research was to claim that improvements to navigation would follow. Navigation meant shipping, shipping meant trade, trade meant money and profits, and profits were something that even the most difficult and unscientifically minded government official could understand. The Royal Greenwich Observatory had been established for the purpose of helping navigation and in particular with the problem of finding longitude at sea. Nearly a century had elapsed since the foundation of the observatory and an enormous volume of astronomical knowledge had been amassed, tables of lunar motion had been published and were now available to navigators. Nevil Maskelyne, the Astronomer Royal, published his method for finding the longitude from these tables and from the precise position of the moon in the sky. The astronomers were reluctant to admit that the method was so involved that nobody except themselves could understand how to use it – as far as the navigators were concerned the problem of finding the longitude at sea still remained unsolved.

The Admiralty would not offer Alexander Dalrymple command of the expedition, but they offered him the position of observer on the voyage. He replied rather pompously that he had 'no thoughts of making this voyage as passenger nor in any other capacity than having the total management of the ship intended to be sent'. His hopes of leading the expedition suffered a fatal blow when his name came before Sir Edward Hawke, the first Lord of the Admiralty – he who could blaspheme as elegantly as any seaman on the lower decks. Sir Edward smashed his fist on the table and declared that he would rather lose his right hand than give command of a King's ship to a landlubber like Dalrymple!

But here was a problem. If the vociferous Alexander Dalrymple was given the cold shoulder then where could the Admiralty find a suitable man, acceptable to Lord Hawke, to lead the expedition? Such a man had to be an experienced naval officer, he required great qualities of leadership. He needed to be highly skilled and experienced in seamanship to be able to keep his vessel away from danger in unknown and uncharted waters. He needed to be an expert navigator who could find his position on the surface of the globe at all times and who could calculate longitudes as well as latitudes. Ideally he needed to be a skilled cartographer so that he could make and supervise maps and charts of the southern continent. He had to be capable of finding fresh water, food and provisions for the ship in the vastness of the Pacific, he also needed to be an astronomer to help with the observation of the transit of Venus. Did such a man exist anywhere with all these exacting qualifications?

The Navy had plenty of good officers, but the main problem with most of them was that they knew their mathematics only by rote. They could follow the procedures laid down for them in the nautical almanac but they did not understand the principles behind the spherical trigonometry of the terrestrial and celestial spheres and they had no knowledge of the triangulation methods required for the surveying techniques. Few, if any, naval officers were capable of mastering Maskelyne's method of finding the longitude unless it could be greatly simplified. A man who satisfied all the Admiralty's exacting requirements must be an extraordinary seaman indeed but, according to Hugh Palliser, such a genius did exist in the Royal Navy. Palliser claimed to know a man who had turned down the command of a merchantman to serve below decks on a naval frigate, he had risen through the ranks in less than two years to become the master of a British man-of-war.

Palliser's protégé was not entirely unknown to the powers at the Admiralty. He already had a reputation as the finest navigator in the service and he could find his position at sea with greater accuracy than any of his peers. When serving in Newfoundland he had helped with the survey and charting of the Gulf of St Lawrence and had produced a chart of exceptional quality which was available for all the Doubting Thomases to see. On his own initiative he had observed and carefully recorded an eclipse of the sun, he had written a paper from his results and sent it to the Royal Society so that the observation could be used to make accurate determination of the longitude of Newfoundland. Hugh Palliser had served with this man in the Bay of Biscay during the blockade of the French coast and knew him well. His name was James Cook.

Ah yes, agreed the Admiralty. James Cook was an exceptional seaman who undoubtedly had some of the qualifications to lead the expedition and there was little doubt that if this unknown southern continent really existed then Cook was the man to find it. He met most of the requirements, even that of being a skilled observational astronomer, but there was still one qualification which he did not have. Cook was not a commissioned officer. This put the Admiralty in a damned embarrassing position because to give the command of a king's ship to Cook was to admit that the Royal Navy had nobody in the higher ranks who was capable of doing the job. It was obviously within their powers to grant him a commission, but Cook was not born of the gentry – his father had been an obscure labourer in a remote part of England and the Admiralty was not in the habit of handing out free commissions to the sons of farm labourers. James Cook was an excellent ship's master and good ship's masters were scarce and valuable men, it made no sense to promote them into sinecures which officers and gentlemen could hold just as well as they.

Palliser argued strongly that this ridiculous snobbery had to be overlooked. Cook was the only man for the job and it was ludicrous to give him the command without making him a post captain at least. The establishment agreed that he should be given the command but argued that he should not be made an officer. In the end it was obvious that a commission must be granted and a clumsy compromise was reached – James Cook was to be made a lieutenant but not a captain. He would be referred to as the captain, he would be captain of the vessel in every sense, but to keep the conservative die-hards happy his promotion would give him only the rank of naval lieutenant.

The origins of the man who unwittingly threw his superiors at the Admiralty into such a dilemma were a long way from the fashionable society and seats of power in eighteenth-century London. James Cook's birthplace was deep in the English countryside, in the northernmost part of one of the northern counties. Whilst the Admiralty and the Royal Society argued about high-minded subjects like unknown continents and solar parallax, the great majority of Englishmen worried only about matters such as the weather and the state of the harvest – mundane matters which made the difference between life and death for them.

On 3 November 1728, in Marton-in-Cleveland, an agricultural village hidden amidst the scenic beauty of the Yorkshire Dales in the rural acres of the North Riding, James and Grace Cook brought their week-old son to the parish church of St Cuthbert for baptism. When the boy grew to adolescence he was apprenticed to a grocer in the nearby fishing village of Staithes. It was there that he felt the first call of the sea – a passion which never left him. He was not prepared to spend his life as a grocer and within eighteen months he moved down the coast to Whitby where he signed on as a deck hand on a Whitby collier.

Cook's progress in the merchant navy was steady but not spectacular. At the age of 26 he was offered his first ship and it was then, for reasons best known to himself, that he took a decisive step in his life and gave up his opportunity of advancement to join the Royal Navy as an able seaman. His talents and his hard-won knowledge soon gained him recognition in the Navy. He obtained his master's certificate in 1757 after serving under Hugh Palliser during the blockade of the French ports and he served in Canada during the siege and the capture of Quebec. It was when he was employed on the charting of the Newfoundland coast and the estuary of the St Lawrence River that he met an army surveyor called Samuel Holland. Within a very short time Cook had mastered the surveying and map-making techniques which Holland taught him.

Cook was a close and silent man and he seldom displayed his feelings to any of his fellows. He was cautious by nature but he was always prepared to take calculated risks. He never dashed into any undertaking without careful scrutiny of the situation. On what became one of his brief visits to England he somehow found time to meet and court a young Essex girl called Elizabeth Batts, his junior by fourteen years. Elizabeth was an exceptional girl for, as far as is known, she was the only member of the fair sex ever to make an impression on James Cook. They married in 1762, a few days before Christmas; James was 34 and Elizabeth 20. They set up home in the East End of London at a house on the Mile End Road. Elizabeth must have been a great influence on Cook's life and it would be of interest to know more about her but Cook was not the man to waste his writings on idle gossip to his wife at home. She must have known from the outset that the sea was his first love and his duty always came before his family. The couple produced children at regular intervals – the bairns saw little of their father but he provided well for them and Elizabeth was not one to complain.

The Lords of the Admiralty were finally agreed about their commander. The next problem was to find a suitable ship and equip it for the expedition. Cook rejected any suggestion that one of the Navy's smart frigates should be used, he was clear in his mind about the type of ship most suitable for the job in hand. He wanted a vessel with a large storage capacity, with good seagoing capabilities and with a shallow draught so that it could sail close to shore in a few fathoms of water. The ideal vessel, he argued, was the 'cat-built' bark used on the North Sea to carry coal from the Tyneside coal-fields to the capital. There were many other makes of vessel which may have fitted the bill, but Cook had learnt his seamanship in the coal trade, he knew the vessels well, he knew their strengths and their weaknesses and he was confident about handling them. The Admiralty agreed readily enough to this suggestion and on enquiry they found three possible available vessels – they were called the *Valentine*, the *Earl of Pembroke* and the *Ann and Elizabeth*. The officers at the Deptford Yard inspected these three and reported their findings to the Navy Board:

The Earl of Pembroke. Mr Thos. Milner, owner, was built at Whitby, her age three years nine months, square stern back, single bottom, full built and comes nearest to the tonnage mentioned in your warrant and not so old [as one of the others] by fourteen months, is a promising ship for sailing of this kind and fit to stow provisions and stores as may be put on board her.

The *Earl of Pembroke* was a classical example of what was known as a three-masted cat-built bark. She was 106 feet in length from stern to bowsprit, she measured 29 feet 3 ins across the beam, she displaced 370 tons burthen and drew only 14 feet of water fully laden. She seemed to meet all the Admiralty's requirements and she was therefore purchased for £2,800. She was refitted, completely re-rigged, given an additional outside skin of thin planking over a layer of tarred felt, and renamed as His Majesty's bark the *Endeavour*.

An unfair notion has been perpetuated which pictures the bark as an ugly squat sailing barge covered in coal dust and creeping sluggishly along the North Sea coast. The time to destroy this image is long overdue and the cat-built bark must be given its proper respect. It is true that by comparison with the naval frigates anchored in the roads at Portsmouth she was built smaller, squarer and rounder. It is true that she was not painted in smart yellow and black bands with rows of scarlet gunhatches on each side like the great three-decker ships of the line. It is also true that she had no figurehead or decoration on the prow below the bowsprit and her stern cabin did not have the lavish external and internal decor of the *Victory*. Naval men were scathing about the lines of the merchant vessels, but the arrangement of masts and rigging on the catbuilt bark was very similar to that of a Navy three-master – an untrained landlubber seeing such a vessel on the horizon would be hard pressed to tell the difference between it and a Navy frigate. The *Endeavour* was robust and well designed for sailing coastal waters, her lines were clean and efficient. She had cabin windows to port and starboard which were tastefully decorated on the outside, and a row of five windows lined the rear of her stern cabin. She was a three-masted tall ship, built entirely to be handled by the brawn and skill of a crew of sailors, propelled by the forces of nature alone. Leaning before the wind in full sail with her ropes taut and her canvasses swelling she was a sight of great power and natural grace. The *Endeavour* was a beautiful ship.

The ship was fitted with twelve swivel guns and ten carriage guns with all the necessary powder and shot. The hold was loaded with eight tons of ballast and with several tons of coal for heating and cooking. There were spare timbers for spars and planking, barrels of tar and pitch, tools for carpenters, canvas for the sail-makers, hemp for the ropes and rigging, a ship's forge, tools and materials for all other shipboard crafts. Twenty tons of ship's bis-cuits and flour were loaded, 1,200 gallons of beer, 1,600 gallons of spirits, 4,000 pieces of salted beef and 6,000 pieces of salted pork, 1,500 pounds of sugar, suet, raisons, oatmeal, wheat, oil, vinegar, malt, 160 pounds of mustard seed, 107 bushels of pease stored in butts, and a staggering 7,860 pounds of a high-smelling fermented cabbage which the Germans called *Sauerkraut* – this was a ration of 80 pounds per man and, if the sailors could be persuaded to eat the stuff, it was thought to keep the dreaded scurvy at bay. The Admi-ralty supplied a copy of Dr Macbride's recently published *Historical Account of the New Method of Treating the Scurvy at Sea*. Into the hold went sacks, hogsheads, casks and barrels of all shapes and sizes. The ship carried with her a good quantity of iron nails, fish hooks, hatchets, scissors, red and blue beads, small mirrors and even a few dolls to charm the natives of the south sea islands and to barter with them for food and provisions.

All these supplies, with the possible exception of the two-and-a-half tons of sauerkraut, were part of the standard rations for a naval vessel. When it came to the equipment for navigation, however, the quality of the instruments was well above the standard supplies for any vessel. Doctor Knight's newly patented azimuth compass of improved construction to find magnetic North was supplemented by a vertical compass to measure the angle of dip. An astronomical brass quadrant of 1 foot radius was supplied together with a high-quality sextant. The quadrant was made by John Bird and the sextant by James Hadley, two of the finest instrument-makers of the times – but even these expensive instruments paled alongside the two carefully packed astronomical telescopes provided by the Royal Society. Both telescopes were Gregorian reflectors with parabolic mirrors of polished speculum metal – each with a focal length of 2 feet. One had an eyepiece fitted with a Dolland micrometer, the other was fitted with a set of moveable cross-wires. Wooden stands made by expert craftsmen were supplied for the telescopes, and they had polar axis mountings suitable for the tropical latitudes of the Southern Hemisphere. There was a portable observatory made of wood and canvas designed by the lighthouse engineer John Smeaton. There were recording devices, an astronomical clock for accurate timekeeping supplied by the Royal Greenwich Observatory, and two thermometers to help with the calibration of the clocks in the heat of the tropics. Mathematical and surveying instruments were carried, a complete theodolite, a plane table, a 2-foot brass scale, a double concave glass and a glass for tracing light rays, dividers, parallel rulers, a pair of proportional compasses, stationery and writing materials.

Then began the process of mustering a crew. Zachariah Hicks, an East Londoner, was chosen as second lieutenant and John Gore, recently promoted from master's mate on the *Dolphin*, was chosen as third lieutenant. William Monkhouse from Cumberland was appointed as the ship's surgeon and his brother Jonathan signed on as a midshipman. Isaac Smith, aged sixteen, cousin to Cook's wife Elizabeth, was also signed up as a midshipman. Above and below decks came a typical assortment of volunteers and pressed men, able-bodied seamen, honest sailors, rogues and drunkards with a colourful mixture of accents and dialects from every corner of the British Isles.

John Satterly was the ship's carpenter with his mate Edward Terral from Spitalfields. Robert Brown, John Charlton, William Howson, William Harvey, Samuel Jones and Thomas Hardman the boatswain's mate were all Londoners. Richard Hutchins, Michael and Richard Littleboy, William Dawson and Benjamin Jordan were local men recruited, or possibly pressed into service, at Deptford. Robert Stainsby was from Darlington. Richard Pickersgill and John Ravenhill came from Cook's own county of Yorkshire, the former from West Tansby and the latter a Hull sailmaker, the oldest man aboard aged forty-nine. Nicholas Young, aged eleven or twelve, appropriately enough, was probably the youngest crew member but he escaped listing in the muster roll. Robert Molyneux from the village of Hale on the north bank of the Mersey, was the only Lancashire man in the crew but he held the key position of ship's master. The west country ports were well represented by Charles Williams of Bristol, John Ramsey of Plymouth and the thirteen-year-old Henry Stephens of Falmouth. A surprising number of the crew came from inland towns: Isaac Parker from Ipswich, Samuel Moody from Worcester, William Peckover from Northamptonshire, Charles Clerk from Weathersfield in Essex, William Collett from High Wycombe, Thomas Symonds from Brentford and Isaac Johnson hailed from Knutsford in Cheshire. Scotland was well represented by Alexander Weir the quartermaster from Fife, Archie Wolf from Edinburgh, John Sewan from Dundee, James Nicholson and Robert Anderson from Inverness, and Forby Sutherland from the distant Orkney Islands. The Welsh contingent consisted of Thomas Jones and Francis Wilkinson, both from Bangor. The Emerald Isle was represented by Joseph Childs of Dublin, Timothy Reardon from Cork and John Reading from Kinsale. Peter Flower was from Guernsey and James Magra came from a rapidly growing port called New York in the American colonies.

There were two widow's men; these were completely fictitious sailors whose salaries were paid into a fund for the widows of dead seamen. Also entered in the muster roll were two very young children called James and Nathaniel Cook aged six and five – they were real people and the captain's children. In reality both were thankfully safe at home with their mother, but James Cook was not averse to following the totally illegal practice of putting their names on the list to give them a few years of extra service towards the day when they might follow their father into the Navy.

An important supernumerary was Charles Green, the official astronomer. He was one of the few men alive who could find the longitude at sea purely from observations of the moon and stars. Green was no stranger to long sea voyages; he had crossed the Atlantic on the important voyage of 1763–4 when John Harrison's fourth marine chronometer was under test. The chronometer was a very expensive instrument, then very much in its infancy, and it is of interest to note that the *Endeavour* carried no such instrument – it was far too valuable to risk on such a voyage. Things changed quickly, however, and it is also worthy of note that in his second great voyage Cook *did* have the advantage of a marine chronometer. Charles Green was the son of a Yorkshire farmer – he was an extremely dedicated and capable man, an excellent teacher and instructor always willing to pass his knowledge on to others but in one respect he was a bad choice for he did not enjoy the best of health. 'He lived in such a manner as greatly promoted the disorders he had long upon him,' wrote Cook – meaning that he suffered from dysentery and made it worse by drinking – a fault which Cook never failed to notice in any of his acquaintances. In the astronomer's case the drinking bouts were occasional and spasmodic events. Charles Green could never have taken all the careful and accurate measurements on the voyage if he had not been completely sober at the time.

Peter Flower, Thomas Hardman, William Howson, John Charlton and Cook's relative, Isaac Smith, were already acquainted – they had served with Cook on the *Grenville* during the survey of Newfoundland and therefore brought useful expertise with them. Richard Pickersgill and Francis Wilkinson were appointed mates to Robert Molyneux, the ship's master. This trio, together with John Gore, also brought invaluable experience with them for they had all served together on the recent circumnavigation of the globe under Captain Samuel Wallis on HMS *Dolphin*. A fifth member of the select party from the *Dolphin* was the ship's goat, an animal which was later honoured by a few lines from the pen of the learned and overweight Doctor Johnson:

Perpetui, ambita bis terra, praemia lactis
Haec habet, altrici capra secunda Jovis.

[The earth twice circled, this the goat, the second to the nurse of Jove, is thus rewarded for her never failing milk.]

The goat was also the Navy's secret weapon for clearing the decks of unwanted boarders – on Wallis's voyage one butt on the unsuspecting posterior of a Tahitian native cleared the decks of boarders as quickly as if the ship had burst into flames!

On 30 July 1768 the *Endeavour* left the Deptford Yard and sailed to Plymouth. The ship behaved well enough on this passage along the English Channel; she steered well and made her best progress with the wind a point or two abaft the beam when she was capable of making 7 or 8 knots. Cook was unhappy about the trim. 'His majestys bark the *Endeavour* under my command Swims too much by the Head, and there being no means left to bring her down by the stern, but taking in more iron ballast abaft,' he complained. 'Please order her to be supplyd with as much as may be found necessary for that purpose.' He also requested that a green baize floor cloth be fitted to the great cabin, and the Navy Board agreed to both requests. Eventually the captain was very pleased with his ship and he wrote that 'No sea can hurt her laying Too under a

Main sail or Mizen ballanc'd. She is a good roader and Careens easy and without the least danger.' When the going became rough she could ride out a storm easily by rolling in the troughs of the waves.

The full ship's complement was originally planned as seventy-two, but this was increased to eighty-five by the inclusion of a detachment of marines, a contingent rightly thought to be indispensable on an undertaking of this kind. John Edgecumbe was a sergeant of marines and John Truslove was his corporal, Thomas Rossiter was the drummer, and there were ten privates. As the final preparations were made at Plymouth, eighteen men, having no desire to be transported around the world, took the option of deserting the ship. This was to be expected for a crew the size of the *Endeavour* and they were easily replaced by volunteers and by the handy expedient of the press gang. The ship's company was still not complete, however, and news arrived that yet another party was expected to embark at Plymouth. The awaited personages are explained in the minutes of the June meeting of the Royal Society where there exists a copy of a letter from the society to the Lords of the Admiralty:

> *Joseph Banks Esq fellow of this Society, a gentleman of a large fortune, who is well versed in natural history, being Desirous of undertaking the same voyage the Council very earnestly request their Lordships, that in regard to Mr Banks's great personal merit, and for the advancement of useful knowledge, he also, together with his Suite, being seven persons more, that is, eight persons in all, together with their baggage, be received on board the Ship, under the command of Captain Cook.*

Joseph Banks, Fellow of the Royal Society and owner of a large fortune, was a gentleman adventurer belonging to that fortunate minority called the English aristocracy. He was a young man of twenty-five who had inherited a sizeable part of Lincolnshire and an income of £6,000 per annum from his estates at Revesby near Boston. Generally speaking the English aristocracy was the most unlikely class of people to exchange the life of luxury on a country estate for months of riding the waves on a long sea voyage and sharing the ship-board food and other horrors with the riff-raff of commoners below decks. But Joseph Banks was no ordinary aristocrat; he did not use his wealth and position to obtain favours at court or to dabble in the world of eighteenth-century politics. He did not belong to the gossiping, philosophising, coffee-drinking circle of Johnson and Boswell. He decided at an early age to devote his life to the study of science and, as a young man, he became a Fellow of the Royal Society. He was not a novice to the rigours of life on board ship, and already he had crossed the Atlantic to Newfoundland on a scientific expedition and had returned from there intact and prepared to undertake a second, much longer voyage.

Unlike Cook and Green, Joseph Banks's idea of science was not the study of Newton's *Principia* or the observation of the stars and planets – he was a collector of flora and fauna of all known species. Since the Swedish botanist Carolus Linneaus (1707–78) had published the system of classification which bears his name, it became possible to classify all botanical specimens by the Linnean system, and Banks's ambition was to find and classify as many new species as possible – for him the voyage was a golden opportunity.

The Linnean system was introduced to England in about 1760 when one of Linnaeus's pupils, Dr Daniel Carl Solander (1736–72), arrived in London to spread the gospel of the system. One of his earliest converts was Joseph Banks. The two collectors saw a great deal of each other and they were both present at a dinner party given by Lady Anne Monson when Joseph Banks brought the conversation round to his intended voyage to the Southern Hemisphere. Banks expounded passionately on his theme and the many new flora and fauna which he felt confident he would find, and Solander was quickly caught up in his enthusiasm. The Swedish doctor could contain himself no longer. He leapt to his feet and announced that he too wished to undertake the voyage to the South Seas. The two scientists embraced each other in delight and practically danced around the dinner table in their enthusiasm. Banks successfully petitioned the Admiralty for the inclusion of his friend in the party – a party which already included two artists, a secretary, four servants and two hunting dogs.

The artists were Sydney Parkinson and Alexander Buchan, the first a fine draughtsman whose job was to draw the specimens which Banks and Solander were going to collect. Alexander Buchan was also a skilled artist, but his talents were those of the landscape artist and, thanks to the Banks entourage, the *Endeavour* thus became well equipped for recording all the details of the expedition. The need for four servants seems rather excessive but since the growth of the African slave trade it was essential for fashionable gentlemen of Banks's fortune to have at least one black amongst their retinue – Banks therefore had two black servants and their names, conferred by himself, were Thomas Richmond and George Dorlton. The other servants were James Roberts and Peter Briscoe from his Lincolnshire estates at Revesby.

The unknown southern continent, argued Joseph Banks, would be rich in hunting and shooting of game. It followed that an English gentleman could not possibly venture on this undertaking without his sporting dogs. There was also a large quantity of baggage to be accommodated – including reference books, tins and jars in which to store specimens, oils and spirits in which to preserve them, reams of paper for drying and preserving purposes. The scientific equipment included an electrical machine – a great novelty constructed of glass discs which were made to rub against felt by the turning of a wheel which thereby generated static electricity.

One feels that the captain must have doubted the value of the electrical machine, but other parties were very impressed by Banks's equipment. 'No people ever went to sea better fitted out for the purpose of natural History, nor more elegantly,' wrote an observer John Ellis to Linnaeus.

> They have got a fine library of Natural History; they have all sorts of machines for catching and preserving insects; all kinds of nets, trawls, drags and hooks for coral fishing, they have even a curious contrivance of a telescope, by which, put into the water, you can see to the bottom at great depth, when it is clear. They have many cases of bottles with ground stoppers, of several sizes, to preserve animals in spirits. They have several sorts of salt to surround the seeds; and wax, both beeswax and that of Myrica; besides there are many people whose sole business is to attend them for this very purpose. They have two painters and draughtsmen, several volunteers who have a tolerable notion of Natural History; in short Solander assured me this expedition would cost Mr Banks ten thousand pounds.

It cannot have been welcome news to Cook when he discovered that this additional party, with all the extra baggage and paraphernalia, had to be accommodated between the already overcrowded decks of the *Endeavour*, especially when one of the party was of such a high social standing that he would undoubtedly expect to get preferential treatment and report any failings of the expedition to the whole of London society. The Banks entourage would expect a large share of the table space in the great cabin and would get in the way of the mapping and charting activities. Joseph Banks and James Cook each claimed to be a scientist, but this was the only common point of contact, their interests did not overlap and they were from the opposite ends of the rigid English social spectrum. It was to the credit of both men, and no small factor in the success of the voyage, that they formed an immediate liking for each other. Banks's journal always referred to Cook in the highest terms as 'the captain' and Cook referred to his aristocratic passenger as 'Mr Banks'.

When at Plymouth, Cook decided to employ the ship's carpenters, together with shipwrights and joiners from the Plymouth yards, to build a platform over the tiller arm. This great wooden lever swept the rear deck of the *Endeavour* behind the mizzen mast; the platform would provide a little more promenading space on deck and would be particularly appreciated by the Banks's retinue. Cook also employed the carpenters to refit the cabins and to build extra storage units to hold books, clothing and equipment. On 14 August Cook was almost ready to sail and it was time to send to London for his two gentlemen adventurers who were living it up in the capital until the last minute. 'Dispatched an express to London,' he wrote in his journal, 'for Mr Banks and Dr Solander to join the ship, their servants and baggage being already on board.'

On the evening of the following day the dispatch was delivered to Joseph Banks. He was enjoying a night at the opera with a lady friend, Miss Harriet Blosset. He had met Miss Blosset at the vineyard nursery of Kennedy and Lee in Hammersmith, where Mr Lee was her guardian. Joseph Banks was very taken with her, she 'possessed extraordinary beauty and every accomplishment with a fortune of ten thousand pounds'. In eighteenth-century courtship it was normal for both sexes to make accurate estimates of the other's worth as early in the relationship as possible. Her fortune apart, he thought her 'the fairest amongst flowers' and was smitten with her charms. According to contemporary accounts Miss Blosset enjoyed the opera and was quite gay, but she was blissfully ignorant of the fact that her wealthy escort was leaving on the morrow for the *Terra Australis Incognita*. Banks was quite prepared to face the perils of a journey to unknown antipodes of the world but he could not bring himself to hurt the feelings of his lady friend. He was quite unable to communicate the news to Miss Blosset and he therefore decided to turn to the bottle to help with his problem. He too became quite gay, but the drink did not loosen his tongue and it was not until the following morning that poor Harriet discovered the news that her escort had departed for Plymouth and the most distant parts of the Earth. Unreliable sources state that they were actually engaged and that he left a ring with her guardian to claim her on his return.

At Plymouth boarding commenced. Cabin space in the *Endeavour* was at a premium and six very small cabins had been built on the quarter deck – each about 7 feet by 5. These were allocated to the captain, Charles Green, Joseph Banks, and three of his party. Banks's cabin was the only one with no porthole, whether or not this was by choice we do not know but there was very little to choose between the cabins in terms of space and comfort – or rather the lack of it! The lower deck was the place where the crew slung their hammocks between the ship's timbers to make a large dormitory when night fell and here were more cabins partitioned off from the deckspace. They were allocated to lieutenants Hicks and Gore, to Robert Molyneux, the ship's master, William Monkhouse, the surgeon, Richard Orton, the captain's clerk and Stephen Forwood who combined his skill as the ship's gunner with a great talent for illegally tapping the casks of rum on the quarter deck. The full ship's complement was increased to ninety-four, and there was precious little space to spare but the sailors did not complain for they knew that they had more inches per man than they would have had on a British man-of-war.

On 19 August the captain assembled the crew and read them the Articles of War, followed by a boring but necessary reading of an Act of Parliament which related to the law of merchant shipping. He ordered a few more stores and waited for a fair wind to help them out of the English Channel. It was not until Thursday 25 August that the wind veered towards the north-west and Cook hoisted a signal for Banks and Solander to embark. The day started off cloudy with a fresh breeze but with clear skies appearing and a lighter wind in the afternoon. The sailors manned the capstan and the anchor was weighed. Able-bodied men scrambled up the ratlines and worked their way out along the yards to unfurl the mainsails. Other sailors followed to set the topsails and yet others climbed to the dizzy heights of the crosstrees to set the topgallants to the wind. Deck hands worked the ropes and hawsers, two seamen stood by the wheel waiting until the ship had picked up sufficient speed to make steerage way. There was a rumble as the wind filled the swelling sails, the clicking of the taut hemp taking up the strain and the creaking of the oaken timbers – the sea lapped against the wooden sides of the *Endeavour*. Sailors shouted to each other above the shrill cries of the scavenging gulls. Swirling eddies and a white wake formed behind the *Endeavour* as she heeled round to catch the wind. With sails billowing and with the Ensign fluttering from her stern the tall ship sailed slowly past Plymouth Hoe, and as she passed Drake's Island some wondered about Drake's great voyage around the world from this same place long ago. The *Endeavour* was out of the harbour, into the vast open sea which encompassed the whole world beyond. She was on her way to the unknown.

CHAPTER 2

CROSSING THE LINE

To 21 January, 1769

JOSEPH BANKS was seasick. The ship rolled so incessantly that Sydney Parkinson was unable to keep his pencil steady enough to make any drawings. The wind freshened from the south-west, the English Channel sank below the horizon and in the Bay of Biscay several black seabirds alighted on the rigging. Banks was well enough to identify them as *Procellaria pelagica* but the seamen assured him they were called Mother Carey's Chickens and that they were a sure sign that a storm was on the way. The *Endeavour* was capable of weathering any storm that the elements could throw at her, but this degree of seaworthiness was achieved at the expense of a deep wallowing roll which was executed with every swell of the sea and was one of the major causes of the seasickness. The sailors were proved right about the heavy weather ahead. 'Very hard gales with some heavy showers of rain the most part of these 24 hours which brought us under our two courses, broke one of our Main topmast Puttock plates,' wrote the captain, and Cook was not a man to reef the topgallants without good reason. A small boat belonging to the boatswain was washed overboard; the ship was still left with three other boats but it was an annoying loss so early in the voyage. Sharing the deck with two dogs, a few sheep, a goat and the ship's cat were some crates containing three or four dozen cackling hens – a supply of eggs and fresh poultry was lost as they too were washed overboard to perish in the Bay of Biscay.

The storm passed over, Cape Finisterre was sighted and passed, the sea became calmer and the ship rolled less violently. Joseph Banks recovered well enough to write up his journal and to take an interest in his all-consuming passion of collecting new specimens. The sailors were greatly intrigued by the grand Mr Banks. Few of them had ever seen such a grand personage on board ship before and they could not understand why he took such a great pleasure and interest in low forms of life such as the worms and insects that were commonplace to the experienced sailor. Two birds became entangled in the rigging, they were caught and presented to Mr Banks and the donors were warmed by the gratitude shown by the aristocratic personage. The birds were a new species to the collectors, so that Banks and Solander found that already they had discovered a species which was unknown to the great Linnaeus.

When the wind dropped and the ship entered calmer waters there was plenty of time to trawl for marine specimens over the side. One of Banks's black servants was given the job of casting a net to fish for sea creatures of any kind, but the net slipped from his grip and was lost to the sea, much to his master's annoyance. Spare nets were stored somewhere in the hold in a very inaccessible place and they could not be recovered easily, but the sailors helped out and solved the problem in their practical fashion by providing an old hoop net fastened to a fishing rod – this kept the collectors happy for a time. Banks and Solander netted a small creature of the salp genus which they called '*Dagysa saccata*'. They thought originally they had netted a single creature but on putting their catch into a glass of seawater the individuals separated and it was seen to consist of several identical creatures clinging together. The Atlantic was found to be rich in uncatalogued sea creatures and they were already discovering new species – one small creature in particular, another species of salp, was so brightly coloured that the naturalists named it after a gemstone:

> *... another insect which we took today was possest of more beautiful Colouring than any thing in nature I have ever seen, hardly excepting gemms. He is of a new genus calld [a blank] of which we took another species who had no beauty to boast, but this which we called opalimum shone in the water with all the splendour and variety of colours that we observe in a real opal; he lived in the Glass of salt water in which he was put for examination several hours; darting about with great agility, and at every motion shewing an almost infinite variety of changeable colours.*

A few days later a large shoal of the opal salps swam right under the stern of the ship. The individuals were only a few millimetres long and a millimetre wide but the bright colours of the shoal could be seen shining brilliantly under the water at a depth of 2 or 3 fathoms.

The wind blew fresher and the ship was able to make more rapid progress. On 8 September Cape St Vincent was sighted and the sailors knew that this was the last they would see of Europe for a very long time. A few days later Porto Santo and the volcanic island of Madeira appeared on the horizon. The island rose up from the sea, its steep slopes clothed in vineyards as high as the eye could see. In the harbour were several merchant ships and the *Endeavour* was greeted by a salute from the naval frigate HMS *Rose*. The new arrival anchored in Funchal Bay and she had to await the formalities of the 'product boat' to give the crew a clear bill of health before anybody was allowed on the island.

Once ashore Cook found that there was plenty of good-quality meat to be purchased at a price and he bought beef and some poultry to replace his losses in the Bay of Biscay. There were fruit and vegetables to be had in abundance, the water casks were replenished and of course there was plenty of excellent local wine for sale. In Madeira horses and mules were the standard form of transport, there were no paved roads and no wheeled carriages, the wine was carried in goat skins which balanced on the heads of the carriers. Cook purchased 3,032 gallons of it!

Banks and Solander went to visit Mr Cheap, the English Consul. They obtained permission to scour the island for botanical specimens but the captain had allowed only five days for revictualling and this meant that the collectors did not have time to visit the whole of the island. They made the acquaintance of Doctor Thomas Heberman, the leading local authority on natural history and he was able to add a few of the rarer specimens to their collection. On one of their five days at Madeira they were honoured by a visit from the Governor but this meant that the impatient botanists were to lose one of their precious collecting days hanging around waiting for His Excellency to arrive. Joseph Banks decided to revenge himself on the Governor and sent to the ship for his electrical machine. It was the first time that such a novelty had been seen on Madeira and Banks turned the handle as everybody watched the glass plates rotate and build up a static charge. The Governor was then invited to touch the terminals and receive an electric shock. It was a new experience which His Excellency found so stimulating that Joseph Banks repeated the performance and 'shocked him full as much as he chose'.

Leaving Madeira behind the next point of interest was the Canary Islands, the peak of Tenerife rose high out of the sea, above the horizon and even above the clouds – standing out impressively against the sunset. The ship sailed on a south-south-west course into the open Atlantic. Migrating swallows alighted on the rigging. A flying fish flew right into the astronomer's cabin. A young shark was baited and caught, it was hauled flapping on to the deck and killed. Banks and Solander ate the shark meat with relish but some of the superstitious sailors found the meat revolting on the grounds that sharks were known to eat human flesh.

Officers and midshipmen exercised on deck with their weapons and Charles Green looked on with amusement. 'They behaved much like the London Trane band with their [arms] sometimes on one shoulder and then on the other,' he observed, referring to an unknown company of musicians who were not noted for their high precision. It was clear that he was not the only person who thought they needed a bit of discipline and a few days later Cook instructed the young officers to clean up the atrocious mess they had left in their berths and to scrape and clean the ship between the decks. Richard Pickersgill refused to carry out this menial task and was ordered before the mast for his insolence.

'The observations of this day are Pretty good, the Air being very Clear,' wrote the astronomer as he calculated the ship's longitude. 'But might have been made more, and better, if proper assistance could have been had from the Young Gentleman on Board, with Pleasure to Themselves; or otherwise their Ob[serva-tio]ns cannot be depended upon, and when made a fatigue instead of pleasure.' Green was dismayed to find that he was the only person on board who knew the correct method of taking a lunar observation – even the captain was incapable of doing it properly. What was the point of the Royal Greenwich Observatory publishing the Nautical Almanac, he grumbled, if the naval officers didn't even know how to take observations? When he was the age of these youths the almanac did not even exist. They hadn't the faintest notion of the labour which had been expended on it for their benefit. They should take a leaf out of the captain's book. James Cook had shown immense interest in the method and mastered it very quickly. By the time they reached Tenerife the captain was just as capable of making a lunar observation as was Green himself and furthermore he knew how to use it to calculate the ship's position at sea. Charles Green was determined to teach the method to at least a few of the young officers before the voyage was much older.

The Nautical Almanac contained tables of the distances from the moon's centre to the sun and to nine selected bright stars. Positions were given for every three hours with instructions on how to correct for atmospheric refraction and for parallax with details of the calculation. In practical terms it required as many as four observers to make an accurate lunar observation and this was one of the main reasons why Charles Green wanted to teach the method to the other officers. The principal observer used a sextant to measure the angular distance between the moon and the sun or a selected star. Two other observers noted the precise time by means of a deck watch – a spring-driven watch with nothing like the accuracy of the marine chronometer but which could be calibrated to obtain a fair estimate of the local time. The method required good instruments and careful observation and the results were rarely more accurate than half a degree of longitude – but this was considered good by the standards of the time.

In the deep darkness of the Atlantic nights the explorers wondered at the luminous glow which they could see on the surface of the sea and the nature of the creatures which caused it. The stars stood out clear and sharp against the firmament. The Pole Star sunk nightly lower in the northern sky and Ursa Major bathed the ocean below the horizon but the Magellenic Clouds, the Southern Cross and constellations invisible from the northern latitudes rose above the horizon to the south. The sigh of the wind in the sails and the rigging, the creak of the masts and spars and the steady lapping of the waters on the prow brought the *Endeavour* steadily closer to the great circle which divided the northern and southern hemispheres – the line where night and day are always equally divided and where the darkness followed light with uncommon haste as the sun dived steeply into the western seas.

Every passing day saw the noonday sun climb a little higher in the sky. A feeling of anticipation grew in the ship as she drew closer to the equator. The young bloods were not to be denied their pleasure on this momentous occasion and every man on board was brought to the quarter deck to determine whether or not this was the first time he had crossed the line. Novices had to be indoctrinated by ducking three times into the Atlantic Ocean from the end of the main yard arm and those who qualified for this initiation ceremony included the great majority of the ship's company. Joseph Banks and all his retinue were eligible for a ducking and so was Captain Cook himself, experienced sailor as he was. It was agreed that some of the candidates would be excused the proceedings – but only on payment of a fine which amounted to four days' ration of spirits and must be surrendered to the remainder of the crew. Cook wisely paid the fine, as did Joseph Banks – but the organisers made it clear that the latter's dogs must pay the fine as well.

Some of the crew opted out of the initiation, but no young sailor could face up to his mates if he did not agree to go through with it. At the end of the day a score of unfortunates had been pressed into the ceremony and it was plenty for a good afternoon's sport. Joseph Banks gives a full account of the proceedings, a ceremony which doubtless varied from ship to ship and which was certainly elaborated by the sailors of later generations. As an eye-witness account of the proceedings in the 1760s it is one of the best descriptions we have:

This evening the ceremony of ducking the ships company was performed as always on crossing the line, when those who have crossed it before Claim a right of ducking all that have not, the whole of the cerremony I shall describe.

About dinner time a list was brought into the cabbin containing the names of every body and thing aboard the ship, in which the dogs and catts were not forgot; to this was affixed a petition, sign'd 'the ship's company', desiring leave to examine every body in that List then it might be known whether or not they had crossd the line before. This was immediately granted; every body was then called upon the quarter deck and examind by one of the lieutenants who had crossd, he marked every name either to be ducked or let off according as their qualifications directed. Captn Cooke and Doctor Solander were on the black list, as were my self and my servants and doggs, which I was oblig'd to compound for by giving the Duckers a certain quantity of Brandy for which they willingly excusd us the ceremony.

Many of the Men however chose to be ducked rather than give up 4 days allowance of wine which was the price fixed upon, and as for the boys they are always duckd of course; so that about 21 underwent the ceremony which was performed thus:

A block was made fast to the end of the Main Yard and a long line reved through it, to which three Cross pieces of wood were fastned, one of which was putt between the leggs of the man who was to be ducked and to this he was tyed very fast, another was for him to hold in his hands and the third was over his head least the rope should be hoisted too near the block and by that means the man be hurt. When he was fasned upon this machine the Boatswain gave the command by his whistle and the man was hoisted up as high as the cross piece over his head would allow, when another signal was made and immediately the rope was let go and his own weight carried him down, he was then immediately hoisted up again three times in this manner which was every mans allowance. Thus ended the diversion of the day, for the ducking lasted until almost night, and sufficiently diverting it certainly was to see the different faces that were made on this occasion, some grinning and exulting in their hardiness whilst others were almost suffocated and came up ready enough to have compounded after the first or second duck, had such proceedings been allowable.

At daybreak on 8 November the coast of South America was sighted and later in the same morning contact was made with a local fishing boat with occupants eager to sell their catch to the *Endeavour*. The fish provided a welcome change of diet for the ship's company, Banks had some Spanish silver with which to barter but to his surprise the fishermen preferred to be paid in English money.

They sailed southwards along the coast and admired the spectacular mountain scenery which in places came right down to the sea. The Brazilian port of Rio de Janeiro was a few days' sail along the coast, and at noon on 12 November the summit of the Sugar Loaf mountain was sighted on the horizon. Another day's sail and the *Endeavour* was approaching Rio in a calm sea and expecting a pilot boat to come out and guide her into the harbour. No such boat appeared so Cook shortened sail and dropped anchor beneath the Sugar Loaf. He sent his first lieutenant Zachary Hicks ashore in the pinnace to find a pilot. Hicks was a long time returning and in due course the pinnace appeared without him and without the midshipman sent with him. Instead came two straight-faced Portuguese officials who boarded the ship and proceeded to ask all sorts of questions regarding her business in these waters.

Another boat came out to the ship. It was a large ten-oared craft carrying about a dozen armed soldiers. The boat rowed sullenly round the *Endeavour* but the occupants refused to converse with anybody or to answer any of the questions which the sailors shouted at them. The officials declined to explain the reasons behind their interrogation, they invited the captain to come ashore and speak to the viceroy but ordered that everybody else was obliged to remain on board the ship.

Cook was angered and confused by this shabby treatment of his ship and crew. After weeks at sea the whole ship's complement was looking forward to setting foot on dry land again, and the gentlemen botanists were champing at the bit to get their hands on the South American flora. He obtained an audience with His Excellency Dom Antonio Rolim de Moura, the Viceroy of Brazil, and explained that the *Endeavour* was a British naval vessel on her way to the Pacific on a scientific expedition. He produced all the necessary papers and documents to support his case and even offered to produce two genuine natural historians to prove his case. He tried to explain to the viceroy about the transit of Venus and its importance to the science of astronomy.

The viceroy was no astronomer and had not the faintest idea of what Cook was talking about – to him the story was a complete concoction. How could a planet like Venus possibly pass through the sun? He announced that he could form 'no idea of that Phenomenon than the North Star passing through the South Pole'. As for the captain's claim that the ship was one of his Britannic Majesty's, the viceroy knew a naval vessel when he saw one and the *Endeavour* was no such vessel. True, she had a few swivel guns and carriage guns aboard, but British ships of war were bristling with sixty guns and more, they should have two or three decks of 32 pounders armed with powder and shot enough to blast their enemies out of the water with one double broadside. The *Endeavour* was not a naval vessel – she was a merchantman. The captain's papers were clever forgeries and his excellency had seen the like on this coast before. The English were very enterprising merchants but they were a very devious nation and the viceroy decided that the real business of the ship was either that of smuggling or of spying on the harbour at Rio. He concluded that the scientific gentlemen were either engineers or spies. He explained to Cook that the ship would not be molested, she was free to leave whenever she chose but no person except the captain was to be allowed on shore. The viceroy also explained politely that he was doing no more than executing his duty – he was acting under the orders of the king of Portugal.

All this was too much for Banks and Solander, they were left fuming in the great cabin with the vista of a whole new continent right before their eyes. They put their heads together and tried to work out a way of slipping ashore without being seen by the guard boat which constantly circled the ship. After a few days the crew had acquired a good knowledge of the bay and harbour and also of the regular movements of their custodians. One night at about midnight the Hon. Joseph Banks Esquire, future President of the Royal Society, and the respectable Dr Daniel Solander, high priest of the Linnaean system of classification, climbed furtively out of the cabin window like two schoolboys and slipped down a rope into a small boat tethered below. The two of them then rowed silently away from the ship and into the town of Rio de Janeiro. The nocturnal adventure was successful and their first landing in South America was made at a quiet spot on one of the least frequented parts of the large harbour.

'The morning after we went ashore,' said Banks, 'my eyes were feasted with the pleasing prospects that opened to my view on every hand.' Perhaps the authorities in Rio witnessed the excursion but decided to turn a blind eye, for nobody could appear less like a smuggler than the crazy Englishman watching a beautiful humming-bird extract the nectar from a bright tropical flower or the engrossed Swede enthusing over a *Mimosa Sensitivia*. Both scientists were very taken with the tropical colourings of the birds and flowers, but their expedition was not entirely confined to botany and Banks could not resist making several purchases during his time ashore. The two botanists managed to slip back aboard unseen, or at least unmolested, but the next day the watering boat returned with the news that there was a search onshore for persons who had landed without the viceroy's permission, and Banks was therefore not prepared to risk making a second expedition. He did, however, manage to send his servants ashore more than once and before leaving Rio his tally of Brazilian species had risen to no less than 245 entries in his pocket book.

The viceroy continued to be polite but firm. He turned a blind eye to the botanical excursion which must have been brought to his notice and he did allow a few exceptions to the rules. A minor concession was that Cook was allowed to purchase fresh food and vegetables so that at least the fare of the seamen was changed from the monotonous salted pork and biscuits. Cook was also allowed to fill the water casks from the public fountain but the water was of poor quality and tasted worse than the water which had travelled all the way from Madeira. The ship's surgeon, William Monkhouse, was allowed ashore regularly to help with the purchase of supplies and on one occasion a request was made for him to administer treatment. The Portuguese were not aware that Monkhouse was the surgeon and it was therefore decided that Dr Solander should go ashore instead, posing as a medical man and by this subterfuge the botanical doctor managed to see a little more of Rio.

The *Endeavour* carried three small boats on deck, all of which were in regular use at Rio. The largest and most strongly built was the longboat and it was used for the carriage of casks and stores to supply the ship; then came the pinnace which was designed primarily for coastal exploration by the captain and the ship's master. Thirdly there was a smaller boat called the yawl which carried only four oars and was a suitable craft for short journeys and small parties. Sydney Parkinson sketched all three boats showing that they all carried sails as well as oars – rowing was used only in cases of necessity.

At Rio the longboat was unloading four casks of rum on to the ship when a hawser broke and the boat was carried off by the force of the tide. The pinnace was already in use at the time and could not be sent to recover the longboat, and the yawl had therefore to be launched to try to bring the larger boat back to the ship again. The effort was wasted, the yawl was too small and had insufficient oar and sailpower to move the heavier boat in any direction. The tidal race carried the longboat progressively further from the ship and out of sight. The last glimpse of the longboat from the decks of the *Endeavour* showed it drifting towards a group of jagged rocks, and later in the day reports came in to say that it had foundered on the rocks and was holed and filled with water.

On the same day as the longboat incident other crew members had gone ashore in the pinnace to purchase supplies and for some unknown reason they were molested by the Portuguese soldiers and bundled unceremoniously into jail. The sailors protested loudly that they had done nothing to provoke the Portuguese but it was all to no avail. They described their prison as a foul dungeon where they spent the night in the company of some poor black wretches who were chained to the walls. It was the learned Doctor Johnson who claimed that shipboard life in his times was worse than being in jail (sir!) because it included the possibility of being drowned – the seamen would gladly have exchanged their prison quarters for the lower decks of the *Endeavour*.

Things could hardly be worse. A dozen seamen held in a Portuguese dungeon; Thomas Foster, an English merchant who had tried to help his countrymen was also thrown into jail on a false charge of smuggling; the longboat was gone and wrecked; the pinnace was captured and held by the Portuguese; the boatswain's boat had been swept overboard back in the Bay of Biscay; and the little yawl was the only one of the ship's boats that remained. The viceroy claimed doggedly that his stringent security applied to all foreign vessels but matters were soon made worse when a Spanish ship arrived from Buenos Aires and Cook indignantly recorded the treatment of the new arrival:

> *This day a Spanish Packet (a small Brigg) from Buenos Ayres put in here in her way to Spain, this vessel belonged to His Catholic Majesty, and notwithstanding the Viceroy had all along pretended that orders he had respecting Foreign vessels were general yet this vessel met with very different treatment from us, no Guard was put over her and her officers and crew went where ever they pleased.*

The irate captain wrote a long and indignant letter to the viceroy asking for the immediate return of his crew and his boat. No explanation or apology was given, but it seems that the viceroy may at last have begun to wonder if the Englishman spoke the truth after all for he seemed to develop a conscience regarding his actions. He was obviously trying to execute his duties correctly but Cook's letter had the desired effect – the viceroy actually relented and the crewmen were released from prison. The pinnace was returned to its rightful owners and to the great surprise of all concerned the longboat was also returned intact. The rumour that the longboat was wrecked proved to be false, and furthermore four barrels of rum, which had never been unloaded, were still aboard. The Portuguese had actually assisted in the recovery.

It dismayed Cook to know that throughout all these problems he had had the alternative choice of avoiding Rio altogether and that he could have called at the Falkland Islands instead to prepare for the passage around Cape Horn. But he knew that supplies at St Egremont were more limited than on the mainland and he also had information that several British ships had been very civilly received at Rio in recent years so that he had no cause to anticipate any problems. He was very conscious of his new commission and he did not expect the long delays and frustrations which he experienced, he was very sensible of his need to do his duty to his superiors at the Admiralty. James Cook, the complete mariner, skilled navigator, cartographer, astronomical observer and mathematician now came face to face with petty officialdom, illogical bureaucracy and international politics. The whole episode frustrated him and he penned a long report to the Admiralty, making far more out of the incident than was really necessary. In the event he did manage to get the ship caulked and cleaned, he was able to repair and replace worn rigging and the coopers repaired his damaged barrels. He was also able to draw some accurate maps and charts of the Rio harbour with detailed plans of the guns and fortifications – a fact which would have given the viceroy real cause for concern had he known about it.

> I shall now give the best description I can of the different Forts that are erected for the defence of this Bay: the first you meet with coming in from the Sea is a Battry of 22 Guns, seated in the bottom of a Sandy Bay which is on the South side of the Sugr Loaf, and can be designed for no other use than to hinder an enemy from landing in that Vally from whence I suppose they may march up to the town, or round by the west side of the Sugar Loaf to attack the Forts that are on that side of the entrance into the Bay, the first of which is seated under the foot of the Sugar Loafe on a low isthmus which Joines the peninsula or point of the bay with the land of the Sugar Loafe, it appears to be a square of Stone work, without a ditch, with Bastions and furnished with cannon.

A little within this fort are two batteries of 5 or 6 guns each, they are design'd to play upon Shipping but nither these Batteries or the Fort are out of reach of a Ship's Cannon.

Rio was obviously very well defended and he goes on to describe Fort Lozio, a hexagonal stone fortress built on a rock at the entrance to the bay, and another battery to the west armed with seventeen cannon. On the east of the bay stood the battery of St Dominica with seven guns and other guns were mounted around the bay at various strategic positions. He did not think Rio was impregnable, however, but he estimated that it would take five or six ships of the line to take the harbour by force and once it was taken he noted that there were seven regiments of regular troops to be overcome within the town.

The re-provisioning and the repairs to the ship were completed, and when the time came to depart there was not a man aboard the ship who was not glad to leave Rio behind. The viceroy, ever polite, provided a pilot boat to guide the ship out of the harbour and into the open sea – he then bid the ship a formal farewell. On the way out of the harbour Peter Flower, one of the seamen whom Cook had known for more than five years, fell overboard and was drowned before any kind of assistance could reach him. He was replaced by a Portuguese volunteer. Then came the final sorry episode of the Rio affair when the *Endeavour* was being towed out of the bay – the fort at Santa Cruz fired two shots across her bows to halt her. It seemed that his excellency the viceroy, in spite of his polite farewell letter, had forgotten to give the fort official notice of the departure and the soldiers were acting under orders not to let any vessel leave without permission. 'Many curses were this day expended on his excellence,' wrote Banks feelingly when the ship found herself becalmed. There was a minor consolation for him, however, when a swarm of colourful butterflies alighted on the ship and settled all over the rigging. On the following day, when lack of wind hindered progress, the keen botanists had time to land on the small island of Raza to collect specimens in the hot noonday sunshine.

The *Endeavour* set sail southwards again, heading towards the southern extremity of the American continent. The days were uneventful except for Christmas Day which was celebrated in the unfamiliar summer climate of the Southern Hemisphere. 'All good Christians, that is to say all hands get abominably drunk so that at night there was scarcely a sober man in the ship,' complained Joseph Banks. 'Wind thank God very moderate or the Lord knows what would have become of us.' The captain admitted in his journal that 'the people were none of the soberest', but it was a festive occasion and the men were allowed their extra ration of rum – Cook had seen many Christmases at sea and the excesses were no worse than normal for the occasion.

There were certainly times, however, when the discipline on board the ship seemed to be lacking. The drunkenness was frequent, the drilling was slack, the officers never tidied their mess and they were slow with their lessons in navigation, the longboat should never have slipped from its hawser and two men had already been lost overboard. Measured by the progress of the *Endeavour* to this point on the voyage Cook had yet to prove himself as the great seaman his admirers claimed him to be – he did not excel in the negotiations at Rio and the progress made by his ship was so far steady but unremarkable.

But Banks the landsman was too critical and upset at having missed his golden opportunity of collecting the Brazilian flora. To date there had been no great tests of seamanship but already the captain was moulding the crew to get the best out of them. On a few occasions he had been obliged to punish both seamen and marines for minor mis-demeanours and he knew that he was expected to give out harsh naval punishment to all who disobeyed orders or broke the rules. But he wanted to gain the respect of the men through example and through administration of justice and fair play on board ship. At Madeira Henry Stephens and Thomas

Dunster were each given twelve lashes for the heinous crime of refusing to eat fresh beef. At Rio Robert Anderson was given twelve lashes for attempting to desert and William Judge, a marine, was given the same punishment for using abusive language to one of the officers. Cook knew that he could not command respect in his ship unless he was seen to come down hard on the offenders.

The health and safety of his men were matters of paramount importance to Cook. He was most upset at the loss of Alexander Weir and Peter Flower and he was annoyed over the incident with the longboat, but standards of safety in the eighteenth century were almost non-existent, life was held cheaply and he had been at sea long enough to know that the number of accidents was on a par for a voyage of this nature. Few, if any, captains would punish men for not eating their food but Cook saw the health of his crew as very important, particularly with the great challenge of the Pacific Ocean ahead of them. The dietary knowledge of the times was full of unproven superstitions and foundered on the difficulties which the experimenters encountered when trying to test out their ideas. Cook knew that the secret behind the cure for scurvy lay in finding fresh food and that certain preservatives helped to prevent the disease. Malt was suggested as a preventative and also citrus juice mixed with cider but the vitamin C had been destroyed by the well-meaning dieticians when the juice was boiled to preserve and bottle it. We begin to see from Cook's actions that he was no ordinary captain – when the seamen turned up their noses at the detested fermenting German cabbage which the ship carried in large quantity, the captain applied an amazing piece of modern psychology:

The Sour Krout the men at first would not eate untill I put in practice a method I never once knew to fail with seamen, and this was to have some of it dress'd every Day for the cabbin Table, and permitted all the Officers without exception to make use of it and left it to the option of the Men either to take as much as they pleased or none at all; but this practice was not continued above a week before I found it necessary to put every one on board to an Allowance, for such are the tempers and disposissions of Seamen in general that whatever you give them out of the Common way, altho it be ever so much for their good yet it will not go down with them and you will hear nothing but murmurings gainest the man that first invented it; but the Moment they see their Superiors set a value on it, it becomes the finest stuff on the World and the inventer a damn'd honest fellow.

With typical reserve James Cook realised that his superiors would read what he had written. He struck out the word 'damn'd'.

Between Rio de Janeiro and Cape Horn lay nearly a thousand leagues (three thousand miles) of ocean. Rio lay near the tropic of Capricorn but Cape Horn was situated in a southern latitude of over 56 degrees. With every degree of latitude the temperature dropped, the wind became colder and harder and the sea rougher and higher. For more than thirty days the *Endeavour* pressed steadily southwards standing well off the South American coast and sailing into progressively worsening weather. The New Year arrived and on 11 January 1769 land was sighted to the south-west. It was Tierra del Fuego, the country which Ferdinand Magellan called the 'land of the fires' with its cold dark mountain ranges and heavy cloud cover. This was the most southerly land of the American continent, the most southerly land in the whole known world – it lay at the very ends of the Earth between Atlantic and Pacific and guarding the passage between them.

It was high summer, however, when the *Endeavour* approached this inhospitable land but the mountain peaks were still covered with snow. The land was well known to be inhabited and the red fires seen by Magellan were seen also by Cook's crew; they knew that very soon they would be making contact with this primitive people. A landing was made at a place where Banks and Solander could collect specimens.

The Fuegians were a nomadic tribe who at some point in their ancient history had crossed from the mainland and evolved into an isolated race on their windswept island. They not only managed to survive in the inhospitable climate but they were so hardy that the men braved the cold almost naked and the women wore little more than a small apron made of leather with an occasional sealskin coat around the shoulders. The Fuegians built rounded huts for shelter, shaped like a beehive with wooden frames and covered by sealskins and brushwood. Alexander Buchan made a painting of one such dwelling, showing the inhabitants huddled around a fire and wrapped in their cloaks, while a woman holds a small baby and a dog scratches on the earthen floor. In the winter they would keep a fire going all the time for warmth – there was no shortage of timber for fuel.

Cook and Banks described the people as dark haired with deep copper-coloured skin and noted that some of the men painted their faces with horizontal bands of black and red pigment. They used shells to fashion bracelets which both sexes wore around the wrists, and the women also about the ankles and legs. It was obvious that although they appeared to have no boats to cross to the mainland, they traded with the coastal settlements to the north for they had arrows cleverly tipped with broken glass and they knew the power of the firearms that the English carried with them. After a cautious start the Fuegians showed signs of friendship – they were delighted with the red beads which Joseph Banks offered as a sign of friendship and three natives offered to go aboard the ship. One of the three seemed to be a priest or wise man of some kind and he exorcised every part of the ship shouting loudly all the time to nobody in particular. The speech of the Fuegians was quite incomprehensible to the Europeans and when they conversed with each other all that Cook was able to hear was a grunting and clearing of throats.

Cook wanted to replenish the ship with wood and water before the next stage of the voyage. Banks and Solander, after all the problems and frustrations of Rio, were more eager than ever to explore the island. They organised an expedition with Banks's four servants plus William Monkhouse, the ship's surgeon, Charles Green the astronomer, Alexander Buchan the artist, a greyhound and two able-bodied seamen to help with the porter-ing. They set out to cross what appeared to be a swathe of grassland but it turned out to be a bog covered by a species of tough birch bush which made it a difficult and very exhausting terrain to cross. About two-thirds of the way through the bog Alexander Buchan, who suffered from epilepsy, threw a fit. The party decided to light a fire for him, thinking that this was the best they could do for his comfort. It was decided that Banks, Solander, Green and Monkhouse should proceed on their own and leave the artist in the care of the rest of the party.

A satisfactory number of new specimens was collected and all went well until the return journey when the weather turned sud-denly cold and flurries of snow appeared. The party was reunited and they decided to make their way back to the ship. It then became very much colder, the snow had started to fall steadily and the ground was soon white with fresh snow. Dr Solander became so exhausted that he insisted on resting in the snow before he would take another step. Alexander Buchan had fortu-nately recovered from his epileptic fit and he went ahead of the party to try to get a good fire going. Thomas Richmond and George Dorlton, the two black servants, were feeling the cold so badly that they too were unable to go any further. Joseph Banks had to leave his servants behind to help his friend Dr Solander to make the fire. When he returned with the seamen to assist the ser-vants he found them in a very weak state. They managed to get Richmond to his feet but he could not put one foot in front of the other. Dorlton lay on the ground as heavy as stone. It was then that the reason why they were insensible was discovered – between them they had managed to consume practically all the supply of rum for the expedition! It began to snow more heavily and it became obvious that the party would have to face the cold prospect of a Fuegean night in the open.

Now might our situation truly be called terrible: of twelve our original number 2 were already past all hopes, one more was so ill that tho he was with us I had little hopes of his being able to walk in the morning, and another very likely to relapse into his fitts either before we set out or in the course of the journey: we were distant from the ship we did not know how far, we knew only that we had been on the greatest part of a day in walking it through pathless woods: provision we had none but one vulture which had been shot while we were out, and at the shortest allowance could not furnish half a meal: and to compleat our misfortune we were caught in a snowstorm in a climate we were utterly unacquainted with but which we had reason to believe was as inhospitable as any in the world, not only from all accounts we had heard or read but from the Quantity of snow which we saw falling, tho it was very little after midsummer: a circumstance unheard of in Europe for even in Norway or Lapland snow is never known to fall in the summer.

The next morning the two black servants were found dead from exposure – only the faithful greyhound which had remained with them was still alive. Joseph Banks had formed a deep attachment to his servants; it was he who had brought them to this place and he held himself largely responsible for their deaths. Peter Briscoe was very ill but thought himself capable of walking. Thankfully Buchan was much better. They had the vulture for breakfast – it amounted to three mouthfuls of hot food per person. At about 8 a.m. a breeze sprang up and the sunshine combined to start a thaw. When visibility improved they found they had not been travelling in a straight line but on a curved path which meant that the ship was nearer than they had feared. The disastrous expedition found the way back to ship without two of its members. 'As soon as they came on Board & Refresh'd they were put into warm beds,' said Robert Molyneux. It must have been a great comfort to find that such luxuries as warm beds existed in the neighbour-hood of Tierra del Fuego.

There was no point in remaining at the scene of the disaster. The ship was rewatered and refuelled. The weather was about as fair as it could ever be in these latitudes. The whole of their courage and resources would be needed for the next stage of the journey. Ahead of them lay Cape Horn, the stormiest and most difficult sea passage on Earth. The captain had no intention of standing out to sea in the hope of finding a smoother passage, he was ready to sail and he was determined to measure the latitude and longitude of the storm-beaten cape at the southern extremity of the known world.

CHAPTER 3

CAPE HORN

To 13 April, 1769

S INCE THE LEGENDARY voyage of 1519 when Ferdinand
Magellan found a passage through South America into an
ocean which he called the Pacific, wooden-walled vessels of
many nations had fought their way through the straits which bear
his name. Sixteenth-century map-makers such as Ortelius show
that for many years it was assumed that Tierra del Fuego was part
of the *Terra Australis Incognita* which, with an optimism typical of
the times, was conjectured to be a great continent stretching
many degrees both west and east of the Straits of Magellan. It
was well known from the outset that the entry into the Pacific was
the most hazardous of sea passages, but this did not deter the
great seamen of Elizabethan England from being amongst the
first of Magellan's followers. Amongst these great explorers were
Drake, Cavendish and Hawkins. In 1578, when Francis Drake
emerged from the Straits of Magellan into the Pacific Ocean he
encountered weather so ferocious that he was driven many
leagues to the south of his planned course, towards the southern
coast of Tierra del Fuego, and it was Drake who first suspected
that Tierra del Fuego was not a new continent but merely an island
at the southernmost tip of America with open sea to the south.
Drake's theory was correct but he was so intent on his plans to
sail northwards and plunder the Spanish Main that he had no time
to prove the truth of his hypothesis.

In 1516 two Dutchmen, Schouten and Le Maire, led an expedition from Amsterdam which arrived at a point on the east coast of Tierra del Fuego where they discovered a narrow strait with land running eastwards which they called Staten Land. They passed through the strait and discovered a scattered group of islands which they named the Hermites. On the southernmost island was a cape which they named after the town of Hoorn in Holland. The Dutch rounded Cape Hoorn and thereby became the first to navigate the infamous passage to open up an alternative route into the Pacific. The new passage proved to be almost as difficult to navigate as the old one, and generations of sailors loved to argue the merits of one route against the other – but in truth very few had the direct experience of both these routes and for centuries the number of mariners who had sailed both passages into the Pacific could be counted on the fingers of one hand.

The immense navigational difficulties and the lack of profitable trade through what was sometimes called the South West Passage meant that in the seventeenth and eighteenth centuries the number of ships entering the Pacific Ocean was still a mere handful. In the case of the English great efforts and resources were diverted towards the more profitable colonisation of North America and it was not until the middle of the eighteenth century that the English began to take a more serious interest in the world beyond America. In 1741 Commodore George Anson doubled Cape Horn on a four-year voyage which took him around the world. He returned with the spoils from a Spanish Manila treasure ship and captured the public imagination by publishing an account of the places and adventures which he encountered on his circumnavigation.

The next British expedition was not until 1764 when John Byron passed through the straits of Magellan with two ships, one called the *Dolphin* and the other the *Tamar*. The *Dolphin* was the first naval vessel to be fitted with experimental copper sheathing on the hull as protection against the ravages of the Teredo worm. The sheathing was a success but the expedition was a failure. It took Byron's ships only two years to circumnavigate the globe but his voyage was marred by terrible suffering amongst the crew. Many died from scurvy and this was the main reason why he did not make any major new discoveries.

The *Dolphin* remained in England only a short time before she headed for the Pacific a second time under the command of Captain Samuel Wallis and accompanied by another vessel called the *Swallow*. Wallis, like Byron before him, was instructed to sail through the Straits of Magellan and he dutifully battled his way against the elements for twelve weeks before he finally fought his way through to the Pacific. He lost touch with his companion ship the *Swallow* altogether and eventually had to return to England without her. His great discovery was a beautiful Pacific island in the latitude of 17 degrees South which he named King George the Third island – a pompous piece of English nomenclature which was dropped in favour of the native name of Tahiti. His voyage, like Byron's, was marred by bad health and he was thus prevented from achieving as much in the way of discovery as he might otherwise have done. Wallis's companion ship the little *Swallow* did not perish in the Pacific after all. She also circumnavigated the world and eventually arrived home a full year later than the *Dolphin*.

It was the knowledge of these recent voyages, as much as anything else, which convinced Cook that if he was going to make any significant discoveries in the Southern Hemisphere then the health of his men and their diet were of paramount importance. By the time the *Swallow* was back in England the *Endeavour* had already sailed from Plymouth carrying with her four men who had served under Wallis on the *Dolphin* – they were Robert Molyneux the ship's master, Lieutenant John Gore, Richard Pickersgill the master's mate and the Welshman Francis Wilkinson. As Cook approached Cape Horn the four veterans of the *Dolphin* hoped to join the select company of sailors who had doubled Cape Horn and also navigated the Straits of Magellan.

The Admiralty had studied the accounts of the voyages of

Byron and Wallis, as well as the earlier experiences of Lord Anson, and they decided in favour of the Cape Horn route for the *Endeavour*. Cook's sailing instructions were very clear on this point and included some good advice for rounding the cape itself: '...we recommend it to you to stand well to the Southward in your passage around the Cape, in order to make a good Westing.'

· A few days after sailing from Tierra del Fuego a cold wind sprang up from the south-east and the temperature dropped rapidly to 48°F (9°C). Coming as it did so soon after leaving the tropics this keen wind seemed an icy blast to the mariners, but colder weather and harder gales lay ahead of them. Joseph Banks donned a warm jacket, a waistcoat and a thicker pair of trousers – the captain decided that the time had come to issue the whole crew with heavy trousers and jackets, called Fearnought Jackets or Magellan Jackets, which had been supplied by the Admiralty as protection against wind and weather. The South Atlantic lived up to its stormy reputation and replied by throwing a howling gale at the *Endeavour*, tossing her like a cork on the angry swell.

Conditions deteriorated throughout the day and when the evening came the storm had become so ferocious that Cook decided to heave to and ride it out. He brought the ship to a halt and reefed all the sails except one mainsail. The goat was removed to the safety of the lower deck, sails were tightly furled, hatches were battened down and everything above was tied and roped securely. Waves smashed violently against the flanks of the ship and the sea poured over the deck breaking into angry white foam as it swirled around mast, rails and rigging. Inside the ship loose articles were thrown everywhere as the *Endeavour* executed her famous roll and combined it with a pitch-and-yaw motion. One wave tossed the ship around so violently that Banks's desk crashed to the floor and his books were thrown off and spread all over the cabin. When darkness came it was impossible to sleep as hammocks swung violently and unpredictably throwing their occupants against the wall with every lurch of the ship:

*In the evening blew strong, at night a hard gale, ship was brought too
under a mainsail; during the course of this my Bureau was overset and
most of the books were about the Cabbin floor, so that with the noise of
the ship working, the books &c. running about, and the strokes of our
cotts or swinging beds gave against the top and sides of the cabbin we
spent a very disagreeable night …*

The sailors knew that the cat-built bark was a ship that could
patiently withstand weather of this kind, but even the experienced hands were impressed with the way the *Endeavour* rode out
the heavy seas. 'The ship during this gale has shewn her excellence in laying too remarkably well,' wrote Banks. 'Shipping
scarce any water tho it blew many times vastly strong; the seamen
in general say that they never knew a ship lay too so well as this
does, so lively and at the same time so easy.'

The next day there followed a brief respite and Cook sent the
sailors scurrying up the ratlines to set the topgallants again.
Banks, who at times loved to extract bits of sea-lore from the
men, gives an interesting little anecdote:

*The ship has been observed to go much better since her shaking in the last
gale of wind, the seamen say that it is a general observation that ships go
better for being what they call Loosnen[d] in their Joints, so much so that
in chase it is customary to knock down Stantions &c. and make the ship
as loose as possible.*

The ship was getting closer to land and bearing down on a narrow
strait called the Strait Le Maire, named after the Dutch navigator
who first discovered it in 1615. This strait separates Tierra del
Fuego from a long barren island running to the east. Charles Green
was trying to take a lunar observation but the sea ran so high that it
filled the quarter deck three times as he tried to get his sighting, the
ship was thrown around so much that even the dedicated Captain
Cook did not try to observe under these atrocious conditions.

The entrance to the Strait Le Maire was flanked by Cape St Diego on the west and by a rocky promontory on the east. It was guarded by a stretch of ferocious breaking sea which smashed constantly against the rocks and threw white spray high into the air. The *Endeavour* sailed into this raging torrent of broken water hoping to make an entry into the strait but the sea decided otherwise and tossed the ship around at will. The stern was thrown high into the air and the bowsprit was forced down so violently that it actually dipped right into the water. At about midday, after enduring about two hours of this punishment, Cook decided to give up the attempt – he retreated and waited for the wind to die down before trying again. At four o'clock in the afternoon a second attempt was made to cross the ferocious stretch of water, again the pitching was just as violent as on the first attempt but this time the *Endeavour* successfully negotiated the worst and was able to pass Cape St Diego and enter into the straits beyond.

It was to no avail. There came a powerful rush of water down the strait, so strong that it drove the ship back to where she came from and the horrific pounding had to be endured all over again.

The rush of water which forced the *Endeavour* out of the Strait Le Maire was a tidal effect created by the narrow channel at the exit to the strait. 'Hauled our wind Point St Diego where in crossing the ripling of a Strong Tide the Ship was so agitated as to pitch the Spritsail yard under several times,' wrote the ship's master. 'And at the same time roll'd surprizeing deep [as] this Curr[ent] took us out of the strait.' The captain hoped to be able to anchor and to give his crew some rest before a third attempt was made. He sent Molyneux to examine a small cove behind Cape St Diego, but the master's soundings showed a hard rocky bottom with nothing for the anchor to hold on to. The ship made a third attempt to enter the strait and was repulsed a third time.

'As we Pass'd the Point we had the Strongest rippling to Pass I have ever saw,' exclaimed Richard Pickersgill. 'Which I immagine was Occaisend by the meeting of the Tides and the Bottom being nothing but Coral Rocks and very uneven.' The ship retreated to behind Cape St Diego where there was sheltered water even though there was no anchorage. It was difficult to see how any vessel could get into the Strait Le Maire let alone get through to the other side and the captain allowed the botanists to go ashore in one of the boats whilst he took stock of the situation and tacked up and down outside the straits. He concluded that the rippling torrent was an effect caused by the arrangement of capes and headlands and by two opposing tidal currents which clashed with each other from different sides of Staten Island. If this theory was correct then the secret was to find the right turn of the tide to get through.

The next attempt was duly made at what was judged to be the right state of the tide. Cook gives no details in the log, but the *Endeavour* finally made it at this fourth attempt. Once inside good progress was made and the ship was able to anchor in the sheltered waters of the Bay of Good Success. It was badly named for Joseph Banks and his party after their disastrous expedition into the interior. Here preparations were made for the final rounding of Cape Horn: guns and heavy items were lowered into the hold to give the ship better stability. It was a tricky operation with a restless sea and the surf breaking heavily on the beach nearby. A kedge anchor was lost when a line broke in a gale. 'The gale broke the hawser and buoy rope and buried the anchor in the sand,' said Wilkinson. 'Squalls of hail, snow and excessive cold. Prepared for sea to the joy of all hands.' In spite of the blustery weather and low temperatures the crew were eager to tackle the task which lay before them.

The skies were overcast and the wind very blustery, but the sailors had become accustomed to the heavy seas and made light of the conditions. As they sailed through the straits Sydney Parkinson gazed with awe at the huge cliffs of Staten Island which towered above the ship as she progressed towards Cape Horn. He was sufficiently moved to call upon his maker:

How amazingly diversified are the works of the Deity within the narrow limits of this globe we inhabit, which compared with the vast aggregate of systems that compose the universe, appears but a dark speck in the creation. A curiosity, perhaps, equal to Solomon's, though accompanied with less wisdom than was possessed by the Royal Philosopher, induced some of us to quit our native land, to investigate the heavenly bodies minutely in distant regions, as well as to trace the signatures of the Supreme Power and Intelligence throughout several species of animals, and different genera of plants in the vegetable system ... the smallest object, seen through the microscope, declares its origin to be divine, as well as those larger ones which the unassisted eye is capable of contemplating ...

The ship sailed out of the Strait Le Maire into the open sea, and the tip of the great land-mass of South America crumbled into a spate of barren islands called the Hermites. They were small craggy outcrops guarded by pointed rocks each one as sharp as a needle and capable of prising open the timbers of any ship unfortunate enough to founder against them. The ship's progress was accompanied by a flock of inquisitive screaming seabirds including several large albatrosses which wheeled effortlessly against the sky, following behind in the hope of picking up scraps of food. Cook wrote up his journal for 25 January when the Hermite Islands lay to windward off the starboard bow. Cape Horn was the tip of the southernmost island in the Hermite group but there was some disagreement as to which island held this honour.

Winds from the South to WNW, the first part fresh gales and squally with some rain, middle little wind with hail and rain, latter fresh gales and hazey with showers of rain ... at Noon the south point of the Southernmost Island bore NWBW dist 3 leagues, having then 55 fathom Peble stones; this point is pretty high and consists of Peeked craggy rocks and not far from it lay several others high above water; it lies in the latitude of 55° 53' South and SW 26 Leagues from Strait Le Mair, and by some on

board thought to be Cape Horn, but I was of another oppinion and with
good reason because we saw land to the southward of it about 3 or 4
leagues. It appeared not unlike an island with a very high round
hummock upon it: this I believe to be the Cape Horn for after we had
stood to the southward about 3 leagues the weather clear'd up for about a
quarter of an hour, which gave us a sight of this land bearing then
WSW but we could see no land either to the Southward or the Westward
of it, and therefore conclude that it must be the Cape, butt whether it be
an Island of itself, a part of the Southernmost Hermites Islands or a part
of Tierra del Fuego I am not able to determine.

The weather relented and the *Endeavour* was exceptionally fortunate to round the Cape in such relatively mild conditions. The good weather held long enough for the bark not only to spread all her three masts of sail to the wind but even to set the studding sails – the sight of so much sail in these regions was one which future mariners would find difficult to believe. There was some fog, but it was very slight and not too misty to prevent the taking of astronomical readings. The captain, some of the officers, and the astronomer took sightings whenever the conditions allowed so that eventually no less than twenty-four sightings had been made from which to calculate the position of Cape Horn. 'I can now venture to assert that the Longitude of few places in the world are better assertain'd than that of Strait Le Maire and Cape Horn,' wrote Cook with pride and almost showing a rare glimpse of his emotions. 'Being determined by several observations of the Sun and Moon, made by both myself and Mr Green the astronomer.'

Another, almost incomprehensible but interesting, account of the longitude made a few days after rounding Cape Horn was given by one of the midshipmen:

... at 3 PM Observ'd longd in sun & moon 90:05 and pr Do Observd
Longd in moon and Star Regulous 91:09 W of Greenwich an Instance of

*the Accuracy of this method of Discovering the Longd and the great
benefit it is to Navigators in thise Long Voyages and in My Opinion
cannot be too much Incourage'd.*

It was young Pickersgill exalting about the method of lunars, he
who had been sent before the mast in mid-Atlantic for grumbling
about cleaning up his berth. Richard Pickersgill also makes an
interesting comment that an occultation of the planet Saturn
passing behind the moon was observed, evidence that the
astronomers never wasted an opportunity to measure the moon's
position. His new enthusiasm must have been a welcome development to Charles Green when he found that his patient teachings
were at last bearing fruit.

Whenever the ship was close to land Cook and Green were
determined to try to establish the longitudes of the headlands
and main features. At the Strait Le Maire Cook discovered that
his own calculations, based on the traditional method of dead
reckoning, differed from those of the astronomer by nearly a
whole degree, of about 55 nautical miles in this latitude. He
concluded that the ship must have been carried westward by a
strong current coming out of the Straits of Magellan to the east.
On this occasion, when the sea washed over the quarterdeck, the
pitch and roll of the ship was so pronounced the astronomer's
observations were no more reliable than the captain's dead reckoning but later in the voyage Cook discovered something which
accounted for part of his error. The speed of the ship through the
water was measured with a 'logg line'. This was a rope calibrated
with knots at regular intervals and with a float fixed at one end.
The float was thrown over the stern and a half-minute sand-glass
was turned. The number of knots unreeled from the line gave the
speed of the ship through the water in knots. Cook discovered
that the knot spacings were too long so that the speed of the ship
through the water was measured as too slow and the log line had
to be recalibrated to correct the error.

Cape Horn was the last sight of land for a long time, many miles of open sea lay before them and Cook made sure that he had plenty of westerly, steering well away from the land, for he knew that the gales could drive him north at any time and it was necessary to get well clear of the end of the continent before tacking northwards again. When he had seen the last of Tierra del Fuego he entered his findings in his journal with comments and advice for future navigators:

> ... we are now advanced about 12° to the westward of the Strait of Magellan and 3h° to the northward of it, having been 33 days in doubling Cape Horn or the land of Terra del Fuego, and arriving into the degree of Latitude and Longitude we are now in without ever being brought once under our close reefe'd Topsails since we left Strait la Maire, a circumstance that perhaps never happen'd before to any Ship in those seas so much dreaded for hard gales of wind, insomuch that the doubling of Cape Horn is thought by some to be a mighty thing and others this Day prefer the Straits of Magellan. As I have never been in those straits, can only form my judgement on a carefull comparison of the different Ship's Journals that have pass'd them and those that have sail'd round Cape Horn, particularly the Dolphin's two last Voyages and this of ours being made at the same Season of the Year when one may reasonably expect the Same winds to prevail. The Dolphin in her last voyage was 3 Months in geting through the Straits not reckoning the time she lay at Port Famine, and I am firmly perswaded from the winds that we have had, that had we come by that passage we should not yet have been in these seas; beside the fatiguing of our people the Damage we must have done to our Anchors Cables Sails and Rigging none of which have suffered in our passage round Cape Horn.

Having firmly declared his preference for the Cape Horn route he thought it necessary to explain why he chose to go through the Strait Le Maire when he had been advised to sail to the east of Staten Island. It is strange that at this point in his journal he makes no mention of the problems encountered in getting into the straits as this would be of value to later navigators, but no doubt he wanted to justify his decision to take that particular route.

> *From what I have said it will appear that I am no advocate for the Straits of Magellan, but it may be expected that I should say some thing of Strait le Maire through which we pass'd, and this is the more incumbent on me as it was ye choise and contrary to the advice given by Mr Walter the ingenious author of Lord Anson's Voyage who adviseth all Ships not to go through this strait but to go to the Eastward of Staten land, and likewise to stand to the Southward as far as 61° or 62° South before any endeavour is made to get to the westward; with respect to the passing of Strait le Maire or going round Staten land I look upon of little consequence and either one or the other to be pursue'd according to circumstances...*

January changed into February and on the first of the month the sea was calm again and Cook allowed Joseph Banks to potter around with his shotgun in one of the small boats. Banks, the avid sportsman and collector, shot about twelve birds. By the standards of later centuries the natural historian could be described as an indiscriminate slaughterer of everything that moved – but Banks would be offended, his feelings for all kinds of wildlife were as sympathetic as any man of his times. He occasionally shot to add a new species to his collection but large birds and animals were difficult to preserve and most of his shooting was the traditional hunting sport of the country gentry. Scientists and seamen alike were always prepared to try out new dishes for the captain's table and the lower decks. Banks had spent many weeks watching the albatross following the ship and he began to wonder what sort of dish they would make. He shot one to find out.

The albatross, according to sailors' folklore, was a sacred bird which embodied the spirit of their dead comrades and Joseph

Banks must have known that they held it in great reverence. His journal proves that he had some respect for the seamen's superstitions even if he did not believe the sea-lore himself. It seems a careless action and one which was bound to upset the sailors – they thought the killing of an albatross could bring only bad luck to the ship.

The next day Banks admitted to feeling unwell, but his illness was short-lived and the albatross was duly served up for dinner and eaten with great relish. He even gives us some useful instructions for those wishing to acquire the culinary art of dressing an albatross:

> *All but calm today: myself a little better than yesterday, well enough to eat part of the Albatross shot on the third, which were so good that every body commended and eat heartily of them tho there was fresh pork upon the table. The way of dressing them is thus: Skin them over night and soak their carcasas in Salt water till morn, then parboil them and throw away the water, then stew them well with very little water and when sufficiently tender serve them up with Savoury sauce.*

In this part of the Pacific the prevailing winds and the ocean currents came from the west so that between them these elements connived to make heavy weather of sailing westwards away from the coast of South America and into the ocean. Previous explorers were well aware of the westerlies and they clung to the coastline for safety and for ease of navigation, making their way northwards to the tropics where the ocean currents ran from the east and took them across the Pacific in warmer latitudes. But Cook's orders were to sail north-west from Cape Horn into the ocean in search of the southern continent. In spite of the contrary winds and currents he adhered closely to his instructions and headed for the uncharted waters. The search for the *Terra Australis* had begun at last, and after a few days the *Endeavour* was sailing through waters where no vessel had ever ventured before.

Day followed day as the *Endeavour* held a north-westerly course. She came to a region of ocean with beautiful sunsets and scarlet morning skies, but each morning when the sun lifted the mist there was nothing on the horizon except a vast empty sea. Sometimes a cloud formation fooled the sailors into thinking that there was land ahead but always the fickle cumulus gave itself away by changing shape and colour as they advanced towards it. Day after day the *Endeavour* crept gradually northwards into the boundless ocean which Magellan called the Pacific. As the days became weeks the grey sea and the skies became tinged with an occasional trace of blue but the great unknown continent did not materialise.

It is said that Cook was the first captain to enter the Pacific and to know the precise whereabouts of his ship on the surface of the Earth. The claim is well founded but it must be remembered that much of the credit on this first great voyage should go to Charles Green. It was he who taught Cook and his officers the method of finding the longitude from the observations of the moon. Green was the only man on board whose enthusiasm for taking observations exceeded even that of the captain; he took readings whenever he could, even in the most appalling conditions when the sea was sweeping over the decks.

Finding the longitude at sea was a problem with a long and chequered history. When no coastline was visible the traditional means of finding a ship's position, used by all the early navigators, was the method of dead reckoning. It involved measuring and recording the speed and direction of the ship through the water at regular intervals. After correction for ocean currents, this data together with the bearing from the compass and the stars, enabled the navigator to estimate the distance and direction of the ship from the last known landfall. A skilled and experienced navigator could use the method of dead reckoning to obtain reasonable results on a short voyage but the speed of the ship could be determined only approximately and the drift due to ocean currents was almost impossible to measure – thus the calculated position was subject to accumulative errors of many kinds. The estimated longitudes of remote islands in the Pacific were notoriously unreliable and the only sure way to find them was to trust to the latitude alone and run down a parallel in the hope that the land would be discovered even if the longitude was out by several degrees.

In the seventeenth century, as international trade with America and the Far East expanded, the need for improved methods of navigation became progressively more apparent. Astronomy was the key to navigation and in 1675 the Royal Greenwich Observatory was founded to help solve the problem of finding the longitude at sea. It was well known that the longitude could be calculated at any point on the Earth by comparing the local time as measured by the sun or the stars with the time at a fixed meridian such as Greenwich. One obvious solution was therefore to carry a clock set to Greenwich time which would keep good time on board ship – but the snag was that it had to be so accurate that over the period of many months on a long sea voyage the clock was not allowed to be in error by more than a few seconds. 'By reason of the motion of a Ship, the Variation of Heat and Cold, Wet and Dry, and the Difference of Gravity in different Latitudes,' said Isaac Newton, 'Such a watch hath not yet been made.' Newton did not say it was impossible but that it was beyond the technology of his times. The Board of Longitude offered a prize of £20,000 to anybody who could construct a clock which could meet all the exacting requirements.

There was, however, an alternative method of finding the longitude, a theoretical method which in the seventeenth century seemed a more feasible proposition than making a clock. In the heavens there already existed a clock for all to see, it was the most familiar object in the night sky – the moon. If the motion of the moon could be calculated and predicted from a set of tables then it would be possible for an observer to find the longitude anywhere on Earth from the observed position of the moon against the background of the fixed stars or against the position of the sun. The only requirement was a table of lunar motion. The motion of the moon, as with the planets, was subject to Newton's universal law of gravitation.

Newton himself worked on the problem for many years. He knew that the forces which kept the moon in its orbit did obey his inverse square law, but the whole problem was made very complicated by the fact that the moon was subject to two gravitational forces – one from the Earth and one from the sun and it did not therefore follow the elliptical type of orbit which Kepler had discovered for the motion of the planets around the sun. The crux of the problem was that it needed not only the genius of a mind like Newton's to formulate the mathematics but also careful observations of the moon over a period of many years before the constants of the orbit could be accurately determined.

In the meantime the French, with their own very characteristic and practical approach, proposed yet another method of finding the longitude by using another clock in the sky. The French method was to observe the positions of the moons of Jupiter – the satellites, each with its own orbit around the giant planet, made it possible to find the time at any chosen meridian from any place where Jupiter was visible. The method was quite practical for the Paris Observatory and for good land-based telescopes but it was an impossible task for a navigator tossing on the swell of the ocean to find and identify an object as tiny as a satellite of Jupiter.

In Britain there were advocates for both the practical method of the clock-maker and the theoretical method of the astronomer, and it happened that both methods became possible at almost the same time. John Harrison, a clock-maker from the remote village of Barrow on Humber, took up the challenge of the Board of Longitude and dedicated his whole life to building a chronometer which would keep good time at sea. He built four superb timepieces and his fourth model was so successful that on a test voyage to Jamaica it predicted the ship's position with an error of less than 1 nautical mile. On a second voyage to Barbados in 1764 Charles Green was present as the official astronomer and Harrison's chronometer gave an error of about 10 miles under very stringent conditions. It easily met the conditions stated for the £20,000 prize and the Board of Longitude grudgingly paid Harrison half the prize money. Ten thousand pounds was enough to make the clock-maker into a very wealthy man but he rightly claimed that the whole of the twenty thousand should be his. After a long quibble in which even the king voiced his support for Harrison, the miserly Board of Longitude was forced to pay Harrison, then an old man of eighty, the other half of the prize money. (An exact copy of Harrison's fourth chronometer was made by the London clockmaker Kendall and used by Cook on the second of his voyages to the Pacific.)

When the *Endeavour* sailed from England in 1768 no chronometer was available for use on the voyage but the Astronomer Royal, Nevil Maskelyne, had published his method of lunars in the first edition of the *Nautical Almanac* and the longitude problem had therefore been solved by the theoreticians. The voyage of the *Endeavour* was in a navigational sense unique for it was the very first voyage on which the method of lunar observation was successfully used to establish longitude and this was a great advance over the method of dead reckoning. Yet the new method was itself obsolete by the time the voyage was over – by then Harrison's chronometer had been copied by other craftsmen and the method of lunars had been superseded by the easier and more accurate method of the marine chronometer.

Every new sunrise found the *Endeavour* bark penetrating further into the unknown waters of the Pacific and every dawn the captain knew his precise coordinates on the surface of the globe. Every morning the man on watch at the masthead scanned the horizon for a sign of land. The navigators knew that according to the map they were right in the middle of the hypothetical *Terra Australis Incognita* but still no land had been sighted. Soon it was 1 March and although it was autumn and not spring which was approaching the ship was getting into more temperate zones and Joseph Banks was able to discard his waistcoat. 'I began to hope that we were now so near the peacefull part of the Pacific ocean that we may almost cease to fear any more gales,' he ruminated. The position of the ship showed that there was no current carrying her westwards and Cook knew from experience that the lack of a current implied that there was no land nearby:

> ... *this must be a great sign that we have been near no land of any extent because near land are generally found Currents: it is well known that on the east side of the Continent in the North Sea we meet with Currents above 100 Leagues from land, and even in the Middle of the Atlantic Ocean between Africa and America are always found Currents, and I can see no reason why currents should not be found in this Sea Supposing a Continent or lands lay not far west from us as some have imagine'd, and if such land was ever seen we cannot be far from it, as we are now 560 Leagues West of the Coast of Chili.*

The days grew warmer but no land appeared, the latitude was down to 25 degrees and the longitude 130° west of Greenwich. Joseph Banks makes a few interesting comments on the absence of land and allows himself a well-earned dig at the armchair philosophers reclining safely back at home:

> *I cannot help wondering that we have not yet seen land. It is however of some pleasure to disprove that which does not exist but in the opinion of Theoretical writers, of which sort most are who have wrote anything about these seas without having themselves been in them. They generally supposd that every foot of sea which they believd no ship had passd over to be land, tho they had little or nothing to support that opinion but vague reports, many of them mentiond only as such by the very authors*

who first published them, as for instance the Orange Tree of the Nassau
fleet who being separated from her companions and drove to the westward
reported on her joining them again that she had twice seen the Southern
continent; both which places are laid down by Mr Dalrymple as many
degrees to the eastward of our track, tho it is probable that he has put
them down as far to the westward as he though that she could go.

Banks goes on to decry other interesting theories which the Dalrymple school put forward to support their hypotheses of the
unknown continent. At the same time he displays his own igno-
rance of the solar system by describing a pre-Copernican view of
the Earth in space. Astronomy was not his strongest point:

To strenthen these weak arguments another Theory has been started
which says that it is Necessary that so much of the South Seas the authors
of it call land should be so, otherwise this wor[l]d would not be balnc'd
as the quantity of the Earth situated in the Northern hemisphere would
not have a counterpoise in this. The number of square degrees of their
land which we have already changed into water sufficiently disproves this,
and teaches me at least that till we know how this globe is fixd in that
place which has been since its creation assigned to it in the general system,
we need not be anxious to give reasons how any one part of it counterbal-
ances the rest.

The long voyage was beginning to take its toll on the men: Banks
complained of swollen gums – a sure symptom of the scurvy. The
ship carried a small keg of lemon juice mixed with brandy but
the keg was damaged and some of the juice had leaked out
although the remainder was edible. Banks took about 6 ounces
every day and within a week his gums were back to normal again.
But the sailors had been three months at sea since the landing at
Tierra del Fuego and the monotony and melancholy solitude of
the empty sea around them day after day depressed some men
more than others. One Sunday morning one of the marines was

reported missing. He was William Greenslade, a raw young man of about twenty-one, described as a quiet and industrious fellow. On the previous day he had been on sentry duty at the cabin door where a sailor was cutting pieces of sealskin to make into tobacco pouches. Greenslade asked if he could have one of the pouches for himself but his request was refused. He therefore took the opportunity of stealing part of the sealskin from the very cabin he was supposed to be guarding on his sentry duty. The fact soon came to the ears of his fellow marines and they rightly thought he had committed an inexcusable crime which blackened the honour of their corps. John Edgecumbe, sergeant of the marines, thought the crime sufficiently serious to be brought to the notice of Captain Cook and at about seven in the evening he called for the marine to accompany him to the captain's cabin. Greenslade was seen slipping off to the forecastle, but that was the last time anybody saw him and he never got as far as the captain's cabin. Cook was forced to the conclusion that Greenslade was so depressed that he was unable to face up to the consequences of his crime and he committed suicide by jumping overboard.

The suicide cast a shadow over the whole crew but by this time the ship had reached a latitude of less than 19 degrees; the longitude was estimated at 139° 29′ west of Greenwich and the land could not be far away. It was a Tuesday morning in April and Peter Briscoe, one of Banks's servants, was on the second watch when they heard the cry they had all been waiting for. Briscoe had spotted land! It was only a tiny island, just a speck in the mighty ocean, but it was a sign of greater things to come. An atmosphere of relief and excitement spread through the whole ship. Some of the sailors climbed the rigging to get a better view, those on deck grasped at the rail and shaded their eyes with their spare hand. The officers trained their telescopes on the speck of land as every eye on board strained to see the welcome sight of a tiny island.

The land was several leagues to the south of the planned course but the ship altered direction a little and by noon it was only a mile away. The men at the masthead could make out the island to be no more than a circular rim enclosing a large lagoon. It was less than 2 miles in diameter and was covered with trees and other vegetation. Two tall coconut trees stood out above the smaller trees with their palm fronds streaming like flags in the breeze. There was no suitable anchorage, but in any case Cook did not wish to stop until he reached Tahiti. Most interesting of all was that this tiny island had people on it even though they were not permanent residents, and the islanders ran down the shore to get a better view of the ship. Twenty-four natives were counted, eleven of them walked along the beach abreast of the ship – each native wore a covering over his genitalia and carried a long pole or club in his hand. As the ship sailed by the natives retired to a point higher up the beach and seemed to reappear dressed in white clothing – but Cook thought the clothed natives were the womenfolk who had remained hidden in the trees. The islanders had built a few huts under the shade of a clump of palm trees and they had cleared the ground to make a pleasant opening. 'Pleasanter groves can not be imagined,' said Banks meaningfully. 'At least so they appeared to us whose eyes had so long been unus'd to any other objects than water and sky.' They named the place Lagoon Island.

Soon there appeared another small island; it was round and bushy with vegetation hanging shaggily over its cliff edges. It had neither palms nor inhabitants and Cook named it Thrum Cap from its appearance. There followed another island, similar to Lagoon Island but so small that it was no more than a narrow arc of a circle – it was given the name of Bow Island. Then came two groups – an assemblage of smaller islands joined only by reefs – it was followed by Bird Island which was named after its only inhabitants, followed by another group joined by reefs and named Chain Island.

Soon there appeared Osnaburg Island which was shaped like a high crowned hat, and expectation in the ship mounted because it fitted the description and position given by Samuel Wallis and this meant that King George's Island (the meaningless and short-lived name given to Tahiti) could not be far away. The ship sailed easily in pleasant weather making good progress along the parallel which would bring them to Tahiti.

On 10 April Joseph Banks and several others were at the mast-head straining their eyes to the west for all they were worth. At one o'clock some claimed to be able to see the faint outline of mountains on the horizon. A verbal dispute divided the ship's company as to whether or not they had sighted Tahiti or a cloud formation in the distance. At sunset the skies had clouded over, it grew misty and became impossible to see very far. A shark swam to the stern of the ship and attacked a net which was being towed behind thereby stealing the next day's dinner which was being stored in the water to keep fresh.

The variable winds slowed the ship down, but it soon become obvious that it was indeed the mountains of Tahiti which lay on the horizon. It was only a matter of time before the ship would be safely at anchor again. By the standards of the times it was a magnificent piece of navigation which had brought them here – to sail for nearly three months with no sign of land and to reach their destination in good time was a great achievement. Cook's weather-beaten sailors knew that soon there would be firm dry land to walk upon, fresh food to eat and pure water to replace the stagnant contents of the casks. There would be contact with a brown-skinned and dark-haired people who ranked amongst the friendliest and most generous races on Earth. What thoughts passed through the minds of the men who had fought their way around Cape Horn and had beaten into the wind for more than eighty days across the endless Pacific, men who had not set foot on shore since the icy bay in Tierra del Fuego? On 13 April the *Endeavour* was sailing into the harbour at Matavia Bay, the volcanic peak of Orofena towered high above the ship with its steep flanks clothed in forest and lush green vegetation down to the waterfront. Here was Tahiti, with its bright colours bathed in tropical sunshine. Tahiti, an emerald jewel surrounded by a coral reef set in an azure sea. Tahiti, island of slender wild-crowned coconut palms and bountiful breadfruit trees. High-prowed Tahitian canoes came out to welcome the ship, their occupants chattering excitedly as they offered tropical fruits and island delicacies for barter. Tahiti charms included its lightly clad and clean-limbed maidens waiting onshore to welcome the foreign sailors. Was there a man on board whose blood did not rise and whose pulse did not race at the sight of the Tahitian girls, uninhibited by western prudery and eager to bestow their favours on the men in return for a ship's nail or a string of beads? These were dusky maidens with large smiling eyes, soft lips and fine white teeth and with the scent of the South Pacific in their long dark hair. To the men of the *Endeavour* Tahiti was worth every second of their long hard voyage. It was an Arcadia, the very essence of a South Sea Paradise.

CHAPTER 4

TRANSIT OF VENUS

To 3 June, 1769

T HE HONOUR of being the first European vessel to anchor at Tahiti did not belong to the *Endeavour* but to the *Dolphin* which had anchored in Matavia Bay in the summer of 1767, about two years earlier than Cook. Samuel Wallis was too ill to make the landing himself so he sent his first lieutenant Tobias Furneaux to make the first contact with the islanders. The initial reaction of the Tahitians was hostile, in fact Furneaux was greeted with a shower of stones in an assault which was so determined that the *Dolphin* was forced to use her great guns to deter the attackers.

The startling thunder and fire-power of a broadside was something which the Tahitians had never witnessed before and the guns had the desired effect – the opposition melted away and the islanders were forced to respect the new arrivals. It is greatly to the credit of Wallis and his crew that after this uncompromising start they were able to convince the natives that their intentions were friendly. The warm-hearted Tahitians more than atoned for their initial reaction and their subsequent behaviour was characteristically excitable but civil and friendly. Trade was soon established and Queen Oborea was invited on board the ship, the island pigs were exchanged for beads and other small items, and the women of the island willingly conferred their favours on the crew of the *Dolphin* for the price of a ship's nail. The sailors took so readily to the amorous approaches of the girls that the *Dolphin* was soon in danger of falling apart as ship's nails, the price of love, were illegally extracted from their rightful places in the ship's fabric.

Other nations were close behind the British. A French vessel commanded by the famous explorer Chevalier de Bougainville called at Tahiti the following year and found an anchorage on the east side of the island. The Frenchmen were not slow to gain the attention of the Tahitian maidens and almost as soon as Bougainville's ship dropped anchor a lascivious native girl climbed on to the open hatch and slowly stripped herself of what little clothing she had whilst the men worked the capstan below. Bougainville's capstan sped up to a hitherto unattainable angular velocity. Bougainville, like Cook, was the leader of a scientific expedition and he carried an astronomer and a botanist on board his ship. The botanist was a woman, Jeanne Beret, who had fooled the Frenchmen into thinking that she was a man but who didn't fool the Tahitian women for one moment.

The *Endeavour* was therefore the third European vessel to anchor at Tahiti within the space of two years. Cook and the more humane people of the western world were well aware that the islands and the peoples of the Pacific were open to exploitation and even to slavery by the European nations. This was the age when the African slave trade had reached its height: blacks were transported by force across the Atlantic to work as slaves in the sugar plantations of the West Indies where they were often treated with no more respect than beasts of burden. The more liberally minded whites were already trying to put a stop to this inhumane traffic but the trade was highly profitable and contained many vested interests and it still had many years to go before it was suppressed. With these factors in mind Cook was determined to make it clear from the outset that the people of the island were to be treated with the greatest respect and with all possible humanity, and he resolved to punish any man who did not obey his instructions to the letter.

Cook's insistence on fair treatment of the natives was to some extent merely a reiteration of the views of the more enlightened of his superiors at the Admiralty, but this respect for the customs and property of primitive peoples became his first principle in dealing with newly discovered races and was one of his finest human attributes. He was also an immensely practical man and he knew that the *Endeavour* had to stay in Tahiti for an indeterminate length of time, certainly until well after the transit of Venus took place, and the feeding of over eighty extra mouths for three months was bound to make a sizeable inroad into the island food supplies. Cook thus wanted to make certain that relations with the inhabitants of this Arcadia remained as cordial as possible throughout the whole of the stay. One of his first actions was to issue a set of rules of conduct to be observed by every man on the ship.

RULES *to be observe'd by every person in or belonging to His Majesty's Bark the Endeavour, for the better establishing a regular and uniform Trade for Provisions &c with the Inhabitants of George's Island.*

1ST *To endeavour by every fair means to cultivate a friendship with the Natives and to treat them with all imaginable humanity.*

2D *A proper person or persons will be appointed to trade with the Natives for all manner of Provisions, Fruit, and other productions of the earth; and no officer or Seaman, or other person belonging to the Ship, excepting such as are so appointed, shall trade or offer to Trade for any sort of Provisions, Fruit, or other productions of the earth unless they have my leave so to do.*

3D *Every person employ'd a Shore on any duty what soever is strictly to attend to the same, and if by neglect he looseth any of his Arms or working tools, or suffers them to be stole, the full value thereof will be charged against his pay according to the Custom of the Navy in such cases, and he shall recive such father punishment as the nature of the offence may deserve.*

4TH   *The same penalty will be inflicted on every person who is found to imbezzle, trade or offer to trade with any part of the Ships Stores of what nature soever.*

5TH   *No Sort of Iron, or anything that is made of Iron, or any sort of Cloth or other usefull or necessary articles are to be given in exchange for any thing but provisions.*

J. C.

Before the *Endeavour* had dropped anchor she was surrounded by the distinctive Tahitian canoes. Some of these were vessels 60 or 70 feet in length with a double hull spanned by a cabin, with decorated high prows and fitted with sails and outriggers. The occupants traded their breadfruit, coconuts, fish and apples in exchange for beads and pieces of cloth. One Tahitian offered a pig for sale – he wanted a hatchet in exchange but Cook declined on the grounds that hatchets were few and if the bargain was sealed he would never again get a pig for less than the cost of the first sale.

The ship's boats were lowered and manned. Soon a landing party set foot ashore. Hundreds of islanders crowded around to see the hairy faced, fair-skinned and strangely attired arrivals from the unknown and incomprehensible world beyond their horizon. One of the first natives to greet them came creeping 'almost on his hands and knees' and offered a green bough or palm frond as a token of peace. The new arrivals each plucked a frond of their own to carry with them as a symbol that they came in peace to the island. The party arrived at an open space where one of the leaders threw his green bough to the ground and made signs for the others to do the same. Tahitians and British followed his example and the pile of boughs sealed and agreed the peace between them.

The newcomers walked several miles on their first outing at Tahiti, enjoying the feel of *terra firma* beneath their feet after many months at sea. They were followed everywhere by a train of excited chattering natives. They passed through groves of coconut and breadfruit trees each laden with its own fruit; the ship had arrived at the harvest season and there seemed to be an excellent crop of ripe fruit ready to be gathered in. The laden trees created quite an impression on the landing party. 'The scene we saw was the truest picture of an Arcadia that the imagination can form,' remarked Joseph Banks. He was very taken with the beauty of the island and the friendly innocence of its people.

But the old hands from the *Dolphin* were not so happy – it was not easy to put their finger on the problem but they knew that something was wrong and that things had changed since their previous visit to the island. They could find none of their old acquaintances and they looked in vain for Oborea (Oborea is often referred to as Queen Purea. The British had great problems with Tahitian names. The islanders had no form of writing and pronounced names had to be written as the journalists thought best), the queen of the island who had treated the crew of the *Dolphin* with such fine hospitality. They searched for the queen's house and the homes of the leading dignitaries and discovered that the houses they remembered were deserted. In two years they had been reduced from their former glory to ruin and decay. At one place where a house used to stand was a great carved pillar of native craftsmanship. The carvings showed four or five men standing on each other's shoulders – it lay discarded on the ground:

> *Hogs and Fowls about the Houses ... found a few temporary Huttes with a few of the inferior sorts of the inhabitants who seem'd to be looking after their master's property. In several places [where] there had been fine houses we found a field of the Cloth Plant, in others nothing but grass and some Pillars of the Houses remaining.*

Robert Molyneux searched in vain amongst the Tahitians to find old friends from his visit in the *Dolphin*. 'I look'd out diligently for some of my old Accquainteaince,' he complained. 'But could not find more than 3 that I could recollect with certainty – one of which was an Elderly man [called Owhaa] with his Son whom we had dress'd & christn'd jack. The other was a young Women about 19. With these three I was very Happy, but still I could hear no news of the Queen.' Molyneux particularly wanted to see Queen Oborea again, but none of the islanders seemed willing to help him find her. Pickersgill and Gore were also puzzled and disappointed with the findings of their second visit to Tahiti: the pigs which had been so abundant were now hardly anywhere to be seen. It became apparent that there had been a revolution of some kind since they had left two years ago and Queen Oborea had been deposed. If she was still alive she was living somewhere in exile. One problem which the revolution had created was that nobody seemed quite sure who had replaced Queen Oberea as the new leader of the people. It presented Cook and his officers with something of a dilemma for they did not know who had what authority and with whom they should be negotiating.

A few days after the arrival at Tahiti, Alexander Buchan, the landscape artist, suffered another epileptic fit. This time the attack was so bad that he did not recover and in the early hours of 17 April he died on board ship. Buchan was part of Joseph Banks's suite and was employed to draw the people and landscapes with which Banks planned to impress his friends in London:

> I sincerely regret him as an ingenious and good young man, but his Loss to me is irretrievable, my airy dreams of entertaining my friends in England with the scenes that I am to see here are vanishd. No account of the figures and dresses of men can be satisfactory unless illustrated with figures: had providence spared him a month longer what an advantage would it have been to my undertaking …

Banks understated the problem, the loss of Alexander Buchan was a loss to posterity and although Banks could not have been aware of it, even another month would not have given the artist time to record more than another fraction of the voyage.

'Mr Banks thought it not so adviseable to Enterr the Body a shore in a place where we was utter strangers to the Customs of the Natives on such Occasions,' wrote Cook. 'It was therefore set out to Sea and commited to that Element with all the decency the circumstance of the place would admit of.' The death of Buchan put a heavy load on the shoulders of Sydney Parkinson, who was employed principally as a draughtsman to draw animals and botanical specimens, but Parkinson rose to the challenge and his landscape sketches were full of detail and interest. The presence of the artists on board was entirely due to the Banks retinue but it prompted many of the officers to try their hand at sketching and even the captain himself tried a few sketches when he had time. A wide variety of paintings eventually found their way back to England. The majority of the sailors' drawings would have been more at home on the schoolroom wall than at the Royal Academy but they still have value as a record of real events of the voyage.

A serious problem arose when it was discovered that Tahitian ideas of property and ownership were quite different from western ones. Put bluntly the Tahitians were skilful and determined thieves intent on carrying off anything of value which they could lay their hands on – they even went to the lengths of stealing the glass from the ship's portholes and the top of the lightning chain. 'I have so long omitted to mention how much these people are given to thieving,' wrote Banks after a few days on the island.

I will make up for my neglect however today by saying that great and small chiefs and common men are firmly of opinion that if they can once get possession of an thing it immediately becomes their own. This we were convinced of the very second day we were here, the chiefs employd in stealing what they could in the cabbin while their dependents took every thing that was loose about the ship, even the glass ports not escaping them of which they got off with 2.

The captain's sentiments were in complete agreement. 'It was a hard matter to keep them out of the Ship as they clime like munkeys,' claimed Cook. 'But it was still harder to keep them from Stealing but everything that came within their reach, in this they are prodiges expert.'

Tahiti was a Stone Age society in which metal and glass were unknown, so the natives were fascinated by any item with a degree of craftsmanship in it. Sydney Parkinson discovered that an earthen vessel had been pilfered from his cabin, the surgeon lost a snuffbox picked from his pocket and even the meticulously careful Dr Solander had his spyglass stolen. These thefts came to light as Joseph Banks was being entertained at the house of one of the local chiefs and when he was busy making advances to a beautiful young native girl. When he was told about the thefts he struck his gun on the ground with such a show of anger that the girl and practically all the other natives ran from the house like a flock of sheep. The chief's wife, however, described by Banks as 'ugly enough in all conscience', was one of the few who did not take flight and she took advantage of her rival's absence to make her own advances to the unwilling Englishman.

The local chieftain, whom the classically educated Banks called Lycurgus because of the even-handed justice which he executed on his offending subjects, kindly offered his guests Tahitian cloth or any other object in his house in exchange for the stolen property. Lycurgus was described as 'a middle-aged man of a cheerful, though sedate countenance, with thick frizzled hair and a beard of some kind. His behaviour and aspect had something of natural majesty in them.' When the offerings were firmly refused Lycurgus followed after the offenders in an effort to retrieve their property. After about half an hour he returned with an empty snuff box and a case which should have contained the spyglass but which also turned out to be empty. He then made further enquiries and took his guests about a mile along the coast where they came to the house of a native woman. He offered her cloth and beads, both of which she refused to accept, but greatly to the relief of everybody concerned she produced the stolen spyglass and gladly returned it to the rightful owner. The incident ended very amicably when Dr Solander had a present of cloth forced upon him as compensation for his trouble. The Tahitian lady was likewise presented with the beads which she had politely refused.

Not all the disputes ended with such good humour. The next day a great rumpus broke out when one of the natives struck down a marine on sentry duty, picked up his musket, and ran off with it. In the heat of the moment, as the native was running off with his prize, the youthful Jonathan Monkhouse ordered the other marines to open fire and the thief was killed. Sydney Parkinson, who had heard the shots rattle in the branches above him, was very upset by the conduct of the marines:

A boy, a midshipman, was the commanding officer, and, giving orders to fire, they obeyed with the greatest glee imaginable, as if they had been shooting at wild ducks, killed one stout man, and wounded many others. What a pity that such brutality should be exercised by civilised people upon unarmed ignorant Indians

Other natives who had crowded round to watch were immediately dispersed by the shooting and news soon spread around the island. The result was that the Tahitians refused to come near the ship to trade.

Joseph Banks was also very dismayed by the incident. In spite of the petty thieving he knew that the natives were basically an innocent and friendly race. 'If we quarrelled with those Indians, we should not agree with angels' was his comment. But Cook was not displeased with Jonathan Monkhouse: he saw him as one of his most trusted officers and he knew that something had to be done to curb the thieving and to prevent the natives from getting their hands on the firearms.

For a time old Owhaa, Molyneux's friend from the *Dolphin*, was the only native to remain on speaking terms. It was he who persuaded a party of about twenty natives to come back and parley with Cook and to explain to them the reason why the man had been killed. The talks lasted all afternoon until sunset, but at the end of the day the natives seemed satisfied and willing to reopen trade. It was probably as a result of the incident that a few days later Owhaa, who remembered the hostilities when the *Dolphin* first arrived at Tahiti, arrived excitedly to tell Cook he must fire the ship's great guns in four days' time. The reason for the request was apparently so that the old man could fulfil a prophesy which he had made to his people – Cook had no intention whatsoever of humouring him in so far-reaching a matter.

Within a few days of arrival Cook and Green had set about trying to establish the longitude of Tahiti by observing the moons of Jupiter. Their first attempt was thwarted by cloud cover but they managed to obtain good readings when the skies were clear again. When the longitude was established another more important priority was to make the necessary preparations to observe the Transit of Venus. A suitable spot at the northernmost end of Matavia Bay was chosen for the observatory.

The chances of the natives turning against the ship were small, but Cook did not trust their light fingers. He was determined that the observing site must be well fortified for otherwise valuable equipment would surely be stolen and the measurements of the transit would be hindered by crowds of excitable Tahitians. He was careful to obtain permission from the right person to use the part of the bay to build his fort and he also asked consent to fell trees in the area and to build a stockade around the observatory. The natives, not realising that they themselves were the reason for the stockade, happily helped with the preparations. High breastworks were built at each end of the fort and the palisades at the front and the rear were guarded by a river and a line of water casks. Zachary Hicks described the inside arrangement:

Our Works was finished the two Ends having a Wall of Turf and Mudd the Front Pallasaded the back a line of Water Cask; two four Pounders pointed to the Country & 6 Swivel to flank the Walls. In the front of West side Mr Banks's Bell Tent & two Markies No[rth] end the Observatory, NW Corner Armourers Forge, Oven & Cook Room the So[uth] end a Tent for the Ships Company, East Side a Tent for Capt Observer and Officers, without the Works a Tent for the Cooper and Sailmaker to Work in ...

Cook himself made a sketch of Fort Venus showing the high spiked palisade guarding several ridge tents inside and the bell tent with a union flag flying from the top of its high pole. The swivel guns were installed at each corner of the fort and the two heavy carriage guns from the ship were trained on the woods to cover the unlikely event of an attack by the natives from that quarter.

During the construction of the fort the Tahitians came to trade and visit from all parts of the island. Joseph Banks was entertaining some women visitors in his tent when Robert Molyneux entered. The ship's master fixed his eyes on one of the women and declared that she was Oborea, the queen of the island whom he had known from his first visit two years ago and whom he had been seeking ever since his arrival. Oborea and her attendants recognised him and greetings were exchanged all round. Molyneux was delighted and the crew of the *Endeavour* took a lot of interest in the deposed queen of the island. 'She appeard to be about forty,' said Banks. 'Tall and very lusty. Her skin white and her eyes full of meaning, she might have been handsome when she was young but now few or no traces of it were left.' Cook also estimated her age at forty but he was more grudging in his praise and described her as very masculine – this was, however, a description which he wrongly applied to all the women of Tahiti. Sydney Parkinson was generous, describing her as fat but a 'bouncing good-looking dame'. Oborea may have been past her prime and she was no longer queen of the island but she was still full of life and spirit, she had a lusty native lover aged about twenty-five who shared her bed, and her age did not prevent her from making passes at the Englishmen. In addition to her male gallant and her female attendants she was accompanied by an intelligent young man called Tupia who claimed to be a priest in exile from the island of Raiatea some distance towards the setting sun. The English were destined to see much of Tupia. He was a man with a great deal of local knowledge and quicker than any other to pick up a strange language and communicate with the English.

On 28 May Cook decided to visit a chieftain called Tootaha who lived near the coast about 8 miles east of Matavia Bay. The main reason for the visit was the promise of a supply of island hogs with which to feed the crew. He wanted to take the longboat for the expedition but he found that the keel was eaten away by the Teredo worm and the pinnace had to be used instead. It was not possible to get all the way by boat, and the party was obliged to cover the second half of the journey on foot. Night had fallen by the time they arrived and Tootaha offered them a pig by way of hospitality. Cook felt the slaughter of a whole pig on their behalf was a great waste and he diplomatically negotiated to purchase the pig and take it back to the ship with him.

It became obvious that it would be necessary to stay the night with Tootaha and there arose the problem of where to sleep. Joseph Banks was offered a place to sleep in Oborea's canoe and this included the company of the lady herself. He diplomatically declined on the grounds that the canoe was too small – Oborea could no longer command the royal double-hulled canoes with a cabin built across them. James Cook was less fortunate, his guests chose to entertain him with a little music and the captain did not wish to offend his hosts. 'Tootaha came to the Hutt where I and those with me lay and entertain'd us with a consort of Musik consisting of three Drums four Flutes and singing.' It was no music of the spheres and to the uninitiated it sounded like a monotonous repetition of about four notes. He added he was very glad when it was over.

The next morning the inevitable had happened. Banks discovered that his best white waistcoat and his jacket with the silver frogs on the shoulders was missing. Joseph Banks intended to cut a fashionable figure even at this distance from London society, but the Tahitians also coveted handsome white jackets and gleaming silver frogs. Pistols and other clothing were also missing, the midshipmen had their jackets stolen, and as usual there was a great fuss and commotion to get them back again.

On the return journey, near the point where the pinnace had been moored, there was a high surf breaking offshore. To every seaman breaking water was a hazard to be avoided and it never occurred to them that it was something which could be enjoyed. Banks was fascinated by the sight of natives riding their canoes in the surf:

It was in a place where the shore was not guarded by a reef as is usualy the case, consequently a high surf fell upon the shore, a more dreadfull one I have not often seen: no European boat could have landed in it and I think no European who had by any means got into [the surf] could possibly have saved his life, as the shore was covered with pebbles and large stones. In the midst of these breakers 10 or 12 Indians were swimming who when ever a surf broke near them divd under it with infinite ease, rising up on the other side; but their chief amusement was carried on by the stern of an old canoe, with this before they swam out as far as the outermost breach, then one or two would get into it an opposing the blunt end to the breaking wave were hurried in with incredible swiftness. Sometime they were carried almost ashore but generally the wave broke over them before they were half way, in which case the[y] divd and rose on the other side with the canoe in their hands, which was towed out again and by the same method repeated. We stood admiring this very wonderful scene for a full half hour, in which time no one of the actors attempted to come ashore but all seemed most highly entertaind with their strange diversion.

Thanks to the generous assistance of the native labour force Fort Venus was soon finished, the telescopes were safely installed in Joseph Banks's tent, and other equipment was kept in the captain's own quarters. With the marines guarding the entrances to the fort, Cook felt confident that all the valuable astronomical equipment would be safe inside. He was wrong. Everybody underestimated the cunning of the natives, and no sooner had the observatory been set up and the instruments taken ashore than the large box in Cook's tent which was supposed to contain the astronomical quadrant was found to be empty!

Nobody could work out how the natives even knew about the existence of the quadrant, still less how they had managed to enter the fort from under the noses of the sentries only 5 yards from the tent and get clean away with it. The only possible explanation seemed that the thief had seen the box carried ashore on the previous day, and must have waited until sunset when Cook left his tent for a few minutes which happened to coincide with the sentry walking round the works beating a tattoo on his drum as a signal to call everybody into the fort. The thief had entered the tent for a brief few seconds when the drummer's back was turned and managed to take the quadrant from the box and escape with it unseen. Cook was now very angry: if the quadrant was not found then they might just as well have stayed home in England for all the value of the observation. He immediately sealed off the bay so that nobody could escape by sea. He made enquiries of the local people and seized some of the protesting chiefs to hold as hostages until the quadrant was returned. The thunder in Cook's face was very evident and the Tahitians knew that it would be the worse for them if the quadrant was not found.

In the event it was Banks and Green who saved the day. They had both made some excellent and trusted contacts amongst the natives and Banks went straight to his friend Tubourai for information. The Tahitian chieftain knew exactly who the cunning thief was and co-operated by going from house to house shouting out his name. The occupants came out to help and pointed readily to the direction in which he had fled. Banks, Green, Tubourai and one of the midshipmen set off in hot pursuit. There followed a long hot chase in temperatures of over 90 degrees for several miles across Tahiti until Tubourai brought them to the spot where they thought the thief was hiding. The excitement of the chase attracted many of the islanders and so many milled around that Banks was nervous about a confrontation. The only arms he had with him were two small pocket pistols and he therefore took the precaution of sending the midshipman back to the ship to summon reinforcements.

A little further on one of Tubourai's people appeared carrying a part of the stolen quadrant in his hand. This was a welcome sight which proved that they were on the right trail but it did little to improve matters for it showed that the thieves had taken the instrument apart and instead of looking for one item they now had several pieces to find. If the quadrant had been taken to pieces then it also increased the likelihood of damage. Soon Banks and Green were surrounded by hundreds of chattering Tahitians – so many that they could easily overpower the Englishman. Banks nervously took out his pair of pistols to show them that he had firepower.

There was no need to be alarmed. The Tahitians knew all about the devastating effects of firepower and at the sight of the pistols the natives behaved 'with all the order imaginable'. Soon a stolen box was produced, followed by a pistol case which did not contain a pistol but had a reading glass inside! On further inquiry the horse pistol belonging to the case was produced and the co-operative natives then humbly returned all the stolen property including at last the missing parts of the quadrant.

Charles Green looked over the instrument very carefully to see if any part had been damaged. He discovered that it had suffered only minor damage from its adventures and the pieces were care-fully packed into their box and padded with grass to cushion them for the return journey. The heat of the day was over, it was almost sunset and the two men knew that they had been fortunate to retrieve everything before nightfall. They headed back to Fort Venus and soon met with Cook and a strongly armed party of marines on their way to assist them. 'All were, you may imagine, not a little pleased at the event of our excursion,' said Banks with a gift for the understatement.

A few days later another theft occurred at Fort Venus which showed again the cunning of some of the thieves and the lengths to which they were prepared to go. Cook described the incident in his journal:

> *Between 2 and 4 o'clock this morning one of the natives Stole out of the Fort an Iron rake made use of for the Oven, it happend to be sent up against the wall and by that means was Visible from the outside and had been seen by some of them in the evening as a Man had been seen lurking about the Fort for some hours before the thing was miss'd. I was informed by some others of the Natives that he watched an oppertunity when the Centinal back was turn'd and hooked it with a long crooked stick and ha[u]led it over the wall*

An iron rake was hardly the same value as the quadrant, but it was the last straw and by this time Cook's patience was at an end. He had been sorely tried by all the previous incidents and he was now determined to teach the natives a lesson which would stop the pilfering once and for all. He seized all the canoes he could lay his hands on and refused to return any of them to their owners unless he got back the stolen rake. Within a day the rake was returned but for once Cook was not satisfied. He was normally a patient and considerate man but on this occasion he still held on to the canoes and he insisted that all the other stolen property should be returned — a musket, a pair of pistols and a sword were still missing. Joseph Banks pointed out that the canoes did not belong to the thieves and that Cook's action was not even-handed justice.

Perhaps Cook's judgement for once was unsound for the result of his action was that the Tahitians refused to trade again with the *Endeavour*.

Fortunately for the expedition there was a set of watchmaker's tools on board ship which enabled Herman Spöring, who had experience as a watchmaker, to repair the damaged quadrant. The final preparations were made for the transit of Venus and as the day drew near it was agreed that the third lieutenant John Gore should take the longboat to Moorea, an island which the English called York Island, some distance to the west but easily visible from Fort Venus. Gore was accompanied by Banks, Spöring, the Monkhouse brothers and two Tahitians. They rowed all through the night and at daybreak discovered a rocky island with a long band of white sand in the middle, large enough to set up the tent for the observatory. (Beaglehole identifies the rocky island as Irioa, almost at the north-west point of Moorea.) The next day the second lieutenant, Zachary Hicks, was despatched in the pinnace to find a suitable island to the east. He was accompanied by Charles Clerk, Richard Pickersgill and Patrick Saunders. They discovered a small but suitable island for the observation and called it Lord Moreton's Island – the native name was 'Taaupiri'. It lay in the bay where the Frenchman Bougainville had landed in the previous summer, and Hicks discovered evidence of the landing. The crew of the *Endeavour*, who knew about Bougainville only from the Tahitians, wrongly identified the ship as Spanish. The error was largely the fault of Tubourai who chose the Spanish ensign from a book of flags, claiming that it was the ensign carried by the visitors.

These minor expeditions were precautions designed to minimise the chances of obtaining a nil result from the observation if the weather proved to be cloudy and unfavourable. Both parties were supplied with suitable instruments to observe the transit but their telescopes and timing mechanisms were not as accurate as the main instruments sited at Fort Venus. The transit was to take place on 3 June. The sense of anticipation rose as the day of this very rare astronomic conjunction came nearer.

The reason for observing the transit of Venus went beyond the bounds of the Earth and into the realms of the Solar System. The astronomers of the ancient world knew that the radius of the Earth could be estimated from accurate measurements of the distance between two points at different latitudes on the surface. Eratosthenes of Alexandria had measured the Earth's circumference very accurately in the third century BC. The distance from Earth to Sun, a unit which determined the dimensions of the Solar System was known as the astronomical unit. It was a far more difficult dimension to measure but if the dimensions of the Earth were accurately known then the astronomical unit could be calculated provided that a fixed point in space could be seen by two distant observers and used for the triangulation. The planet Venus was exactly the reference point which the astronomers needed. Once the dimensions of the Earth's orbit were known then the distances of the fixed stars could be calculated by using the Earth's orbit as a baseline. Attempts were already being made at Greenwich to measure the parallax of the nearest stars but to find their distances from Earth the length of the astronomical unit had to be known; the transit of Venus was thus the key to the very dimensions of the universe.

The first person to see the planet Venus on the face of the Sun was a young Englishman, Jeremiah Horrox, who made the observation from the south bank of the Ribble estuary in Lancashire. Horrox was the first person in England to make use of Kepler's laws of planetary motion and it was thus that he was able to predict an event which did not happen again for 122 years. The year was 1639, before the birth of Newton and long before the Royal Society and the founding of the Royal Greenwich Observatory. Horrox actually used his observation to calculate the distance of the Sun and he arrived at a very accurate figure for the times – but his work was based on an incorrect and long-forgotten theory that the size of each planet is proportional to its distance from the Sun. Horrox's premature death at the age of twenty-one, and the outbreak of the English Civil War, caused his works to be neglected by the scientific community but to the connoisseur he is the father of English Astronomy.

Many years after the death of Horrox, in a paper to the Royal Society, Edmund Halley proposed a method of measuring the solar parallax from the transit of Venus, a measure that was directly related to the distance of the Sun from Earth. The solar parallax was the angle by which the Sun moved against the fixed stars, as seen by an observer carried round by the rotation of the Earth. It was a very small angle and very difficult to measure, not least because the stars were never visible at the same time as the Sun. Halley's method was based on the fact that Venus is a point between the Earth and the Sun. If the transit was viewed from places on Earth at widely different latitudes then the observers would see slightly different results. From the different times taken for the two transits it was possible to work out by triangulation the distances between Earth, Venus and the Sun. It is ironic that Halley is remembered for the comet which bears his name and that he knew he could not live long enough to see the return of the comet which he successfully predicted. We now discover another of Halley's ideas which again he could not live long enough to observe, the measurement of the astronomical unit. This then was the reason why the *Endeavour* had made the long journey to Tahiti for an astronomical observation from the Southern Hemisphere which could be used in conjunction with observations from Europe. It was the precise timing of the transit, from the moment that the dark spot of Venus appeared on the face of the Sun, to the moment it left the Sun, which had to be measured as accurately as possible.

In a paper to the Royal Society James Cook described the preparations made for the observation:

The astronomical clock, made by Shelton and furnished with a gridiron pendulum, was set up in the middle of one end of a large tent, in a frame of wood made for the purpose at Greenwich, fixed firm and as low in the ground as the door of the clock-case would admit, and to prevent its being disturbed by any accident, another framing of wood was made around this, at the distance of one foot from it. The pendulum was adjusted exactly the same length as it had been at Greenwich. Without the end of the tent facing the clock, and 12 feet from it, stood the observatory, in which were set up the journeyman clock and astronomical quadrant: this last made by Mr Bird, of one foot radius, stood upon the head of a large cask fixed firm in the ground, and well filled with heavy wet sand. A centinel was placed continually over the tent and the observatory, with orders to suffer no one to enter either the one or the other, but those whose business it was. The telescope made use of in the observations were — Two reflecting ones of two feet focus each, made by the late Mr James Short, one of which was furnished with an object glass micrometer.

'The day of the Observation now approaches,' wrote Banks on 31 May from Moorea. 'The weather has been for some days fine, tho in general since we have been upon the Island we have had as much cloudy as clear weather, which makes us all not a little anxious for success.'

Two days later Molyneux described the scene at Fort Venus: '… the Captain and Mr Green is entirely employ'd getting every thing compleatly ready. I was order'd to prepare for observations & had a Telescope ready accordingly, every thing made quiet and all Hands anxious for Tomorrow.'

The long-awaited day dawned at last. The weather was perfect. 'This day prov'd as favourable to our purpose as we could wish, not a Clowd was to be seen the whole day and the Air was perfectly clear, so that we had every advantage we could desire in Observing the whole of the passage of the Planet Venus over the Suns disk.' The Tahitians were kept at a safe distance, the day was the hottest so far with the thermometer climbing to a swel-

tering 119°. On York Island the weather had been misty throughout the night but the sun rose bright and clear. Joseph Banks,
whose science was more of the microscope than the telescope, left
the observing to the naval officers and made for the neighbouring
island of Moorea where he hoped to do a little botanising and bar-
gaining for provisions.

For the vast majority of people 3 June 1769 was an ordinary day
and they were totally unaware of anything unusual about the sun
– but for the astronomers all over the globe it was a day which
happens only once or twice in a whole century. On this occasion it
was not the astronomers' normal night-time vigil, but an observation in broad daylight of the sun itself. It was not the common
solar eclipse, it was a less spectacular but a much rarer event, one
which the vast majority of humankind would never notice but
one which the astronomers at Tahiti had travelled halfway around
the world to observe. All over the Earth telescopes were aligned
in the direction of the Sun and the bright circular image was projected on to a screen for observation. The planets continued in
scrupulous obedience to the laws of Kepler and Newton, but time
seemed to slow down and stand still as the observers waited to see
the Sun's second and third planets align themselves. They held
their breath and watched for the first contact of a small, dark, circular object on the face of the Sun.

....

CHAPTER 5

SOUTH SEA PARADISE

To 14 July, 1769

THE 1769 EVENT was the third observation of the transit of Venus. The first observation, as we have seen, was long ago in 1639 but the second was only a few years previously in 1762, when the transit was observed from Capetown, St Helena, and from many places in Europe. In St Helena the Astronomer Royal was thwarted by cloud cover and there seem to be very few reliable observations from that time – in the light of subsequent events this was unfortunate for it should have been possible to warn the 1769 expedition of some of the problems to be encountered.

The astronomers knew that something was wrong at the very moment the silhouette of Venus first touched the disc of the Sun. They could not agree on the time of first contact, neither could they agree on the time when contact with the edge of the solar disc was broken (i.e. the planet fully entered on the Sun's disc):

> … we very distinctly saw an Atmosphere or dusky shade round the body of the Planet which very much disturbed the times of the Contacts particularly the two internal ones. Dr Solander observed as well as Mr Green and my self, and we diffr'd from one another in observeing the times of the Contacts much more than can be expected. Mr Greens telescope and mine were of the same magnifying power but that of the Dr was greater than ours. It was nearly calm the whole day and the Thermometer expos'd to

Captain James Cook. Oil on canvas
by George Nathaniel Dance ©
National Maritime Museum, London
2003

Captain Hugh Palliser. Oil on canvas
by George Nathaniel Dance ©
National Maritime Museum, London
2003

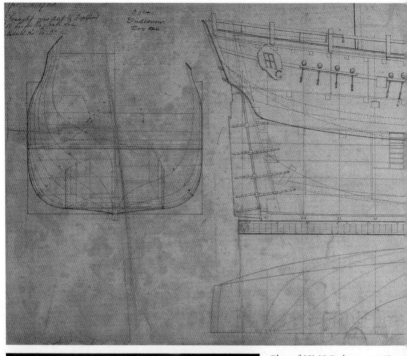

Plan of HMS *Endeavour* 1768
© National Maritime
Museum, London 2003

Sir Joseph Banks. Oil on
canvas by Sir Joshua
Reynolds © Bridgeman
Picture Library 2003

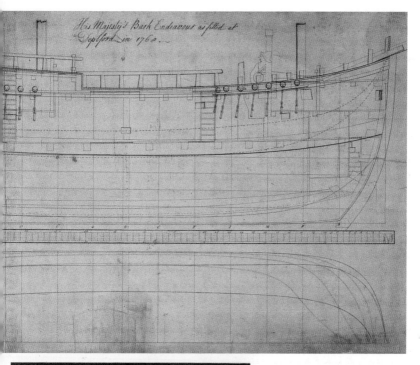

His Majesty's Bark Endeavour as fitted at
Deptford in 1760.—

Daniel Carl Solander, Swedish
botanist. Oil on canvas by Johann
Zoffany © Bridgeman Picture
Library, Linnean Society, London
2003

Sydney Parkinson. An engraving by James Newton © National Library of Australia 2003

View of the Town of Rio de Janeiro from the Anchoring Place (November to December 1768). Drawing by Alexander Buchan © British Library Picture Library 2003. The letter key shows (c) Fort St Sebastian; (d) Careening Place; (e) The way the boats went into the town; (f) The guard boat; (g) The Old Ambuscade; (h) Benedictine Convent

A VIEW of the Town of RIO JANEIRO from the Anchoring-Place.

Inhabitants of the island of Tierra del Fuego (January 1769). A field drawing by Alexander Buchan © British Library 2003

A view of the *Endeavour*'s Watering Place in the Bay of Good Success (1769). Gouache by Alexander Buchan © British Library 2003

'A Point of land we saw in lat. 56 or near & which we took for Cape Horne' (January 1769). Pencil and wash drawing by Sydney Parkinson © British Library 2003

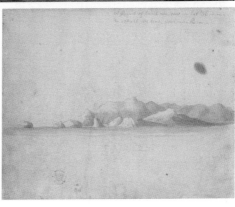

APRIL 1767.

Diſtances of ☽'s Center from ⊙, and from Stars weſt of her

Days.	Stars Names.	12 Hours.			15 Hours.			18 Hours.			21 Hours.		
		°	′	″	°	′	″	°	′	″	°	′	″
1	The Sun.	40.	59.	11	42.	34.	44	44.	9.	51	45.	44.	35
2		53.	32.	7	55.	4.	24	56.	36.	16	58.	7.	45
3		65.	39.	18	67.	8.	27	68.	37.	14	70.	5.	39
4		77.	22.	36	78.	48.	58	80.	15.	1	81.	40.	46
5		88.	45.	20	90.	9.	27	91.	33.	21	92.	57.	0
6		99.	52.	6	101.	14.	34	102.	36.	52	103.	59.	1
7		110.	47.	42	112.	9.	6	113.	30.	25	114.	51.	40
6	Aldebaran	50.	36.	10	52.	4.	5	53.	31.	57	54.	59.	44
7		62.	17.	43	63.	45.	10	65.	12.	34	66.	39.	57
8	Pollux.	31.	25.	48	32.	53.	11	34.	20.	40	35.	48.	12
9		43.	7.	5	44.	35.	4	46.	3.	8	47.	31.	15
10	Regulus.	17.	51.	57	19.	20.	36	20.	49.	26	22.	18.	27
11		29.	45.	36	31.	15.	26	32.	45.	26	34.	15.	35
12		41.	48.	49	43.	19.	55	44.	51.	10	46.	22.	36
13		54.	2.	11	55.	34.	36	57.	7.	12	58.	39.	59
14		66.	26.	28	68.	0.	18	69.	34.	20	71.	8.	33
15	Spica ♍	25.	4.	34	26.	39.	23	28.	14.	26	29.	49.	44
16		37.	49.	37	39.	26.	14	41.	3.	5	42.	40.	8
17		50.	48.	40	52.	26.	59	54.	5.	31	55.	44.	15
18		64.	1.	2	65.	41.	3	67.	21.	18	69.	1.	48
19	Antares.	31.	37.	14	33.	19.	7	35.	1.	13	36.	43.	32
20		45.	18.	29	47.	2.	10	48.	46.	5	50.	30.	12
21		59.	14.	6	60.	59.	31	62.	45.	11	64.	31.	2
22		73.	23.	37	75.	10.	43	76.	58.	2	78.	45.	31
23	δ Capri-corni.	33.	17.	26	35.	4.	38	36.	52.	4	38.	39.	45
24		47.	41.	9	49.	29.	53	51.	18.	44	53.	7.	40
25	α Aquilæ.	65.	57.	35	67.	29.	54	69.	2.	36	70.	35.	39
26		78.	24.	51	79.	59.	9	81.	33.	29	83.	7.	45

The Tree on One Tree Hill (Matavia Bay). An engraving after Barralet copied from pen and wash by Sydney Parkinson © National Library of Australia 2003

Musicians of Tahiti (June 1976). Pencil, wash and watercolour thought to have been done by Joseph Banks © British Library 2003

Telescope from Cook's expedition intended for observing the transit of Venus © National Maritime Museum, London 2003

Vessels of the Island of Otaha (August 1769). Wash by Sydney Parkinson © British Library 2003

the Sun about the middle of the day rose to a degree of heat (119) we have not before met with.

Others were more optimistic. 'If the Observation is not well made it is intirely owing to the Observers,' said Pickersgill. The final analysis of the results still lay in the future but Cook and Green already knew that their disagreement over the exact timings made the results very suspect and incapable of giving the accurate figure for the solar parallax which the astronomers so much wanted and for which they had waited so long. They had been given to expect that Venus would appear as a sharp and perfectly circular disc – but a 'dusky shade' or blurred edge around the planet was a feature for which they were not prepared. The telescope used by Jeremiah Horrox in 1639 was too primitive to show the effect but observers of the transit of 1762 should certainly have seen and recorded it.

Astronomically speaking the observation still had some value. The discovery of an atmosphere around Venus, if such was the cause of the blurred image, was still a new and interesting piece of scientific knowledge, but this information could easily have been discovered by staying at home rather than sailing halfway round the world to see it. The perfectionist James Cook felt that his first commission had been a disaster. Firstly he had failed to discover the great southern continent or any other land mass in the Pacific and now this, the second object of the voyage had also turned out to be a failure. Cook was not to blame for either of these failures but they continued to haunt him and whatever achievements lay ahead of him he would never forget his disappointment.

There was no time to mope. Able Seaman Archibald Wolf had broken into one of the store rooms and stolen some spike nails – he had to be punished with two dozen lashes. The bread had to be taken out of the hold and aired to keep it fresh and to sift out a few weevils and maggots. The ship was in need of repairs and maintenance. The longboat was completely unseaworthy with her bottom so ravaged by the Teredo worm that the naturalists were using it to study the honeycomb texture of the worm cells. The worst blow of all was a disease which had broken out amongst the ship's company and the women of the island. Cook was mortified to think that his ship might have been responsible for bringing this disease to the innocent islanders of the Pacific. His notes are confused but the message is clear:

> *We had not been here many days before some of our people got this disease and as no such thing happen'd to any of the Dolphins people while she was here that I ever heard off, I had reason (notwithstanding the improbability of the thing) to think that we had brought it along with us which gave me no small uneasiness and did all in my power to prevent its progress, but all I could do was to little purpose for I may safely say that I was not assisted by any one person in ye ship, and was oblig'd to have the most part of the Ships Compney a Shore every day to work upon the Fort and a Strong guard every night and the Women were so very liberal with their favours, or else Nails, Shirts &c were temptations that they could not withstand, that this distemper very soon spread itself over the greatest part of the Ships Compney but now I have the satisfaction to find that the Natives all agree that we did not bring it here.*

The records show that he exaggerated about the number of men involved – it was in fact only about one third. It was generous of the natives not to blame his ship for the infection – but this was small comfort to Cook in view of the fact that it seemed indisputable that a European ship had brought the disease to the island. He goes on to expand his feelings further on the matter:

> *However this is little satisfaction to them who must suffer by it in a very great degree and may in time spread itself over all the Islands in the South Seas, to the extent the greatest pains to discover if any of the Ships Company had the disorder upon him for above a month before our arrival*

here and ordered the Surgeon to examine every man the least suspected who declar'd to me that only one man in the Ship was the least affected with it and his complaint was a carious shin bone; this man has not had connection with one woman on the Island.

The introspective Cook once more blamed himself for what he rightly judged to be a terrible sin against the peoples of the Pacific. Again Cook did not know the full facts. The evidence has been examined by medical experts who have studied the various descriptions from the journals and other sources and it now seems likely that what Cook thought was syphilis was probably yaws, a disease which was endemic in the Pacific islands. (The incidence of venereal disease in the Pacific islands is discussed in detail by S. M. Lambert, *A Doctor in Paradise*, London 1942.) It was no wonder that 'the people bear [it] with as little concern as if they had been accustomed to it for ages past'.

It cannot be denied that at some time in the late eighteenth century a European ship did bring venereal disease to the Pacific Islands. It is also a fact that James Cook, more than any other European explorer before or after him, opened up the Pacific to European nations. At this point in time only three ships had visited Tahiti and all three of their captains – Wallis, Bougainville and Cook – took scrupulous care to inspect their crews for signs of the disease. The belief that Cook was responsible for the spread of venereal disease in the Pacific is to make him the scapegoat for a crime which belongs to the whole of Europe. In the case of Tahiti, however, Cook was prepared to take the blame even though he was probably innocent.

On the morning of 26 June Cook and Banks set off on a journey around the island. They set out in the pinnace accompanied by two or three natives – an indication that they thought they had nothing to fear from the islanders to the south and also showing the strong bond of friendship and mutual respect which had formed between the two men. The Englishmen tried to walk along the coastline wherever possible, leaving the natives to manage the boat which was always available for their use whenever the going became difficult over land.

One of the first places of interest which they encountered was the bay where Bougainville had landed in the previous year. The post holes of his tents were still visible. Cook noted that it was good anchorage with 20 to 24 fathoms of water, with offshore reefs and coral rocks offering some shelter from the open sea, but he thought it a lesser anchorage than Matavia Bay where the *Endeavour* was moored.

The island of Tahiti was shaped like a figure of eight with the two parts connected by a narrow isthmus less than 2 miles wide. The two parts were known by the native names of Opooreonoo and Taiarapu, the latter lying south-west of the former – it was a smaller but no less interesting region. Soon they arrived at a part of the coast, near the isthmus, which was very marshy and impossible to cross on foot. They called for the pinnace to cross the waters to Taiarapu. At this point their Tahitian guide Tituboaro advised against travelling further because his people had been at war with the people of Taiarapu. The English loaded their muskets and after some persuasion their guide was reassured and agreed to take them further. Tituboara's fears proved to be unfounded and they received a very cordial reception from the people of Taiarapu.

The last thing Cook and Banks expected to find at Taiarapu was something from their homeland, but the natives proudly showed them two 12 pound shots which had been fired from the decks of the *Dolphin* on the long-remembered day when she fired her great guns across the bay. The cannon balls were not the only souvenirs – at another point on the journey the explorers found to their amusement an overfed English goose and a waddling turkey strutting around the Tahitian houses. Both birds were very fat and tame; they had been left behind by the crew of the *Dolphin* but the Tahitians would not kill them, preferring to keep them as pets and looking after them with pride and care.

The journey was full of interest regarding the Tahitian culture but because of language and cultural differences Cook and Banks never fully understood the Tahitian customs and beliefs. In many places throughout the island they discovered memorials called *marae* which the Tahitians raised to their dead. Sometimes the *marae* seemed to be no more than a rubble of rough stones but more elaborate structures were built from worked coral stone with steps leading up to a kind of altar and with carved wooden posts set into the stone. The carvings were figures of men and animals or birds and in at least one instance the birds were coloured with red and yellow pigment to give colour to the feathers. The *marae* were supposed to be burial grounds, but it was common to find human bones, skulls and jawbones lying around them in confusion – the natives were not very forthcoming about the human bones and claimed they were the remains of their enemies killed in the great conflict which had taken place about two years ago.

In the Papara district of Opooreonoo the explorers came across the largest *marae* in Tahiti. It was shaped like the roof of a house with eleven huge steps leading to a platform at the top and with each step measuring 4 feet in height. It was not unlike a step pyramid with the base dimensions of 267 by 87 feet tapering to a ridge of 250 by 8 feet at the top. The stones were of white coral and beautifully worked and finished. The *marae* was a great and laborious achievement built by men working with Stone Age tools. Another part of the *marae* consisted of a paved square measuring 118 paces by 110 and with steps up to it on each side and a structure like a sundial or fountain erected at the centre. They discovered images of a bird carved in wood and a broken stone carving of a fish. It seemed that this great *marae* belonged to their acquaintance Queen Oborea and the visitors were given an account of the rising in which the queen was overthrown from her position as ruler of the island – she had been forced to flee into the mountains whilst the invaders burnt down all the houses and made off with livestock and other trophies. It seemed that the goose and the turkey were war trophies as were the jawbones and human remains which the Englishmen had found lying around.

The journey took about six days and the two men met with hospitality everywhere, spending most nights sleeping as guests of the islanders. They had difficulty getting supplies in some parts of Taiarapu where it seemed that the breadfruit tree was not so abundant as in the northern districts. Banks was interested in the geology of Tahiti; he speculated quite correctly that it was volcanic in origin and recorded some second thoughts regarding the southern continent:

> *The stones everywhere shewd manifest signs of having been at some time or other burnd; indeed I have not seen a specimen of stone yet in the Island that has not the visible marks of fire on it ... Possibly the Island owes its original to a volcano which now no longer burns; or Theoretically speaking, for the sake of those authors who balance this globe by a proper weight of continent placed near about these latitudes, that so nesscessary continent may have been sunk by Dreadfull earthquakes and volcanos 2 or 300 fathoms under the sea, the tops of the highest mountains only still remaing above water in the shape of the Islands: an undoubted proof that such a thing now exists to the gret emolument of their theory, which was it not for this proof would have been already totally demolished by the Course our ship made from Cape Horn to this Island.*

Tahiti had no towns or villages; the people lived in houses dotted round the coast where the fertile land and fresh water flowed down from the slopes of the volcanic peaks. As well as the bread-fruit they were able to grow coconuts, bananas, yams, sweet potatoes, a yellow apple or Brazilian plum, sugar cane and plan-tains – all of which could be grown with the minimum of labour. The fertility of the soil and the abundance of fruit was something which never failed to impress the visitors. 'In the article of food these people may almost be said to be exempt from the curse of our fore fathers,' wrote Banks. 'Scarcely can it be said that they earn their bread with the swet of their brow, benevolent nature hath not only supplied them with the necessarys but with abundance of superfluities.'

The people fished for shellfish and lobsters, they had a taste for seafood and for a species of jellyfish. On land they kept hogs and island dogs. Cook had to overcome some revulsion at eating a dog but he quickly acquired the taste and likened it to English lamb. There were also birds for the table but he thought the Tahitian fowls were not so tasty as English chicken. The drink seemed to be limited to water and coconut milk, with no intoxicating liquors – a few of the islanders were given spirits from the *Endeavour* and quickly became very drunk from their excesses – but they wisely refrained from repeating the performance. Cook soon discovered that in polite society there existed a *tapu* ('Taboo' is an Anglicised version of the Tahitian word 'Tapu') against men and women eating together. Occasionally some of the women were persuaded to eat on board ship where the great cabin of the *Endeavour* with its carved chairs and large table was a great attraction to them. They agreed readily enough but they took care not to let their own people know they had indecently eaten in the company of the opposite sex.

Their method of making cloth was distinctive and interesting. Bark was peeled from a tree in strips and laid together with a fine paste. It was then beaten flat with a hard wooden tool and other strips of bark were laid crosswise over it and also beaten. The cloth was sometimes dyed in red, brown and yellow pigments. Cook thought the finished product very fine although of quite different texture to European cloth. He noticed that the Tahitians also wove matting which was of a finer and better quality than anything he had seen in Europe. Other manufactures included nets for fishing, ropes which were as thick as 1 inch in diameter, fishing lines and finer threads used to sew parts of the canoes together. There was a wide variety of tools ranging from stone axes to fishing hooks and barbs.

The Tahitians had not developed any form of writing and consequently they had no written laws and no history beyond their folklore. The way in which they had created a hierarchical society with evident social distinctions was of great interest. According to Banks they had 'a system evidently formed to secure the Licentius Liberty of a few while the Greater part of the Society are unalterably immersed in the most abject Slavery' – this was an interesting comment from an English aristocrat at a time when the English had such an appalling record on slavery. They had no written history but they had a great many myths and legends which were passed from mouth to mouth much as Homer and the travelling poets and musicians had done in the Hellenic world. Banks spent a lot of time trying to discover more about their beliefs but his lack of vocabulary made it impossible for him to understand fully their superstitions and religious philosophy. The source of most of his information was Tupia who was not in fact a Tahitian by birth but came from the neighbouring island of Raiatea to the west. Amongst Tupia's many folklore stories was that of a race of gods called Mauwe who inhabited the Earth before the creation of man. They were represented as giants with seven heads, immense strength and superhuman ability.

Tupia and other Tahitians readily attended a divine service every Sunday at Fort Venus. William Monkhouse performed the service and a vast concourse of natives attended. 'They understood perfectly that we were "*Paroweing the Etuah*", that is talking to God,' said Molyneux. 'This they easily comprehended as they themselves worship an Invisible & Omnipotent Being.'

The natives used a decimal system for counting and made signs with their fingers to represent numbers. They had a name for all the numbers from 1 to 10 and a word for 20 – with this vocabulary they could express numbers up to 20,000. Only the simplest methods of calculation existed but they had a calendar based on the lunar cycle of thirty days, each day of the month had its own name and the annual cycle consisted of counting thirteen lunar months. The day was divided into increments of about two hours. Their astronomy was quite advanced: they had names for the planets and all the major stars and they were quite capable of navigating between islands using the stars for guidance.

The people had their own forms of music based on a very simple scale of extremely few notes. All the natives seemed very fond of music; they loved singing and dancing and they had developed two musical instruments. The first was a drum made from hollow black wood and with a membrane of shark's skin stretched across the hollow; the musicians beat the drum with the palms and knuckles of their hands. The second instrument was a kind of flute made from a hollow bamboo cane about 15 inches long. It was not blown by mouth but by the novel method of using one nostril – the technique was to block the unused nostril with the thumb. The flute had four holes and seemed to produce only four notes, allowing for a very limited number of tunes, and some of the English thought Tahitian music consisted of only one monotonous tune. Cook expressed his dislike of the flute and drums, but Tahitian music was an acquired taste and Sydney Parkinson drew a marvellous picture of Tayeto playing his flute with one nostril. Parkinson mentioned a third simple instalment, a clapper made from two mother-of-pearl shells. The Tahitian dancing was full of life and vigour – all but the most staid members of the crew thoroughly enjoyed watching both sexes perform their traditional rhythmic steps.

Delicate matters, like male and female eating together, were not referred to in polite conversation but, in other matters concerning the differences and attraction between the sexes, the Tahitians were very uninhibited, often to the embarrassment of the British. 'Both sexes express the most indecent ideas in conversation without the least emotion,' wrote Cook prudishly. 'And they delight in such conversation beyhond any other.' He described the dance performed by the girls of the island. 'The young girls when ever they can collect 8 or 10 together dance a very indecent dance which they call Timorodee singing most indecent songs and using most indecent actions in the practice of which they are brought up from their earlyest childhood.' He was forced to admit that 'in doing this they keep time to a great nicety'. Sydney Parkinson describes a dance which was probably the Timorodee:

On the 27th [of June] we saw a favourite game, which the young girls divert themselves with in an evening, dividing themselves into two parties, one standing opposite to the other, one party throws apples which the others endeavour to catch. The right of the game I am not acquainted with; but now-and-then one of the parties advanced, stamping their feet, making wry mouths, straddling with their legs, lifting their cloaths, and exposing their nakedness, at the same time repeating some words in a disagreeable tone. Thus are they bred up to lewdness from their childhood, many of them not being above eight or nine years of age.

The words and actions of the Timorodee may have seemed very indecent to European eyes when in fact they were normal to the natives who had been brought up to their own culture. It was the youth of the girls which upset Cook for they were certainly not very old – he admitted that when they arrive at maturity, and as soon as they form an attachment to one of the opposite sex, they left off dancing the Timorodee. The journals do not say much about children, but Parkinson noted that both sexes were remarkably kind to one another and if they were given any present or treat they would, if at all possible, divide and share it without friction. The men also had their own characteristic dance: it was a kind of war ceremony in which they circulated around each other in a crouched wrestling pose and made grimacing faces through their warpaint. The wrestling was described in some detail by Joseph Banks: it was a male sport and was dominated by male spectators. The old men loved the sport – they shouted and sang encouragement to their favourites:

> The diversion began by the combatants, some of them at least, walking round the yard with a slow and grave pace every now and then striking their left arms very hard, by which they caused a deep and very loud noise, which it seemed was a challenge to each other or any one of the company who chose to engage in the exercise. Within the house stood the old men ready to give applause to the victor and some few women who seem'd to be here out of compliment to us, as much the larger number absented themselves upon the occasion.
>
> The general challenge was given as I said, the particular one soon follow it by which any man singled out his antagonist, it was done by joining the finger ends of both hands even with the breast and then moving the Elbows up and down. If this was accepted the challenged immediately returnd the signal and instantly both put themselves in an attitude to engage, which they very soon did striving to seize each other by the hands hair or the cloth they had round their middles, for they had no other dress. This done they attempted to seize each other by the thigh which commonly decided the contest in the fall of him who was thus taken at disadvantage; if this was not soon done they always parted either by consent or by their friends interferd in less than a minute, in which case both began to clap their arms and seek anew for an antagonist either in each other or some one else.

The Polynesian people were quite different from the Africans, the Fuegians and other primitive races whom the sailors had encountered. They were lighter skinned with some Asian characteristics but they were clearly a separate identifiable race. To the European sailors, many of whom had only ever experienced contact with the opposite sex in the filthy back alleys of a British sea port, the uninhibited girls with their brown, sun-tanned limbs, dark shining hair, dusky angelic faces and their huge bright eyes were irresistible. Amongst the Tahitians a fair skin was looked upon as a favourable attribute; they were therefore fascinated by the visitors and there was a lot of mutual attraction between the races. The Tahitian women on their home ground were, if anything, more likely to start an affair with the sailors than vice-versa.

The morals and ideals of the female Tahitians were quite different from those in far-away Europe. During the whole of the time that the *Endeavour* stayed at Tahiti there was hardly a single case of a jealous husband, unless we count the case of the escort of the flirtatious Oborea who did not like her advances to Joseph Banks. The good-natured tolerance with which the Tahitian males allowed their womenfolk to fraternise with the foreigners says much for the generous disposition of the people. 'The women were very kind to us,' wrote Cook, adding that they were 'very liberal with their favours'. A ship's nail or a sailor's shirt was the price of love. Within a few days of arrival the flirtations had become so prolific that Cook forbade his men to go over One Tree Hill at the far end of Matavia Bay.

Cook tolerated the whole situation. It obviously did wonders for the morale of his crew and as long as no actual breach of discipline was involved he was prepared to let it be. It was obvious to the Tahitian women who the important members of the expedition were and Cook himself was approached by some of them. It must have done something for his ego but there was no question of him getting involved with them, not only did he have a wife at home to whom he was unswervingly faithful, but he also had to set an example to his men and had his own duty and reputation to think about. Even had he been a single man he was well into his forties and his iron self-control was more than adequate to resist the advances of the island maidens however seductive they might be. On top of all this he had a great respect for other races and it would be quite out of keeping for a man with the character of Captain James Cook to seduce or be seduced by a Pacific islander.

The same principles did not apply to the honourable Joseph Banks. He had no wife at home even if Miss Blosset did feel she had some hold on him and it was obvious from his fine clothes and bearing that he was an important personage. He was much younger than Cook and his desires were readily fired by the Tahitian maidens. He was able virtually to pick and choose from the whole female population of the island, but there were a few occasions when his popularity landed him in trouble, and on at least one occasion he had to declare himself otherwise engaged to avoid the amorous advances of the bouncing Queen Oborea.

Banks and Solander were the two people who did most of the trading for supplies with the Tahitians. On one occasion when they came to trade articles from the ship in exchange for island cloth they were given a full sales treatment with the assistance of three seductive young women. The sales presentation started with the showing of the samples which were first laid upon the ground. In Banks's account it is difficult to know when he is describing cloth and when he is describing the ladies:

> ... *the foremost of the women, who seemed to be the principal, then step upon them and quickly unveiling all her charms gave me a most conven-ient opportunity of admiring them by turning herself gradually round: 3 pieces more were then laid and she repeated her part of the ceremony: The other three were then laid which made a treble covering of the ground between her and me, she then once more displayd her naked beau-ties and immediately marchd up to me, a man following her and doubling up the cloth as he came forward which she immediately made me under-stand was intended as a present for me. I took her by the hand and led her to the tents acompanied by another woman her friend, to both of them I made presents but could not prevail upon them to stay more than an hour.*

The reasons behind the ceremony were not clear – the cloth was presented as a gift and the whole performance seemed to be a special honour on his behalf. The girls seemed to have no inten-tion of staying the night after their performance but there were plenty of others who were only too willing. On the day of the transit of Venus Banks described another incident when his party was visited by three girls from the island of Moorea:

> *Soon after my arrival at the tent 3 hansome girls came off in a canoe to see us, they had been at the tent in the morning with Tarroa, they chatted with us very freely and with very little perswasion agreed to send away their carriage (Banks presumably meant this word to mean an escort of some kind) and sleep in the tent, a proof of confidence which I have not before met with upon so short an acquaintance.*

Again, when Joseph Banks was entertained by the chief whom he called Lycurgus his host's wife lost no time in trying to seduce him. According to Banks she was 'ugly enough in all conscience' and she received no encouragement but without any invitation she squatted down on the mat close to him. No sooner had she done so than Banks spotted amongst the crowd a very pretty girl 'with fire in her eyes' whom he had not seen before. His desires were fired and, ignoring his companion, he beckoned the girl over and persuaded her to sit on his other side. 'I was then desirous of getting rid of my former companion,' he said. 'So I ceas'd to attend her and loaded my pretty girl with beads and every present I could think pleasing to her: The other shewd much disgust but did not quit her place and continued to supply me with fish and cocoa milk.'

Queen Oborea was another suitor who lost no time in making her advances to Joseph Banks. She was a very direct lady in her approaches and told him she had simply dismissed poor Obadee, her native lover and gentleman attendant. In the evening, however, Obadee came by torchlight to her house in the woods where he usually spent the night with her. She sent him away and claimed to be 'satiated with her lover [and] resolved to change him at all costs'. The glamorous Joseph Banks, with the white waistcoat and silver frogs, was to his dismay the person chosen by

Oborea to succeed Obadee. Banks did not wish to offend Oborea but he was put on the defensive and produced the weak and time-honoured excuse that he was otherwise spoken for. It must have seemed a hollow defence when all the island knew he had been chasing after the girls. 'Indeed was I free as air her majesties person is not the most desirable,' he confided. Oborea was not to be put off by small trifles. 'She had resolution enough to insist upon sleeping in Mr Banks's tent all night and was with difficulty prevaild upon to go to her Canoe altho no one took the least notice of her,' observed Cook.

Two of Oborea's attendants, according to Sydney Parkinson, were just as forward as their mistress in making their advances:

> [They were] very assiduous in getting themselves husbands, in which attempt they, at length, succeeded. The surgeon took one and one of the lieutenants the other: they seemed agreeable enough till bedtime: and then determined to lie in Banks's tent, which they did accordingly: but one of the engaged coming out, the surgeon insisted that she should not sleep there, and thrust her out, and the rest followed her, except Otea Tea, who wined and cried for a considerable time, till Mr Banks led her out also. Mr Monkhouse and Mr Banks came to an eclaircissement some time after; had very high words, and I expected they would have decided it by a duel, which, however, they prudently avoided.

Here then was one of the few occasions when friction broke out between crew members of the *Endeavour*. Neither Cook nor Banks mention the incident but there is little doubt that Parkinson was telling the truth and that the incident very nearly became a duel of honour. The antagonism was short-lived and two weeks later we find the botanist and the surgeon fully reconciled and under-taking an inland expedition together to try to find the source of the river which provided their water supply. (Banks's journal refers to 'Mr Monkhouse and myself' undertaking the expedition but it was William the surgeon not Jonathan the midshipman so the reconciliation was complete.) This was one of very few expeditions to the interior of Tahiti and the two men managed to travel only about 6 miles inland. There was plenty of habitation near the coast but very soon they came to a gorge about 100 feet deep where a waterfall had carved out a pool so deep that the locals said they could not get beyond it. Ropes made from long pieces of bark hung from the slippery cliff and the natives used them to scramble from ledge to ledge and climb higher. Where the sailors might easily have scrambled up, Banks and Monkhouse were not prepared to risk their necks for what they judged to be a very small contribution to human knowledge and they retreated back to the ship.

When taken over the whole duration of the visit, inevitable frictions broke out over the thieving and love-making, but this contact between two very different cultures was surely one of the happiest, the most productive and momentous meetings ever to take place. In the evenings when the two cultures came together and the Tahitian girls danced their Timorodee and the men displayed their wrestling prowess the events would remain in the memories of the sailors. Under the sunshine, blue skies and the ever-breaking sea of the South Pacific, the smiles of the girls and the loud rhythms of the native drums all combined to captivate the hearts of the simple English seamen.

We know that sea shanties must have been sung by the sailors as they worked the ropes and strained at the capstan of the *Endeavour* but their songs were considered too commonplace for the journalists to record – we do not know the names or the words of any of the shanties which they sung as they went about their daily tasks. There was one memorable moment at one of the gatherings when the Tahitian musicians asked the sailors to sing an English song. The sailors readily agreed and for one poignant moment their thoughts turned from their South Sea Paradise to the cold foggy island on the far side of the world, an island which they called home. Accents and dialects from every corner of the

British Isles joined for a time in a rough harmony as the sound of the sea shanty echoed round the hills and bays of Tahiti. The sailors gave it all they had and the natives were spellbound at the strong rhythms of the song; they did not know the words but they listened in awe to the passion and fervour of the sailors. When the song had ended there was a hushed silence – an event very rare on Tahiti – then the generous islanders broke into a sudden, spontaneous and rapturous applause. The sailors grinned through their beards and found themselves embarrassed at their new-found talent. One of the Tahitian musicians asked for a passage back to England so that he could learn to sing!

When July came the ship was fully serviced and provisioned. Queen Oborea presented the captain with four of the island pigs which she knew he would greatly appreciate. Tupia, who was one of Oborea's train of followers, begged to be allowed to travel back to England with the ship. Cook considered this request carefully:

> *This man had been with us the most part of the time we had been upon the Island which gave us an oppertunity to know some thing of him: we found him to be a very intelligent person and to know more of the Geography of the Islands situated in these seas, their produce and the religion laws and customs of the inhabitants than any one we had met with and was the likeliest person to answer our purpose; for these reasons and at the request of Mr Banks I received him on board together with a you[n]g boy his servant.*

If anybody at all was to be taken away with the ship then Tupia was the ideal man, not only because he could guide them to other islands but also because of his skill as an interpreter. He had picked up a good understanding of the English language in his few months' acquaintance with the crew. Banks was more than willing to take responsibility for Tupia when he arrived in England. 'I do not know why I may not keep him as a curiosity,' he pondered. 'As well as some of my neighbours do lions and tygers at a larger expence than he will probably ever put me to.' His motives were typically eighteenth century and he saw the Polynesian as a curiosity even more exotic than the black servants he had lost in Tierra del Fuego.

On 9 July it needed a fair wind for the ship to leave Tahiti. When the roll-call was taken two marines were found to be missing; they were Samuel Gibson and Clement Webb. From the gossip it was easy enough to discover the reason for their absence – they had decided to desert the ship and to remain on Tahiti with two native girls to whom they had formed strong attachments. This was an unexpected but not altogether surprising turn of events. There must have been much talk below decks about the attractions of the island and the beauty of the girls – it would be very surprising if the seamen had not gossiped together about the idea of exchanging the hard discipline of Navy life for that of a South Sea islander. But Cook knew his duty. The incident was a very serious breach of discipline and it put him in an extremely vulnerable position. If he did not find the deserters and punish them he feared that in a few days' time he would be left with less than half of his crew.

Cook's action was dramatic and swift. He took Queen Oborea, Tootaha and seven other innocent protesting hostages whose only crime was that they were unfortunate enough to be near the ship at the time the men deserted. He kept them prisoner on the ship with orders that they were not to be released until the two marines were found and returned.

Robert Molyneux, in his capacity as ship's master, was closer to the men than was the captain and he heard much talk of desertion during the caulking and refurbishing of the *Endeavour* – he knew that the marines were only scapegoats for an action which nearly every man aboard, including the officers, had openly discussed out of earshot of the captain. Molyneux recorded earlier talk of desertion in his journal:

> *[7 May] … this day I accquaintd the Captain with some Mutinous words spoke by some of the People. The fact being prov'd the Captain was going to*

Proceed to Punish the delinquents, I interpos'd & a pardon was granted on
Promise of better Behaviour for the future. I had many reasons for doing
this as I well knew the spring which caus'd these commotions.

'Webb is a sober man & was steward of the Gunroom,' added Molyneux. 'Which offence he faithfully perfom'd, but being extravagantly fond of a young women with whom he has been connected for some time. Gibson is a wild young man & a sworn Brother to Webb he has no other reason than the pleasure of living in a fine Country without controul. They both had large promises from some the Principal men & was to have Lands & servants assighn'd them.'

It was impossible for Gibson and Webb to remain hidden for long on an island as small as Tahiti, but it was an unenviable task for their fellow marines to track them down and force them to return to the ship. The deserters were found very quickly and brought back under arrest. Everybody thought that Cook would punish them severely for their offence, but the captain was humane and he transmuted the punishment a little and reduced the charges from desertion to that of disobeying orders. He was still very angry with the situation. He had worked hard for months to establish a good relationship with the natives and now, right on the eve of departure, he blamed the deserters for the fact that they would be leaving Oborea and other native chieftains in an indignant and disgruntled mood. They rightly felt that they were not responsible for what had happened.

Cook reasoned:

Thus we are likely to leave these people in disgust with our own behaviour
towards them owing wholy to the folly of two of our own people for it
doth not appear that the natives had any hand in inticeing them away and
therefore were not the first aggressors ...

However it is very certain that had we not taken this step we never
should have recover'd them.

Banks saw the hostages shortly after their release. 'I met them from the boat,' he said. 'But no sign of forgiveness could I see in their faces, they looked sulky and affronted.'

The bower anchors were raised from the bottom of Matavia Bay. They were so badly eaten by the worms that one of them broke into pieces when it was heaved up and the carpenters had to fashion another anchor before the ship could sail. At last everything was ready for a sad departure, the decks were cleared of all the clutter which had accumulated during the stay, and the *Endeavour* prepared to weigh anchor at Tahiti. They were leaving on a bitter note after winning the friendship and the confidence of the people and the island they had enjoyed so much. It was true that there had been problems of thieving. There had been the embarrassing episode when the seamen had started to pull down a sacred *marae* to use as ballast for the ship. There was the time when Cook had ordered a man to be stripped, bound to the rigging and flogged for an outrage against a Tahitian woman – the woman had burst into tears and tried to prevent the bloody inhuman naval punishment. Parkinson remembered the insects finding a way through the mosquito net to land and stick in his vivid colours as he struggled to paint. He remembered the occasion when a light-fingered native stole one of his bright colours and applied it to a sore on his backside. But these problems were as nothing compared with the happy memories which they had shared together: the contact between Polynesian and English; the fraternisation with the opposite sex; the good-natured bartering of goods and food; the time when John Gore challenged a native to an archery contest only to find that he had to shoot for distance and not at a target. Everybody remembered the rare flash of wry humour when the captain presented Oborea with a doll which he assured her was the likeness of his wife in England. A delighted Oborea clasped the doll to her breast, grasped the captain by the hand and happily displayed the present to the crowd of people present.

But the worst fears of the English were unfounded. As the ship headed out of the bay a canoe appeared from round the headland. It was followed by another and soon by a small flotilla of native craft. Then came a large familiar canoe with the bouncing and happy Queen Oborea aboard. After the unfortunate problem of the deserters the most forgiving race in the world was not going to let the *Endeavour* leave without a proper Polynesian send-off. Soon the ship was surrounded by canoes and excited Tahitians who scrambled aboard as they had done on the day months ago when the ship first arrived in their waters. 'The inhabitants seeing us prepared to sail Flock'd to us from all Quarters,' said Molyneux movingly. 'Every Body now is preparing Presents for his friends & they on their part are preparing Presents for us.' The natives shouted until they were hoarse, they waved cheerfully at the departing ship, some made loud lamenting noises and others simply burst into tears. It was an emotional forgiveness, perhaps there would never again be such a warmth of contact between two such widely different races. It was an historic parting which could never quite be repeated again:

We had Oborea, Othethea, Tayoa, Nuna, Tuanna Matte, Potattou, Polotheara &c on board when the anchor was weighed; they took their leaves tenderly enough, not without plenty of tears tho intirely without that clamourous weeping made use of by the other Indians, several boats of whoom were about the ship shouting out their lamentations, as vying with each other not who should cry most be who should loudest — a custom we had often condemnd in conversation with our particular friends as savouring more of affected rather than real grief.

Tupia shed a few tears at his decision to leave his friends in Tahiti. He and Joseph Banks climbed to the topmast head where the ebullient Tahitian and the aristocratic Englishman stood for a long time side by side, staring back at the magnificent peaks and tropical foliage of the south sea island, waving to the natives as the canoes and their occupants reluctantly fell away one by one and the ship sailed further into the sunset and the open Pacific Ocean.

CHAPTER 6

New Zealand

To 14 January, 1770

THE ENDEAVOUR SAILED towards the western horizon where the sun set into the Pacific. For Tupia it was a journey back to his homeland. He took his new duties very seriously and the next day when the wind was light and the ship's progress was a little sluggish he gazed out of the stern window of the great cabin, jumped to his feet and shouted fervently '*O Tane, ara mai, matai, ora mai matai*'. This was a prayer to the weather god Tane, asking the god to send the ship a fair wind. The prayer was answered immediately as a favourable breeze caught the sails and speeded the ship on its way. Tupia boasted loudly about success but others were cynical about his efforts.

'Our Indian often prayed for a wind,' said Joseph Banks, 'and as often boasted to me about the success of his prayers, which I plainly saw he never began till he saw a breeze so near the ship that it generally reachd her before the prayer was finished.'

After a short journey of only two days they reached a group of islands which Cook called the Society Islands. The group contained four main islands of which the nearest was Huhine with the islands of Raiatea and Tahaa a few leagues beyond. The latter islands were situated so close together that they were encircled by the same reef. To the north-west lay the smaller island of Bolabola – this was a kind of Polynesian Sparta and was much renowned and feared by the other islands for the ferocity of its fighting men.

Tupia was very happy and at home in his native islands. He enjoyed showing off his new friends. Raiatea was his birthplace where he had been a priest before being forced into exile at Tahiti after one of the many battles with the aggressive Bolabola men. He was the perfect interpreter: he assured his people of the good intentions of his friends the white men and he quickly made all the right contacts for trade and information. He maintained that his people did not steal like the Tahitians and he persuaded some of them to come on board ship so that he could prove his words to be true. The trading was good, it tended to be rather prolonged by the natives' annoying habit of consulting a group of twenty or more people before making up their minds, but eleven pigs were acquired in one day and the next day a number of hogs plus an unlimited supply of breadfruit and coconuts. Tupia sent a native diver beneath the ship to examine the rudder and to report on the amount of water which she drew. He seemed to have a good knowledge of the waters around his native islands and he became greatly alarmed about the safety of the ship when she entered water where the depth was less than about 5 fathoms.

The islanders, as might be expected, were a very similar race to the Tahitians and they had plenty of trade, cultural contact and intermarriage with their neighbours. On the island of Raiatea there was a large *marae* built from huge coral stones. It was ornamented with wooden poles set in an upright position and carved throughout their whole length with figures of men and animals. Here a large hog weighing about 80 pounds had been sacrificed for the benefit of the visitors.

Subtle local differences existed between the cultures of Raiatea and Tahiti. The native dancing was if anything more vigorous and exciting than on Tahiti. Sydney Parkinson gives an excellent account of the men's dance:

> *A large mat was laid upon the ground, and they began to dance upon it, putting their bodies into strange motions, writhing their mouths, and*

shaking their tails, which made the numerous plaits that hung about them
flutter like a peacock's train. Sometimes they stood in a row one behind
another, and then they fell down with their faces to the ground, leaning on
their arms, and shaking only their tails, the drums beating all the while,
with which they kept exact time. An old man stood by as prompter, and
roared out as loud as he could at every change. These motions they contin-
ued until they were all in a sweat; they repeated them three times
alternately, and, after they had done, the girls began.

Between the intervals the men performed another dance of their
own, a traditional saga of some kind which had words and a story
to it. It was unfortunate that the British could not follow the
drama because their grasp of the language was inadequate. For
the women's dance the girls wore their hair plaited with flowers of
gardenia making a head-dress which Banks thought 'truly
elegant'. They wore low-cut dresses of black island cloth with
bare arms and with a bunch of feathers on each shoulder. A
pleated skirt in brown and white cloth reached their feet, it was a
very long garment for the native type of dance they performed,
but according to Banks their skill was such that they managed the
skirt 'with as much dexterity as our opera dancers could have
done'. The music was loud and rhythmic, accompanied by the
native drums, the dance was exciting and provocative with the
dancers making full use of limbs and body:

In this dress they advanced sideways keeping excellent time to the drums
which beat brisk and loud; they soon began to shake their hips giving the
fold of the cloth which lay upon them a very quick motion which was con-
tinued throughout the whole dance, they sometimes standing, sometimes
sitting and sometimes resting on their knees and elbows and generaly
moving their fingers with a quickness scarce to be imagined. The chief
entertainment of the spectators seemd to arise from the Lascivious
motions they often made use of which were highly so, more indeed than I
shall attempt to describe.

Joseph Banks was always an appreciative observer of the native girls and he noticed one dancer who wore three pearls in her ear. One pearl was rough and of no value but he thought the other two so fine that he offered the wearer the equivalent of four hogs plus anything else he could supply in exchange. The girl was tempted by the charms and the wealth of the white man but she refused to part with her pearls.

During the festivities at Raiatea there was much talk of the feared Bolabola men and the Raiateans wanted Cook to use the ship's great guns to help defeat them – a request which the captain very rightly refused to honour. Two days later Cook received a present of hogs and fowls from the dreaded king of Bolabola – his majesty had obviously heard the news of their arrival and wanted to come and meet them. On the day appointed they waited apprehensively for the arrival of his majesty, but a great warrior did not appear as promised. In his stead came 'three handsome lively girls' who chatted happily all morning and 'took of all regret for the want of his majesty's company'. The girls invited the visitors to come back with them to their island of Bolabola to meet the king. It transpired that his majesty was not in the least the fearsome warrior they expected to find:

> In the evening all went to see the great king and to thank him for his civil-
> ities particularly of this morning. The King of the Tatatoes or Club men
> who have conquered this and are the terror of all other islands we
> expected to see young lively hansome &c &c, but how were we disap-
> pointed when we were led to an old decrepid half blind man who seemd to
> have scarce reason enough left to send hogs, much less galantry to send
> ladies.

The exploration of the south sea islands was extended a few weeks by this pleasant interlude in the Society Islands. Cook was pleased to be able to map and chart the islands but he was not pre-pared to spend any more time than necessary exploring them.

The main reason was that he had to get back to his business of continent-hunting in the vast unexplored regions of the southern Pacific. After leaving Tahiti he opened the Admiralty's secret instructions which had been placed in a sealed package when the ship left England. The package contained no great surprises:

> You are to proceed to the southward in order to make discovery of the Continent above-mentioned until you arrive in the Latitude of 40°, unless you sooner fall in with it. But not having discover'd it or any evident sign of it in that Run, you are to proceed in search of it to the Westward between that Latitude before mentioned and the Latitude 35° until you discover it, or fall in with the Eastern side of the Land discover'd by Tasman and now called New Zealand.

The crew of the *Dolphin* claimed to have seen the mountains of the *Terra Australis* to the south of Tahiti. Tupia denied the existence of a great landmass to the south, but there was still more than enough uncovered ocean for the continent to exist and if any large landmass was found then it would take many months to chart and survey. The ship was in the tropics but it would soon be spring further south and Cook wanted to start very early in the season to make sure he was not caught by darkness and bad weather at the end of the summer months. Thus, on 9 August he weighed anchor and unfurled his sails again. He pointed the bows of the *Endeavour* southwards. The tropical islands with the blue lagoons and surf-washed reefs, the breadfruit and coconut trees, the frail king of the Bolabola men with his handsome ladies sank slowly beneath the northern horizon.

A few days' sail brought them to the island of Ohetiroa, also known as Hiti-roa or Rurutu. The position of this island was correctly predicted by Tupia who exhibited great skill in navigation and showed that he could find his way by reading the stars. The reception at Rurutu was not friendly and there was little point in trying to land or to spend much time there. The *Endeavour* therefore sailed southwards again and crossed the Tropic of Capricorn. Joseph Banks, with the help of the invaluable Tupia, used the days to write up his log and detailed account of the 'Manners & Customs of South Sea Islands'. Together with Cook's detailed account of the people this valuable record of 25,000 words describes the island and the people as they were before their native culture was permanently destroyed by the western world. It represented one of the most valuable studies in anthropology ever written.

The *Endeavour* continued to sail south and the journals once more tell only of winds, latitudes and longitudes, the weather and the routine monotony of life at sea. On 25 August a piece of Cheshire cheese was taken from a locker and a bottle of porter was opened. 'We lived like English men and drank the healths of our friends in England,' wrote Banks. It was exactly a year since the day they had left Plymouth harbour.

On 28 August John Reading, the boatswain's mate, was found to be so drunk that he was rendered speechless and had 'scarce any signs of life' in him, His excess proved fatal and an hour after he was discovered in this stupor he became the next casualty of the voyage. On enquiry it was discovered that he had consumed about three-and-a-half pints of rum given to him quite legally 'out of mere good nature' by the boatswain. With so much liquor on board it was perhaps no great mystery how the men always managed to get hold of it in quantity and Cook decided to take an inventory and have all the casks checked. Many were found to be only one third full and quite a few were empty – conclusive evidence that the men had been tapping them throughout the whole voyage. The only consolation was that the men had not stooped to the common trick of filling up the casks again with sea water. After so many years at sea Cook was very philosophical about the matter and his journal mentions little regret and no action on his part to find the men responsible – he was much more interested in a comet which appeared in the sky between the star Aldebaron and the constellation of Orion, just above the eastern horizon. The comet was seen and observed in Europe and followed an orbit which took it east of the bright star in Orion's foot. Charles Green, the professional astronomer, first thought the observers were mistaken and that it was only a nebula which they could see – after three nights, however, he agreed that it was indeed an unusually bright comet and in the excellent visibility of the Pacific night Cook claimed, surely with some exaggeration, that the tail covered an astonishing 42 degrees. It seems that in Polynesian folklore as well as in European, the comet was taken as a harbinger of war, and Tupia declared that his people would have to fly into the mountains for the Bolabola men would interpret the starry messenger as a sign to invade and kill the people of their neighbouring island.

The mariners sailed hopefully onwards and further south. The naturalists noted many species of birds about the ship but all were sea birds and there was no sign of the fabled southern continent. Soon it was September and the monotony was broken a little when the weather began to deteriorate and Cook complained of a very strong wind from the west and a great storm brewing. At six o'clock in the evening the sea was so high that he brought the ship to. The latitude was 40 degrees and a number of sailors were beginning to suffer from the cold – some thought conditions to be as cold as the seas around Cape Horn.

We had hard piercing gales and squalls from the W and NW [wrote Parkinson] *with violent showers of hail and rain. The sea ran mountain high, and tossed the ship upon the waves: she rolled so much that we could get no rest, or scarcely lie in bed, and almost every moveable object on board was thrown down, and rolled about from place to place. In brief, a person, who has not been in a storm at sea, cannot form an adequate idea of the situation we were in.*

The violent storms became sharper and more frequent, but they were not as prolonged as the weather in the neighbourhood of Cape Horn – they seldom lasted for more than one or two days and the hardened sailors hardly noticed them. Between were pleasant interludes of weather but always with a heavy swell on the sea which implied that they were a long way from land. There was an occasional false alarm when a cloud formation resembling land was spotted but it was obvious to the experienced seamen that there was no southern continent within many leagues of the ship. There came a point where the ship had reached the latitude of 40 degrees and there seemed little to be gained by sailing further south. Cook therefore followed his instructions to steer westwards where he knew that Tasman had made a landfall at a latitude of about 38 degrees but there were still many leagues of ocean to cover before they would be anywhere near Tasman's longitude. All through September the *Endeavour* sailed an erratic westerly course against the prevailing ocean currents. One day a seal was seen near the ship. Seaweed came floating past and the botanists eagerly netted it for examination. Occasionally a barnacle-encrusted log floated by. The water appeared paler in colour but the lead-line could still not find the bottom. It seemed that there must be land somewhere in that great southern ocean. Banks philosophised a little in his journal:

> *Now do I wish that our friends in England could by the assistance of some magical spy glass take a peep at our situation: Dr Solander setts at the Cabbin table describing, myself at my bureau journalising. Between us hangs a large bunch of seaweed, upon the table lays the wood and barnacles; they would see that notwithstanding our different occupations our lips move very often, and without being conjurors might guess that we were talking about what we should see upon the land which there is now no doubt we shall see very soon.*

It was October and there was another hopeful sighting. 'Our old enemy Cape fly away entertained us for three hours this morn,' wrote Banks. 'All which time there were many opinions in the ship, some said it was land and others clouds.' It was clouds again. But the signs of land grew more frequent, expectation grew and the captain offered a gallon of rum to the first person to sight real land and promised to name part of the land after him. It is difficult to know which of the two promises was the greater incentive. It was on 6 October at one-thirty in the afternoon when a shrill and excited voice at the masthead shouted the call they had all been longing to hear. The voice was that of Nicholas Young, affectionately known by the crew as Young Nick, one of the youngest sailors aboard.

Within a few minutes all hands had gathered on deck to see if this was another false alarm. Tension mounted as the general consensus sided with Young Nick and, not wishing to be outdone, all those on deck claimed to see land clearly when they were looking in the wrong direction. But Young Nick's eyes did not deceive him, the land was high and at first appeared like a single island – but later in the day from the masthead a range of mountain peaks appeared like a group of islands over the horizon and there was a great number of them. James Cook stood on the quarterdeck gazing westwards for all he was worth and thought he could just see the land in the dying rays of the sun. The *Endeavour* continued westwards through the night. The sun rose on yet another Pacific dawn. The morning mist cleared with an agonising slowness and Cook could see the land clearly from the level of the deck. The ship became top heavy as the masthead became a popular vantage point. Excitement rose as it became evident that this time the land was not another group of islands but a single large landmass. Tension mounted as throughout the day the ship sailed nearer:

In the Evening a pleasant breeze. At sunset all hands at the mast head; land still distant 7 or 8 leagues, appears larger than ever, in many parts 3, 4 and 5 ranges of hills are seen one over the other and a chain of Mountains over all, some of which appear enourmously high. Much difference of opinion

and many conjectures about Islands, rivers, &c, but all hands seem to
agree that this is certainly the Continent we are in search of.

'Certainly the continent we are in search of.' In his ecstasy Banks
forgot all his previous reservations about the existence of the
southern continent and his estimation of Alexander Dalrymple
rose overnight. His pulse beat faster as he became convinced that
this was the greatest moment of the voyage, the great *Terra Aus-*
tralis Incognita really did exist and they were now gazing at its
coastline. The land had white cliffs and sandy bays, it stretched to
the horizon in both directions, the slopes of the hills were heavily
wooded and clothed in green. Wide river valleys could be seen fed
by streams of fresh water running down to the sea. Behind the
wooded slopes rose majestic purple mountains, some so high that
the snow lay white in the cracks and crevices near their summits.
Behind the nearer range rose yet more mountains higher and
fainter on the skyline. It was a beautiful and fertile country full of
awe-inspiring vistas, dazzling sunsets, fast-running rivers and
green valleys.

But James Cook was more cautious about the continental
theory: the reason for running down this latitude was because of
Tasman's account of the land called 'New Zealand'. The direction of the coastline did not seem to fit the continental theory
and he felt sure that this was the east coast of a large island which
Tasman had discovered and described many years ago. It is of
interest that Tasman called his discovery Staten Land in the optimistic but mistaken belief that it was part of a continent
stretching all the way to Staten Land east of Cape Horn. Soon
after Tasman's voyage the latter was proved to be no more than an
uninhabited rocky island and Tasman's discovery was therefore
renamed New Zealand.

Tasman's journey did not rule out the possibility that New
Zealand was part of a southern continent, however, and the opti-
mists soon pointed out that it could be a large promontory of the

main continent which lay to the south of them. Cook resolved that he would know the answer to these questions before the next summer of the Southern Hemisphere was over. The country was populated, a column of smoke rose from the woodlands and as they came nearer there was much speculation about a man-made edifice on one of the headlands where a fortification surrounded by a high fence implied a human habitation of some kind. At four o'clock on 8 October the *Endeavour* dropped anchor about 2 miles offshore and the boats were prepared for a landing.

Two boats, the pinnace and the yawl, were used for this first landing. Cook was very anxious to make friendly contact with the people. The natives ran down to the beach but scurried off when the boats landed. Cook and his party followed them to their huts – a distance of 200 or 300 yards – and left four boys from the ship in charge of the yawl. Then came an unfortunate incident: four natives appeared from the trees and attacked the boys, apparently with the intention of stealing the boat from them. The men in the pinnace, realising the danger, fired their muskets over the heads of the aggressors. This did not seem to deter them and when one native made ready to throw his spear at the boys he was shot and killed by a musket ball.

William Monkhouse was amongst the party who followed the trail of blood to find the body of the Maori who had been hit by the shot. Monkhouse gave an excellent medical description of the first Maori to be seen at close quarters – he was very interested in every aspect of the native, his tattoos and his clothing:

He was a short, but very stout bodied man – measured about 5f. 3i. Upon his right cheek and nose were spirals of tattoo or punctuation of the skin – he had three arched tattaous over his left eye drawn from the root of his nose towards the temple; each arch about four lines (12 lines = 1 inch) broad – the interval between each about a line broad; this was an exceeding new and singular appearance and seem[ed] meant to give a fierceness to the visage; his hair, coarse and black, was tied upon the crown of his head — his teeth were even and small but not white — his features were large but proportional — his nose well formed — ears bored — his beard short. He had on him a dress of singular manufacture — the warp consisted of small parcels of the fibres of some plant not twined or formed into thread, but the cross threads were properly twined, and ran into parcels of two or three together with an interval of about four lines between each parcel; a strong selvage thread run along each side but the ends appeared as if cut out of the web of manufacture — this cloth might be about four feet by three — descended from his neck to the buttocks, compleatly covering the back — its upper corners were turned back and tied — from the upper angle of this reflected part on each side went a string which tied across the neck before — the lower part was brought across the hips and secured with a kind of sedge leaf passed round the loins.

'The ball had passed from the sixth rib on the left side thro' the right shoulder blade,' added Monkhouse with a touch of professional accuracy. The killing of the Maori was a most unwelcome development. Cook's party met and debated amongst themselves what they should do next. They retired back to the ship where in the still of the night they could hear the natives on shore, about 2 miles away from them, talking loudly about the incident. It was decided that another attempt to gain the confidence of the natives had to be made on the morrow.

On the second attempt all three ship's boats landed with a strong complement of seamen and marines. A high surf ran along the beach. The natives came forward to meet them and the two parties faced each other across a shallow river. The natives had arrived fully armed with long spears and strange weapons of polished stone. Tupia now proved his worth and to the surprise of all concerned found that he could communicate with them in his own language. He explained the need for fresh water and provisions and exhorted them to lay down their arms. The talk seemed to have some effect and one man waded across the river unarmed.

Again it is William Monkhouse who gives the best description of this tentative meeting between two distrusting cultures:

> ... *he landed upon a rock surrounded by the tide, and now invited us to come to him. C. Cook finding him resolved to advance no farther, gave his musket to an attendant, and went towards him, but tho' the man saw C. Cook give away his weapon to put himself on a footing with him, he had not courage enough to wait his arrival, retreating into the water, however he at last ventured forward, they saluted by touching nose, and a few trinklets put our friend into high spirits — at this time another was observed to strip and enter the water but he very artfully concealed his weapon under the water — he joined his countryman and was presently set a dancing striking his thighs, and shewing the baubles he had received to his friends on the other side. The ice was broke, and we had in moment six or eight more over with us all armed, except the first visiter, with short lances — a kind of weapon we took for a paddle — and a short weapon which was fastned by a string round the wrist, was about 18 inches long, had a round handle and thence formed into a flat elliptic shape: this weapon, we afterwards learnt, was called Pattoo.*

Up to this point things were going well, but the Maoris grew over excited about their gifts. 'Active and alert to the highest degree; overjoyed with the presents they had received, but their desires by no means sated, they were incessantly upon the catch for everything they saw.' The natives snatched at the gifts of iron and beads but parted with only a few feathers in return. They attempted to snatch the arms from the marines but met with no success until one of them got hold of a short sword called a hanger, carried by Charles Green. The thief waved it around his head in triumph and set up a cry of exhaltation. His success caused the natives to become bolder and more insolent. It became obvious that if the man with the hanger was not punished then other weapons would be snatched by the natives. Firing broke out. The man with the hanger was killed and Green's property was recovered. Some natives were wounded by small shot and this caused them to retreat before the musket fire. The whole episode was a very unsatisfactory confrontation and when the incident was over relations were left in a worse state than before the day started.

The next day Cook was even more determined to put things to rights. He took a boat to land at the other end of the bay where he hoped to find a supply of fresh water. The surf was heavy again and the boats could not land, but they saw two native canoes to seaward of them and decided to try to establish contact with the occupants and invite them on board the ship. Tupia called out to the canoes shouting that they would not be hurt, but the natives were afraid and attempted to escape. Cook then showed what was clearly a rare error of judgement on his part and he ordered the muskets to be fired in the hope that this would cause the canoes to stop. The natives turned to face the boat and started to remove what little clothing they had on. They looked ready to jump into the water but the shedding of their clothes was a preparation for battle and as Cook's party came nearer, the natives brandished their weapons and fought like demons to overpower the boat which they thought was going to attack them. There followed a heated and violent exchange, with the natives throwing a large stone, sticks, paddles and anything they could lay their hands on at the English, and the defenders using their firepower in defence. Cook's men over-reacted and fired so effectively that four of the natives were killed by the shots. The other three were captured and taken back to the *Endeavour*.

Cook and Banks were dismayed and horrified by the latest turn of events and by yet more slaughter. That the first contact with a new people should be so violent and blemished by yet more bloodshed was the very last thing that anybody wanted. Both men were fully aware that in their times far worse atrocities were committed daily on the west coast of Africa but this was no comfort to their troubled consciences – the thrill of discovery was clouded by an unnecessary loss of human life. 'I am aware that most humane men who have not experienced a thing of this nature will censure my conduct in firing on the people in this boat nor do I myself think that the reason I had for seizing upon her will at all justify me,' wrote Cook in the unhappy knowledge that he had made an error. It was a tragedy which both men felt in their minds and which lay heavily on their hearts. After dark, loud and angry voices could be heard ashore again. 'Thus ended the most disagreeable day My life had yet seen,' wrote Banks with leaden heart. 'Black be the mark for it and heaven send that such may never return to embitter future reflection.'

Cook's dismay was reflected in the name Poverty Bay which he gave to the first landing place in New Zealand. He honoured his promise to Nicholas Young and named the southern headland Young Nick's Head – a happier and more personal choice of name although it has rightly been pointed out that the first land sighted by Young Nick was the mountains in the interior. As a man of honour Cook must also have presented young Nick with the promised gallon of rum which, particularly after the unfortunate demise of John Reading, we may assume he was not allowed to consume without some willing assistance from his shipmates. It is unfortunate that the records show so little of Young Nick: his age is thought to have been about twelve so that he must have been a tender eleven years when the voyage began. He is referred to by Parkinson as the surgeon's boy but his name does not appear on the muster roll until April 1769 by which time the ship was anchored at Tahiti. A boy so young could not have joined the ship on his own account so we must guess that he could have been a Cumberland lad from Penrith, brought along by William Monkhouse the surgeon. After the voyage he became part of the Joseph Banks entourage of greyhounds, scientists, artists, servants and south sea islanders – but had he been an original member of the Banks party this would certainly have surfaced in the journals. ('At half past one a small boy who was at the masthead Calld out Land', Banks, 6 Oct. 1769. Compare with 'At 10 this morn my servant Peter Briscoe saw the land ...', Banks, 4 April 1769.) Practically the one testimony to Young Nick's character is far from complimentary. It appears in a brief passage by John Bootie, a midshipman who contributed very little to the voyage but who kept an erratic journal in which he wrote the cryptic passage: 'Evil communications corrupt good manners – N Young is a son of a bitch.' This was harsh criticism for a lad of twelve and was probably unjust; the affectionate name 'Young Nick' was an almost inevitable consequence of the boy's real name but it still sounds as though he was thought of fondly enough by the jack tars and rough old salts on the lower decks.

In the eighteenth century boys were often taken to sea at a very tender age; indeed there was a theory that if the boy was past puberty then it was too late for him to take to the hard life of being a sailor. In Nelson's navy every gun crew had a powder monkey to scamper nimbly around the ship and bring the charge of gunpowder for the heavy ship's cannon. Young Nick was not the only boy on board the *Endeavour* and he was probably not the youngest. Tupia brought with him a servant boy called Tayeto from Tahiti; described as a little boy, he was probably under ten years of age. On one encounter with the Maoris trade had been established and a native canoe came alongside the ship to exchange fish for cloth. Little Tayeto was employed to reach over the side, to hand the goods to and fro for exchange, and to scramble up and down the ship's ladder. One of the natives cheated Cook out of a piece of red cloth and in the exchange which followed another of the Maoris seized hold of little Tayeto and dragged the boy down into his canoe. The kidnappers paddled off with their terrified prize and it was fortunate that the marines were ready with firearms loaded to fire on the canoe. The firepower frightened the paddlers sufficiently to loosen their grip on Tayeto and the boy seized his opportunity to jump over the side and into the water. Another canoe then tried to recapture Tayeto but the marines kept the kidnappers at bay with shots. In the meantime one of the ship's cannon was prepared and fired over their heads to frighten them further. 'We sent a boat to take the boy up who was brought on board half dead with fright and the fatigue of swimming,' said Molyneux. Tayeto escaped frightened but unhurt from the ordeal – he became instrumental in the choice of name for the headland which was called Cape Kidnappers. Cook thought originally to call the whole bay Kidnapper's Bay but, perhaps because he had already damned one bay with the name of Poverty, he relented and named the bay instead after Lord Hawke of the Admiralty.

The ship worked further south along the coast but Cook was undecided about whether or not the south was the better direction to sail. The next day, seeing no likelihood of a suitable harbour, he decided it would be more productive to sail northwards. He named the headland Cape Turnagain and turned the ship back towards Poverty Bay where the first landfall had been made the previous week. The *Endeavour* sailed back again past the recently named Isle of Portland and two days later she was back at Young Nick's Head and sailing northwards to explore the other direction.

Poverty Bay was left behind and soon the ship arrived at a bay called Anaura by the natives. News of the frictions at Poverty Bay had spread along the coast, but here the natives were more approachable and gave fish and a quantity of sweet potatoes in exchange for cloth and beads without trying to cheat on the exchange. Cook discovered fresh water but the terrain made it difficult to load the casks and for this reason he resolved to find another watering place. The winds were now against him so he retraced his steps a little and on the advice of the natives he landed at Tolaga Bay to the south. Here he was still very cautious about going ashore and he took good care to take a strong party of marines with him. It happened that these precautions were quite unnecessary. Tolaga Bay was a place which turned out to be one of the most successful landings in New Zealand. The natives were friendly and co-operative, potatoes and crayfish were exchanged, the officers rambled about the surrounding countryside and Parkinson found it:

> ... *agreeable beyond description, and, with proper cultivation, might be rendered a kind of second Paradise. The hills are covered with beautiful flowering shrubs, intermingled with a sort of tall and stately palms, which filled the air with a most grateful fragrant perfume.*

Near the bay was a magnificent natural rock arch standing 40 or 50 feet high and 30 feet wide which aroused the romantic enthusiasm of Banks and Parkinson. One of the young officers even claimed to have attracted 'The ministrations of a beautiful young girl,' and to have been carried ceremoniously over the ditches and rivulets by the natives. Tupia chatted happily with the Maoris and was such a success with his stories of Polynesian folklore that newborn infants were later named after him.

Cook stayed seven days at Tolaga where he obviously had a good opportunity to discover more about the natives. He wanted to stay longer but there was no shelter in the bay. The ship was re-watered and the explorers were anxious to settle down to the joys of discovering and charting the new coastline. On the last day in October the *Endeavour* rounded another cape and found the coast beyond running westwards instead of north. 'This point of land I have called East Cape,' said Cook, 'because I have reason to think that it is the Easternmost land on this whole Coast.' His uncanny intuition was correct again.

The *Endeavour* sailed across a wide north-facing bay. Cook called it the Bay of Plenty and showed one of his rare flashes of humour as they approached a group of rocks which he called the Mayor and the Court of Alderman. Joseph Banks filled in a few details, showing that each rock was deemed to resemble some civic dignitary:

Continent appeard this morning barren and rocky but many islands were in sight … at breakfast a cluster of islands and rocks were in sight which made an uncommon appearance from the number of perpendicular rocks or needles (as the seamen call them) which were in sight at once: these were called the Court of Alderman in respect to that worthy body and entertained ourselves some time with giving names to each of them from their resemblance, thick and squat or lank and tall, to some of those respectable citizens.

November had arrived and Cook began to look for another suitable landing place. On 9 November a transit of the planet Mercury was due to take place, an astronomical event which was by no means as rare or as valuable as the transit of Venus, but one which would enable Charles Green to make an accurate determination of the longitude and which would provide a datum for the position of the rest of the *Terra Australis*. A suitable bay was found which afforded fresh water, botanical specimens to keep Banks and Solander happy, and the usual natives who seemed excitable but open to trade and not hostile. This time Cook and Green, assisted by Zachary Hicks, took observations of the transit, and their timings for internal and external contacts of Mercury agreed to within a few seconds. The astronomers made good use of the readings and were able to calculate the longitude of the place where the observation was made to an accuracy down to a few seconds of arc. They called it Mercury Bay.

The troubles with the natives were by no means over. At Mercury Bay John Gore was left in charge of the ship whilst the captain and the first officer were busy observing the transit. The natives came to trade but one of them cheated Gore by taking a piece of cloth without handing over the items of exchange. Gore was angry and the natives began their war dance as if to taunt the lieutenant and to prove that they could cheat him. This was too much for the impetuous John Gore, he levelled a musket at the guilty man and shot him. When news of the shooting reached

Cook he was saddened by what he thought was more unnecessary bloodshed and the whole crew was concerned about the possibility that the Maoris would try to take revenge for the incident. There was no need for apprehension, however, because the Maoris had held their own inquest and decided that the dead man was clearly guilty of the crime and that he deserved the punishment handed out to him.

Mapping and charting of the land continued apace. Further to the north the coast became broken with shoal water, river estuaries and many islands. The ship explored Hauraki Gulf and sailed right down in to the estuary of a river which reminded Cook of the familiar Thames where he had so often guided the *Endeavour*'s sister ships from the North Sea. He was so impressed with the estuary and the natural harbour outside it that he thought this the most suitable place he had yet discovered for a settlement in New Zealand.

The coast to the northwards became very broken with many bays and islands to chart. Molyneux, Pickersgill and others of the officers all tried their hands at the charting. Progress against the wind was slow and the ship tacked and re-tacked to try to make headway. At one point the *Endeavour* was caught in a strong eddy current and was swept dangerously along at a great speed near the rocky coast. The sailors almost lost control of the ship and they expected to be hurled on to the rocks at any time. Onshore they were accompanied by a great hoard of shouting natives who could clearly see that the ship was out of control and who ran along the coast eagerly watching for the downfall. Cook ordered the pinnace to be launched so that the ship could be towed out of the current but the pinnace caught against one of the guns as it was being lowered to the water. There was a struggle to free it, with the ship all the time being carried along at the mercy of the current. Then the *Endeavour* stuck hard against a rock with a sickening crash of timbers. Luckily a heavy swell lifted the ship clear and the damage seemed to be minimal, but it was a close call. This was one of the worst pieces of seamanship on the voyage; it seemed that the men responsible for the ship expected the rock to swim away – they thought it was a whale!

As the *Endeavour* worked her way northwards the behaviour of the Maoris continued to be varied and unpredictable. At one place which Cook named the Bay of Islands a very difficult and dangerous situation arose when he landed with a small party. A large gathering of Maoris lay in hiding behind the headlands and they suddenly appeared running towards the landing party brandishing their weapons. Cook estimated that about 200 men had gathered to attack them but the people watching from the *Endeavour* could see far more and estimated their numbers at between 500 and 600. The natives began to chant their war song and to advance, but they did not choose to attack the landing party – they went to steal the boats instead. It was very fortunate that Zachary Hicks, who was in charge of the ship in Cook's absence, was fully aware of the danger. He cleverly manoeuvred the *Endeavour* broadside to the beach so that the ship's cannon could be brought into action. There was a puff of blue smoke and the roar of a broadside thundered out from the ship and across the bay. The shot was deliberately fired well over the heads of the aggressors but the firepower of the big guns and the potential danger of the heavy shot was very obvious to the natives and they fled from the scene in terror. Zachary Hicks's action relieved the situation and saved the day.

It was just as well that Stephen Forwood, the ship's gunner, was sober on this the first occasion on the voyage that the heavy guns had to be used in anger. A few days later he was the ringleader in another case of drunkenness. He and three of his colleagues managed to tap off a huge quantity of 10 to 12 gallons of rum from one of the casks and they were caught red handed in the act of consuming it. 'The three men I punished with 12 lashes each,' said Cook. 'But as to the Gunner who richly deserved the whole upon his back is from his Drunkenness the only useless person on board the Ship.' He decided to stop all their allowances until they had repaid the quantity stolen.

At last the *Endeavour* rounded the North Cape of New Zealand and found herself clear beyond the land and into the open Pacific. Cook knew that it was not Tasman's Cape Maria Van Dieman which he had rounded, but he knew that the latter cape could not be far away. The weather was foul and the ship tried to beat westwards into the gale. She tacked and re-tacked for several days and had to ride out a great swell from the west. Cook put out as much sail as he dared. The days became weeks as he still tacked to and fro, weathering the most atrocious gales. It was not merely a question of doubling the Cape and heading southwards again, the perfectionist James Cook wanted to measure the position of Cape Maria Van Dieman as accurately as possible for the benefit of those seamen who came after him. As usual he was ably supported by the astronomer who was still struggling to teach his methods to the less able officers. 'After I had done obs[ervin]g,' wrote Green, 'I Lent my quadrant to Mr Clerk, Mr Saunders and Munkhouse and they each took a Set, alternately taking Alt[itude] for each other and brought me the results …' He was pleased to find that their measurements differed by only 4 minutes of arc from his own readings but this did not prevent him from grumbling about his helpers. 'This is the first Attempt of the kind these hopeful Youths have made and I wish they may not grow worse instead of better,' he complained. We begin to get the impression that Green was a perfectionist who loved complaining, particularly about modern youth.

The men celebrated Christmas Day at sea with a goose pie and an extra ration of rum; in the evening all hands were 'as drunk as our forefathers used to be on the like occasion'. The next morning 'all heads achd with yesterdays debouch'. But Cook hardly noticed the date. On Christmas Eve he was thrilled at spotting the appropriately named Three Kings Island: this could only be the island first sighted by Tasman on the twelfth night of a

Christmas 127 years ago – at last they were falling into the tracks of the legendary Dutch navigator who passed this way in 1642. Cook was familiar with the account of the voyage and knew of Tasman's small ships the *Heemsberk* and the *Zeehaen*, old-fashioned, primitive, high-sided vessels with overhanging forecastles and sterns. On the next part of the voyage the *Endeavour* should confirm the fragment of coast which had been plotted by Tasman. Cook knew that they were only a few leagues north of Tasman's Cape Maria Van Dieman. He described the heavy weather:

> *The gale continued without the least intermission untill 2 am when the wind fell a little and began to veer to the southward and to SW where it fix'd at 4, and we made sail and steer'd East for the land under the Fore-sail and main-sail but was soon obliged to take in the latter as it began to blow very hard and increased in such a manner that by 8 o'clock it was a meer hurricane attended with rain and the Sea run prodigious high, at this time we wore the ship, haul'd up the Fore-sail and brought her too with her head to the NW under a reef'd Main-sail, but this was scarce done before the Main tack gave way and we were glad to take in the Main sail and lay under the Mizen stay-sail and Balance'd Mizen, after which we reefed the Fore-sail and furl'd both it and the main-sail.*

For Cook actually to admit to a hurricane and a 'prodigious high' sea it must indeed have been an incredible tempest which the elements threw at his ship. But by New Year's Eve the cape was rounded and Cook was satisfied that he knew the correct longitude. Dawn broke on a new year and a new decade but there was no respite for the *Endeavour* as she navigated the treacherous west coast of New Zealand with the winds driving her continually onshore and the powerful ocean currents acting against her. At the entrance to Kaipara Harbour the ship was driven back so far that it took her two days and 30 leagues of hard sailing to regain her position. Cook knew that he was navigating a treacherous coast:

... nothing is to be seen but large Sand Hills with hardly any green upon them and the great sea with the prevailing winds impell upon the Shore must render this a very dangerous coast, this I am fully sencible of that was we once clear of it I am determined not to come near again if I can possible avoide it unless we have a very favourable wind indeed.

Cook would have been very surprised to discover that his was not the second but the third European ship to navigate this coastline. The prophets who had forecast that the French were not far behind were correct, and on 12 December, one of the days that Cook was battling against the elements off New Zealand's North Cape, the *Sainte Jean Baptiste* under the command of Jean Francis Marie de Surville sighted the New Zealand coast in a latitude just south of the bar harbour of Hokianga. The storms which hindered Cook had helped the *Sainte Jean Baptiste* and de Surville rounded North Cape only four days later when the *Endeavour* was 50 miles offshore battling against the high seas to make some progress to the west. Unlike Cook, de Surville's crew was in a dreadful state – he had lost no less than sixty dead and the rest so weak that they could hardly handle the ship. The Frenchman was able to land and procure fresh food and water for his ship but he too had problems with the Maoris. They stole one of his boats and he quickly alienated them by trying to recover it by force. De Surville's voyage ended in disaster when he was drowned in attempting to land off the coast of Peru. The two ships were so near each other that the chances of an encounter were very high. It is fascinating but idle to speculate on what might have happened if they had met.

Neither Cook nor Banks noted the entrance to Manukau Harbour, but to the south they named Gannet's Island, Woody Head and Albatross Point. They came to a spectacular mountain rising to such a height that they were reminded of the great peak of Tenerife. It was so high that the snow still lay near the summit. The peak towered many times higher than any other neighbouring hill and rose through the clouds – Cook named it Mount

Egmont after Lord Egmont. (Parkinson's sketch of Mount Egmont has the interesting title 'Mount Egmont, New Zeland, Australia' – the latter being an abbreviation for *Terra Australis Incognita*.) The *Endeavour* was now making more rapid progress but Cook was badly in need of somewhere to stop and replenish the crew and the ship, and he knew that if Tasman's account was correct then there was a large bay to the south where the Dutchman had tried unsuccessfully to land and water his ship. The Maoris had evidently given the Dutch a welcome even less friendly than they gave to the British, and Tasman had called the place Murderer's Bay because four of his crew were killed by the natives in attempting to land.

Cook found that there was indeed a large bay where he expected. There was a great hollow sweep of land containing many bays. It was full of strong currents and difficult winds and nobody was quite sure whether or not they had found Tasman's bay. Deep inside the large inlet was an area of very broken coastline with little islands and many creeks and sheltered waters – some of the creeks were deep enough to take the ship. The natives as usual greeted the *Endeavour* with shouting and a great brandishing of weapons but the land looked fertile and green, and there was plenty of wood and fresh water. It seemed an excellent spot to stop and careen the ship and to try to discover more about the natives. The *Endeavour* was successfully manoeuvred down to the beach. Cook dropped anchor about 2 cable lengths from the shore. He did not yet know it but he had anchored on the South Island.

CHAPTER 7

THE SOUTH ISLAND

To 1 April, 1770

T HE HARBOUR WAS a sheltered spot with good fishing and fresh water. Cook named the place Ship Cove and the waters nearby he called Queen Charlotte Sound. He resolved to stay and rest his crew for a spell. The reception from the natives at first promised to be just as hostile as that of their first landing on the east coast, and they crowded round the ship brandishing weapons. An old man was persuaded to climb on board, he was treated with great respect and given the usual presents of beads and nails. When he returned to his people they broke once again into their war dance, which seemed to be their standard way of venting their emotions – but it was sometimes difficult to know which emotion they were trying to display. 'Whether to show their friendship or enmity it is impossible to say,' Banks commented. 'We have so often seen them do it on both those occasions.' Banks noted with interest the dress of the Maoris in this region, which he found to be almost the same as that depicted in Tasman's drawing of Murderer's Bay – impressive evidence of the accuracy of the earlier explorer.

The British decided they may as well sit back and enjoy the war dance and the Maoris were persuaded that the intentions of the newcomers were friendly. Here was another opportunity for the explorers to learn more about the native customs and about their civilisation. One of the first discoveries at Queen Charlotte Sound was far from pleasant. It was not strictly news to the crew

The Lad Taiyota, Native of Otaheite, in the Dress of his Country. Engraving by R. B. Godfrey after Parkinson © National Library of Australia 2003

Variola louti. A zoological painting by Sydney Parkinson annotated '*Perca rosea*' © Natural History Museum, London 2003

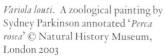

Opposite page top A Morai with an offering to the Dead (July 1769). A wash by Sydney Parkinson © British Library 2003

Bottom The head of a New Zealander © National Library of Australia 2003

This page top A New Zealand War Canoe bidding defiance to the Ship (c. April 1770). Pen and wash drawing by Sydney Parkinson © British Library 2003

Above Sula serrator (Christmas Eve, 1770). An unfinished zoological painting by Sydney Parkinson © Natural History Museum, London 2003

An English Naval Officer bartering with a Maori (1769–). A watercolour thought to be by Joseph Banks © British Library 2003

Patoos used by the New Zealanders. An engraving by Record after J. F. Miller, London 1773 © National Library of Australia 2003

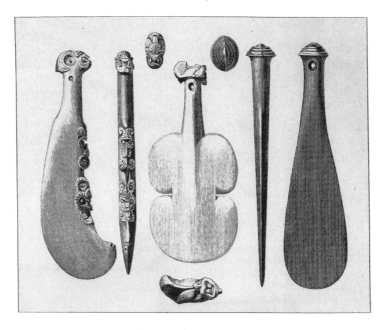

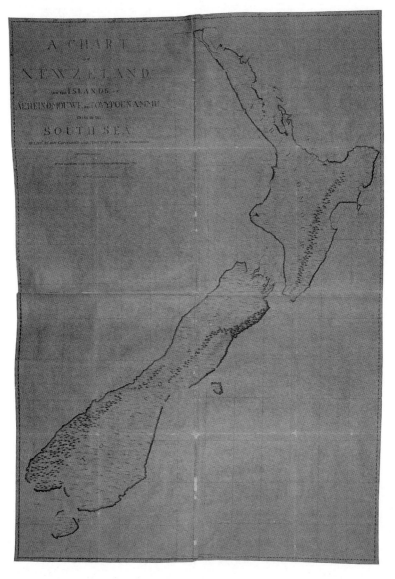

A Chart of New Zealand. Drawn by James Cook c.1770 ©
Public Records Office, London 2003

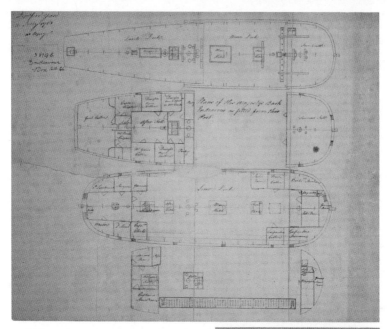

Deck plans of HMS *Endeavour* © National Maritime Museum, London 2003

Australian Aborigines in bark canoes (April 1770). This drawing is thought to have been done by Joseph Banks © British Library 2003

The Calvinistic Church in Batavia.
Engraving and aquatint by Thomas
Medland © Stapleton Collection/
Bridgeman Art Library 2003

List of Officers appointed to the *Endeavour*,
replacing those deceased. By James Cook
1770–71 © Public Records Office, London 2003

A view of the Endeavour River, on the coast of
New Holland, where the ship was laid to shore.
Engraving by Will Byrne, probably after a lost
drawing by Sydney Parkinson © National
Library of Australia 2003

Table Bay by William Hodges (1772) © National Maritime Museum, London 2003

The Triumph of the Navigators. Oil on canvas by Robin Brooks © Blackdog Studios Library 2003

of the *Endeavour*, it merely confirmed a strong suspicion which had been growing since their first contact with the natives. The British had seen plenty of evidence that the Maoris were cannibals but, when challenged on this point, the Maoris always claimed that they themselves were not cannibals but that it was their enemies who ate human flesh. Some claimed that they did not eat the flesh of their own people but only that of their enemies – they did seem to acknowledge some shame, however, in admitting to this fact. Any remaining doubts on the matter were quickly dispelled in Queen Charlotte Sound. Cook discovered a human forearm and other human remains which had recently been picked clean of flesh.

> *There was not one of us that had the least doubt but what this people were Canabals but the finding of this Bone with part of the sinews fresh upon it was stronger proof than any we had yet met with, and in order to fully satisfy the truth of what they had told us, we told one of them that it was not the bone of a man but that of a Dog, but he with great fervour took hold of his forearm and told us again that it was that bone and to convence us that they had eat the flesh he took hold of the flesh of his own arm with his teeth and made shew of eating.*

The crew were sickened and horrified at the thought that they had landed amongst cannibals. Their revulsion can be judged by the fact that a little over a year ago some of the seamen had refused to eat shark's meat on the grounds that sharks in turn ate human flesh. Many seamen resolved to have nothing more to do with the natives, but others had a morbid fascination of the horror of cannibalism and went out of their way to witness the natives in the act of devouring human flesh. They brought their gruesome accounts back to the ship. 'These with several other Instances of Barbarous cruelty these savages is guilty of,' said Sydney Parkinson the artist. 'Ought to make them be abhord by all who may have occasion to tutch at these islands.' Joseph Banks philosophised in his usual fashion at some length and wrote a badly punctuated but fascinating paragraph lamenting the fact that man should stoop to the depths of eating his own species. His passage is a classical example of eighteenth-century scientific thinking and philosophy with overtones of religion and pre-Darwinian ideas about the status of the separate species:

Among fish and insects indeed there are many instances which prove that those who live by prey regard little whether what they take is of their own or of any other species; but any one who considers the admirable chain of nature in which man, alone endowd with reason, justly claims the highest rank and next to him are placed the half reasoning Elephant, the sagacious dog, the architect beaver, &c. in whoom instinct so nearly resembles reason as to have been mistaken for it by men of no mean capacity, from these descending through the less informd Quadrupeds and birds to the fish and insects, which seem besides the instinct of fear which is given for self preservation to be movd only by the stings of hunger to eat those of lust to propagate their species, which when born are left intirely to their own care, and at last by the medium of the Oyster, &c. &c. which not being able to move but as tost about by the waves must in themselves be furnishd with both sexes that the species be continued, shading itself away into the vegetable kingdom for the preservation of whoom neither sensation nor instinct is wanting — whosoever considers this I say will easily see that no Conclusion in favour of such a practise can be drawn from the actions of a race of beings placd so infinitely below us in the order of nature.

The Maoris occasionally ate the island dogs. This and a species of island rat which they caught in a snare were their only sources of meat other than human flesh. The dogs were the only domestic animals which they had and, unlike the Tahitians, they had no pigs or hogs to provide meat. The Maoris were skilled fishermen, however; they constructed traps rather like lobster pots made from twigs, and they were able to make huge seines or trawl nets for bulk fishing. These nets were so large that their construction required the efforts of a whole tribe or village. They had many vegetables in their diet, evidence of agriculture in the North Island where yams, sweet potatoes and other root crops were cultivated in large quantities. William Monkhouse gives an excellent description:

> The ground is compleatly cleared of weeds – the mold broke with as much care as that of our best gardens. The Sweet potatoes are set in distinct little molehills which are ranged in some in straight lines, in others in quincunx. In one lott I observed these hillocks, at their base, surrounded with dried grass. The Arum is planted in little circular concaves, exactly in the manner of our Gard'ners plant melons as Mr. – [Banks] informs me. The Yams are planted in like manner with the sweet potatoes: these Cultivated spots are enclosed with a perfectly close pailing of reeds about twenty inches high. The natives are now [October] at work compleating these fences. We saw a snare or two set upon the ground for some small animal, probably of the Mus tribe [a native rat]. The radical leaves or seed leaves of some of these plants are just above the ground. We therefore suppose their seed time to be about this month. It is agreed that there are a hundred acres of ground cultivated in this Bay (Tolaga bay, North Island) – the soil is light and sandy in some parts – on the sides of the hills it is a black good mold. These, with the Yams, sweet potatoes and Arum are, so far as we know, the whole of what they cultivate.

The natives themselves were of a dark brown colour with thick black hair, their teeth strong and white against their dark faces. Cook was very intrigued by their language which had so many words in common with that of Tahiti, and this caused him to wonder and speculate on a common origin for the two races. The Maoris appeared to be quite distinct from the Tahitians in their physical appearance, there were many characteristic Maori customs, like the tattoos on their buttocks and thighs and the way they decorated their canoes with carvings, which were very reminiscent of the Society Islands. The Maoris took great pride in their canoes and even the prow of a humble fishing canoe was often decorated with a man's face containing a monstrous tongue protruding from it. A twin-hulled canoe had been seen on the North Island, but the single-hulled canoes, carved out of a large solid log, were much more common. A large war canoe, 50 feet long and 5 feet wide with over twenty paddles on each side, could carry up to 100 warriors. These vessels were a fine sight in full power with their great carved stern posts about 12 feet above the water and each with two long light streamers of split feathers blowing behind in the slip-stream. Sydney Parkinson drew a magnificent picture of a war canoe which exactly fits the verbal description given by William Monkhouse:

> The head board was neatly carved – in length about four feet in depth better than two feet – divided into four equal divisions, each filled with spiral carving – the length of this was better than fifty feet, her breadth about five feet: her gunwell was carved – the Stern-post carved with the open Volute – both head and Stern were ornamented with strings of Soot coloured feathers, stript from the racha & wove as it were upon thread, which from the stern post hung down in two pendants, and were not ungracefull when thrown out by the wind.

The Maori cloth was quite different from Tahitian cloth and it impressed the British with its quality. It was made from a plant with the native name of *harkeke* (*Phormium tenax*) which served as flax and hemp. The *harkeke* was very versatile: it could be used to make thick ropes and cordage and could also be drawn out to a very fine thread and woven into cloth. Sometimes the leaves themselves were split into strips and woven into fishing nets and mats. The Maoris knew the art of weaving, and some of their cloth had a woven border 2 or 3 inches wide and worked into a diamond pattern of half black and half white, or sometimes half black diamonds with the other half a brown or cinnamon colour.

Some of the Maori chiefs had cloaks made from dog skins and ornamented with red parrot feathers.

They had stone axes or adzes which they used for building canoes and houses. The common axes were furnished from a polished black stone but the better ones were made from a hard green stone which the natives valued very highly. Cook called this stone 'Green talk', an extremely hard greenstone or nephrite which could be worked to take on a very keen edge.

Houses were designed for a cool rather than a warm climate, they were low built: with a frame of sticks and thatched with long grass; the inside was lined with tree bark to give added insulation. The houses were designed only to give shelter and sleeping accommodation, with a small door usually just large enough for one person to creep through. Cook found the houses to be very weatherproof and warm. Banks described one example of a superior house, representing the acme of Maori architecture, it was about 30 feet long and ornamented with broad planks carved with fantastic spiral designs and contorted faces in the Maori fashion – but the house was unfinished and had been deserted for some time. It was almost certain that some infringement of tapu had taken place during the construction of the house, something which the superstitious Maoris thought would bring them bad luck. The house did not appear to be a temple or place of worship – the people did have some kind of god but as usual the Europeans were confused about the intricacies of the native religion and their tapus. The Maoris had their own folklore and legends about the creation of the world and mankind. They loved to listen to the stories of their people and Tupia, who could converse fluently with them, was able to hold them spellbound with his tales of Tahitian legend and folklore.

At Anaura Bay and Tolaga Bay on the North Island, Joseph Banks was impressed by the cleanliness and the sanitary arrangements. He noticed that every house, or group of houses, had a 'regular necessity house where everyone repairs'. This was a very civilised arrangement and something never seen before in a primitive people. He did not comment on the existence of privies anywhere else in New Zealand but this might well be because he thought it unnecessary to mention such a tapu subject more than once in his journal. There was also a dunghill on which all the waste food was thrown: he wondered if they used it as fertiliser but subsequently discovered that this was not the case.

In many places along the coast were villages of fortified houses called *heppas*, often protected by a wide ditch or moat and by strong fences of wooden palings. The *heppas* were often constructed on rocks or promontories and in one case Parkinson showed a habitation perched on top of a huge arch of rock reaching out to sea – an indication that in some parts of the country there was a perpetual state of war between neighbouring tribes. The fortified villages were found predominantly in the north and west of Aeheinomouwe but in other regions it appeared that the people had no fortifications and lived in a state of peace with their neighbours. In the peaceful parts the inhabitants had finer clothes and more carvings than their more war-like countrymen. In Queen Charlotte Sound Cook and Banks were able to gain the confidence of the Maoris and to visit one of their fortified villages. They discovered that some of the human bones had become items of trade, but they also found that the cannibals had a very approachable side to them:

> Went today to see the Heppah or Town to see our friends the Indians, who received us with much confidence and civility and shewd us every part of their habitations which were neat enough. The town was situated on a small rock divided from the main by a breach in a rock so small that a man might almost Jump over it; the sides were every where so steep as to render fortifications even in their way almost totally useless, according there was nothing but a slight Palisade and one small fighting stage at one end where the rock was most accessible. The people brought us several bones of men the flesh of which they had eat, which they now become a

sort of article of trade among our people who constantly ask for and purchase them for whatever trifles they have. In one part we observed a kind of wooden cross ornamented with feathers made exactly in the form of a crucifix cross. This engaged our attention and we were told that it was a monument to a dead man, maybe a Cenotaph as the body was not there: thus much they told us but would not let us know where it was.

The next day Banks and Solander received an even friendlier welcome. They went on a fishing expedition in the pinnace and met up with a large Maori family who invited them back to their houses. Twenty to thirty natives received the visitors with all manner of friendship including 'numberless huggs and kisses we got from both sexes old and young' – all this was in exchange for a few ribbons and beads.

The natives had their own primitive form of music, created by a selection of wooden flutes and shell trumpets which sounded very inharmonious to European ears. At Poverty Bay when three native boys were taken on board the ship the youths sang a spontaneous song of their own which sounded rather like a psalm tune containing many notes and semitones. William Monkhouse gives a good description of a dance which the three Maori boys performed for the crew of the *Endeavour* on this occasion:

They first prepared themselves by passing some Cloth, which they borrowed for the occasion, round their loins, till now totally without an covering: then placing themselves back to back a little asunder the foremost begins, the others following his motions minutely, with lifting up his right leg, at the same instant raising his arms to a horizontal position, and bending his forearm a little, he trembles his fingers with great quickness – begins a kind of song, and the right leg being raised as above, off they go, beating time and singing & trembling the fingers in the most exact uniformity – the body is now and then inclined to one side or the other – sometimes they bend forward exceedingly low and then suddenly raise themselves, extending their arms and staring most hideously – at

one time they make half turn and face one way, and in two or three
seconds [return] to their former position, in doing of which they bend
forward make a large sweep downwards with both arms, extended, and as
they turn upon the left foot, elevate their arms in the curve, stare wildly,
& pronounce a part of the song with a savage hoarse expiration — this
part of the ceremony generally closes the dance.

The most expressive form of native music, however, was the war
dance which was performed with the whole body and by a shaking
of paddles, jumping and gesticulating. The dance was accompanied by contortions of the limbs and face, the dancers would
thrust out their tongues as far as they were able and widen their
eyes to such an extent that the white could be seen all the way
round. The chant was accompanied by grunting noises and a loud
sigh issued in perfect unison after each chant. Banks described
the war dance as 'an amusement which never failed to please every
spectator'; it was obviously a very fine sight, and one which they
often performed aboard their canoes in exact rhythm with as
many as 100 paddles beating the side of the boat in perfect
unison.

Some members of both sexes had holes bored in their ears from
which they hung adornments of various designs. A favourite decoration was a bunch of down from the albatross; it was snow white
and about the size of a fist. Another ear ornament was a pendant
over 2 inches long and an inch-and-a-half wide: it was made from
the hard green stone, carved in the image of an animal with a
monkey's face. They made head-dresses of black feathers which
were worn on social occasions, and the women sometimes wore
bracelets made from shells or fashioned from the fine bones of
birds. A valuable ornament was the tooth of a whale which was
cut slantwise to resemble a tongue and fitted with small stones for
eyes. Some wore an oval ball the size of an egg around their necks;
it had a distinct perfume which they liked to smell. They had a
method of tattooing their thighs and arms, very similar to the

methods seen at Tahiti. The Maori warriors sometimes daubed their bodies with a dark pigment and painted a broad spiral on each buttock so that their thighs appeared almost covered in black, leaving only a thin line to give an appearance like striped breeches, the amount and design of the decoration varying greatly with individual taste.

The Maoris did not have the bow and arrow for hunting, but they had a long dart lance which was thrown with a stick. Their main fighting weapon was called a *patoo patoo*. This was a short weapon designed for hand-to-hand fighting: it had a blade shaped like a large broad leaf with sharp cutting edges made from the same green stone as their adzes were fashioned from. It weighed 4 or 5 pounds and was a lethal weapon. The warriors took great pride in their *patoo patoos*: they polished the edges, kept them sharp, and they would not readily exchange them for other items of trade.

There was little contact between the European men and the Maori women and Banks thought the females very plain after the exotic girls of the Society Islands. They were not without pride in their appearance but their adornments did not always add to their attractions:

The women were plain and made themselves more so by painting their faces with red ochre and oil which generally was fresh and wet upon their cheeks and fore-heads, easily transferable to the noses of anyone who should attempt to kiss them; not that they seemed to have any objection to such familiarities as the noses of our people evidently shewd, but they were as great coquettes as any Europeans could be and the young ones as skittish as unbroken fillies. One part of their dress I cannot omit to mention: besides their cloth which was very decently rolld round them each wore round the lower part of her waist a string made of the leaves of a highly perfumed grass, to this was fastned a small bunch of the leaves of some fragrant plant which servd as the innermost veil of their modesty.

One of the officers bargained with a native family and agreed on a price in cloth for them to choose a girl with whom he could take his pleasure. The natives sent him off with a youngster who proved to be a boy! When the Englishman complained they gladly exchanged the boy for another youth who also turned out to be a boy and the natives laughed at his confusion. On this occasion the native girls had little or no taste for the white man and they were not prepared to accept any favours. There is very little mention of children in the journals, but at Tolaga Bay Daniel Solander acquired a very interesting child's toy – it was a top 'Shap'd like what boys play with in England' and the natives made signs to him that it should be spun by whipping in exactly the same fashion.

The country was well supplied with good timber which Cook described in seaman's terms as 'fit for all purposes excepting the Ship's Mast'. Banks was much more positive and described the trees around the new River Thames as the finest timber he had ever beheld. It was here that they discovered a giant tree which measured nearly 20 feet in circumference at a height of 6 feet above the ground. A smaller tree of the same species was felled to use for repairs to the ship. The wood was too hard to make a ship's mast but would serve admirably as ship's planking.

Botanically speaking, Banks and Solander were disappointed when their first expedition at Queen Charlotte Sound produced only three new specimens but, by this time, they had made several landings on the North Island and they had collected plenty of interesting specimens of the native flora – certainly enough to keep Parkinson and Spöring busy for many weeks. The fauna was also full of surprises, but the scientists were a little disappointed to discover that, apart from the dogs and the occasional cat or small rodent, they could find no other quadrupeds in New Zealand. Birds, however, were very numerous and, on their first morning on the South Island, the natural historians were awakened by the shrill notes of a glorious dawn chorus in the new land. It seemed the most melodious music they had ever heard.

> This morn I was awakd by the singing of the birds ashore from whence we are distant not a quarter of a mile, the number of them were certainly very great who seemed to strain their throats with emulation perhaps; their voices were certainly the most melodious wild music I had ever heard, almost imitating small bells but with the most tuneable silver sound imaginable to which maybe the distance was no small addition. On enquiring of our people I was told that they had observd them ever since we have been here, and that they begin to sing at about 1 or 2 in the morn and continue till sunrise, after which they are silent all day like

The birds continued to serenade the sailors during the whole of their stay. 'Which we every morning attend to with great pleasure, they sung their time till the sun disturbed them as usual.' On 1 February it rained so hard that the birds were silent and the wind blew so hard that for the first time on the voyage the ship had to put out three anchors to prevent her from being torn from her anchorage.

The last days of January were very wet but, as soon as the rainy spell passed over, Cook took the opportunity to explore the territory inland on foot and along the coast using the ship's boats. The large bay had an inlet which cut very deep into the coastline and he wanted to explore further. Cook set out in the pinnace accompanied by Banks and Solander and a few seamen to manage the boat. The wind blew against them and the men had to row a distance of 4 or 5 leagues. There was no sign of the end of the inlet and he decided to climb a hill to try to see how much further inland it stretched. Visibility was good, and the climb was well worth the effort. From the top was a sight that would stir the heart of any explorer. The view was partly obscured by the neighbouring hills, but before him was a grand vista of wooded mountains and blue seas studded with green islands. It was now obvious that the deep bay off which they had anchored was no mere inlet but a wide strait which swung southwards and ran all the way through the country to the eastern seaboard. In the last two months they had sailed round a large island. The captain recorded a momentous discovery, the existence of the North Island of New Zealand. But what lay to the south was even more mysterious. Was it the mainland of the great southern continent?

> *I took one man with me and climbed up to the top of one of the hills but when I came there I was hindered from seeing up the inlet by higher hills which I could not come at for inpenetrable woods, but I was abundantly rec-ompenced for the trouble I had in ascending the hill, for from it I took to be the Eastern Sea and a strait or passage from it into the Western Sea a little to the Eastward of the entrance to the inlet in which we now lay with the Ship, the main land which lies on the SE side of this inlet appeared to me to be a narrow ridge of very high hills and to form a part of the SW side of the Strait. The land on the opposite side seem'd to trend away East as far as the Eye could see, and to the SE appear'd as oppen sea and this I took to be the Eastern. I likewise saw some islands lying of the East side of the inlet which before I had taken to be part of the Main land.*

A few days later a second expedition confirmed that there was indeed a strait leading to the eastern seaboard. It was what Cook, and Tasman before him, had suspected – the Dutchman had neither the time nor the resources to explore further but Cook determined that he would sail the *Endeavour* right through the straits. He built a conical cairn of stones in which he placed a silver coin with some musket balls and beads, and he left a piece of an old pendant flying from the top of the cairn. He was very taken with this part of New Zealand and, before the ship left the cove, he took formal possession of the country in the name of the king. The ship's carpenter prepared two posts with inscriptions showing the date and the name of the ship. Cook set up one post at the watering place and sought permission of the natives to fix the other post on the outer island which they called Motu-ouru. The natives promised that they would not pull down the post and Cook gave the old men of the village some silver threepenny pieces minted with the date 1763; he also gave them spike nails marked deeply with the king's broad arrow. The union flag was hoisted and a bottle of wine was opened to drink the health of His Majesty King George III. Cook gave the empty bottle to an old man with a tattooed face, a furrowed brow, streaks of red pigment on his face, beard and hair silvered with age, and with earrings of 'Green Talk' and human teeth. The grizzled face broke into a grin and the humble bottle was a present which he knew would please the ancient Maori.

Cook attempted to find out more about the geography of the country from the old man. The information he gained was partly correct: the Maori confirmed the existence of a passage to the Eastern Sea and claimed that the land where they stood was not part of a great continent. His knowledge of more distant parts was fragmentary, however, and it seemed to be no more than guesswork – he said the land consisted of three islands, and that two of these lands could be circumnavigated in a few days but the third would take many moons to sail around.

The repairs to the ship were complete. Cook obtained a last supply of wild celery and the *Endeavour* was warped out of Ship Cove and headed through the straits into the Eastern Sea. The existence of the strait was soon verified but Cook's journal omits to mention the name given to this new discovery. It is Banks who tells us that the passage was christened 'Cook Straits' – the first topological feature to be named after Captain Cook himself. The ship turned northwards along the coast and, after only one day's sail, arrived at Cape Turnagain where the ship had turned to head northwards the previous October. The circumnavigation of the North Island was complete and had taken from October to February – nearly four months. The time had come to explore the rest of the unknown continent.

Southwards along the coast the business of charting and mapping continued. It was almost certainly Banks who insisted on naming Cook Straits so that, when a large offshore island appeared, the captain insisted that it be named 'Banks Island'. The *Endeavour* rounded the island to seaward and continued south – not realising that it was not an island at all but very firmly connected to the mainland. The error might have been spotted but the impetuous John Gore declared that he could see land to the south-east. Cook did not agree, but he was resolved that nobody could accuse him of leaving a single stone unturned in the search for land and he headed in the direction indicated by Gore. No land was found and a little of Cook's chart lost its accuracy. The latitude was approaching 46 degrees and Banks was full of optimism regarding the extent of the continent. He quoted the false rumour about the extent of later Dutch discoveries which indicated that it continued far to the south:

> *We had soundings a great way off and the land appeared very high, so that we once more cherished strong hopes that we had at last compleated our wishes and that this was absolutely a part of the Southern continent; especially as we had seen a hint thrown out in some books that the Du[t]ch, not contented with Tasman's discoveries, had afterwards sent other ships who took the land and followed it to the Southward as high as Lat 64° S*

Banks chose to ignore the fact that the number of inhabitants seemed to have dropped very noticeably. Probably he did not consider this to be significant – the smoke from the fires was still sometimes visible in the night but with ever-diminishing frequency. He remained optimistic, however, as the ship's company divided into continental and island factions and the continentals had the majority. 'Land seen as far South so our unbelievers are almost inclind to think that Continental measures will at last prevail.' The weather had driven the ship far out to sea again and it took a few days to regain the coast. On 9 March she was bearing down on a ledge of rocks with the sea breaking very high against them. Cook had to tack to the east to clear them and he thought the rocks such a danger to shipping that he called them 'The Traps'.

Inland they could see the sun glinting off the bare granite of the Fraser Peaks on Stewart Island, and there was much speculation about the mineral resources of the country. There was an obvious change in the direction of the coastline: the land seemed to have fallen right away and by the next day a southern cape had been rounded. There was much discussion as to whether or not the southernmost land (Stewart Island) was detached from the mainland, and Cook had reasons for thinking it was a peninsula. Molyneux's chart, which was greatly inferior to his captain's draughtsmanship, showed the land as an island, and Hicks, too, was convinced that it was not connected to the mainland. 'At Sun sett the North Eastermost Land bore NE 5 leagues, a point NbW from which there is the appearance of a Passage,' wrote Hicks on 6 March. Five days later he recorded seeing the western opening of the straits: 'The passage at N 69° E to N 72° E, the extreme of the Large Island which is ye Southern Land of the streights at S 72° E to S 41° E; distance from the shore 3½ leagues.' As they sailed round Stewart Island there was a great swell from the south-west.

> I began now to think that this was the southernmost land and that we should be able to get round it by the west, for we have had a large hollow swell from the SW ever since we had the last gale of wind from that quarter which makes me think that there is no land in that direction.

Cook never really believed that they had found a continent, but it was as they rounded Stewart Island that the dream of a world was destroyed. It was in a sense the saddest point on the whole voyage. The *Terra Australis Incognita*, which had filled the maps of the southern seas for centuries, was sadly depleted. If this was the continent which they were charting then it had shrunk to a size no larger than the British Isles. The continent-mongers were totally demoralised: they had sailed halfway round the world and had ridden the great swells of the South Pacific for too many months not to know that the swell meant there was no more land for hundreds of leagues to the west.

'Blew fresh all day but carried us round the Point too the total demolition of our aerial fabric calld continent' – Banks expressed his feelings very succinctly. New Zealand was a major discovery of two large temperate and habitable islands but it was not the great continental land-mass which filled their horizon and which they had sailed the seven seas to find.

> *Fresh gales still and wind that will not let us go to the northward. We stood in with the shore which proved very high and had a most romantick appearance from the immence steepness of the hills, many of which were conical and most had their heads coverd with snow, on their sides and bottoms was however a good deal of wood, so much we could see and no more and the wind baulking us would not let us stand nearer the shore than two leagues.*

Cook set a wide course: he took his ship well out to sea and had difficulty doubling the treacherous west cape but, having once rounded it, he was able to make good headway along the western coast with a strong following current. He found a rocky coastline guarded by steep cliffs. In ideal weather it would have been possible to take the ship into one of the sheltered inlets, and Banks was very keen to land so that he could botanise and study the mineral deposits he could see from the ship. Cook very rightly refused to risk the ship and its crew. It was a dangerous rocky coastline with unpredictable winds and currents near the land. Banks knew that he had to accept the captain's decision.

The mountain scenery was at its most spectacular. The lower slopes were green and wooded and the hills rose steep behind with range upon range of mountain scenery. The peaks were covered in pure white snow, smooth and untrodden and freshly fallen in great quantities. Autumn was approaching fast and there was much rain and mist so the tops of the mountains were not always visible. It was a beautiful and virgin land which they were charting and it was almost untouched by man with hardly any signs of habitation. The wind blew fresh from the open sea and the ship responded with a good rate of knots. Progress was rapid except along the coast near Cape Foulwind where contrary gales set the ship backwards from the planned course. It was only a temporary set-back and soon the *Endeavour* came again to that part of the coast where Tasman made his first landfall. They sailed north-eastwards until they came to the cape at the end of the South Island. They were in familiar waters as the ship tacked into a bay they identified as Tasman's Bay and headed again for Queen Charlotte Sound where Cook knew he could replenish the supplies of fuel and water and feed his crew on the scurvy grass before heading for the open sea again.

It was the end of March and the time had come to make a decision about the remainder of the voyage. Stocks of sugar, salt, tea and tobacco were low but the supplies were judged sufficient to last for another six months at two-thirds' allowance, and this left three alternatives open to them.

Cook, in his journal, admitted that he wanted to return home via Cape Horn so that he could cross the Pacific in the high latitudes and prove once and for all the existence or otherwise of the diminished southern continent in which some of his crew still tenaciously believed. But the southern winter was fast approaching and the state of the sails and rigging was very worn after the beating they had taken in rounding the capes of New Zealand. The Cape Horn route was considered too dangerous and that left two alternatives – either to proceed directly to the Cape of Good Hope, keeping to the south of Van Dieman's land and to sail the empty stretch of ocean already crossed by Tasman in the previous century, or to steer down the latitudes of New Holland in the hope of discovering the unknown east coast of that country which Cook knew must exist somewhere. It was completely out of character for Cook to follow Tasman's route when he knew that no new discoveries could follow. He convinced his crew that they must search for the east coast of New Holland and follow it as far northwards as possible. This plan was unanimously agreed. It would take many months of sailing but, by this route, he hoped to arrive at the islands discovered by Quiros in 1606 and to prove that a strait existed between New Holland and New Guinea, and to make his way home by way of the Dutch East Indies.

The next day there was a moderate breeze from the east. The *Endeavour* weighed anchor and the sailors set her sails to take her out of the bay and into the open sea. Both the islands of New Zealand had been circumnavigated. Cook and several of his officers were busy preparing their charts of the new land. As the breeze filled the sails, they thought of the places they were leaving behind them: of Young Nick's Head, Cape Kidnappers, Mercury Bay, Mount Egmont, Cape Palliser, Queen Charlotte Sound. On the South Island were many mementoes of the voyage – Banks Island, Cape Saunders, Solander Island, Cape Foulwind and the last headland, which they called Cape Farewell, retreated into the haze. The story of the voyage was written everywhere on the coastline and mountains of the land they had discovered for posterity. They talked of colonising the land and of the best places for harbours and settlements. Cook worked at his chart of New Zealand and called the main islands by their native names of Aeheinomouwe and Tovypoenammu. He produced a masterpiece of eighteenth-century cartography.

The chart which I have drawn will best point out the figure and extent of these islands, the situation of the Bays and harbours they contain and the lesser Islands lay about them. And now I have mentioned the Chart I shall point out such places as are drawn with sufficient accuracy to be depended upon and such as are not, beginning at Cape Palliser and proceed around Aechei no Mouwe by the East Cape &c. The Coast between these two capes I believe to be laid down pretty accurate both in its figures and Course and distance from point to point ... From Cape Maria Vandieman up as high as Latitude 36°15' we seldom were nearer the Shore than from 5 to 8 leagues and therefore the line of the Sea Coast may in some places be erroneous; from the above latitude to nearly the length of Entry Island we run along and near the shore all the way and no circumstance occur'd that made me liable to commit any material error ... but I cannot say so much for Tovy-peoammu, the Season of the year and the circumstance of the Voyage would not permit me to spend so much time about this island as I had done at the other and blowing weather we frequently met with made it both dangerous and difficult to keep upon the coast. However I shall point out the places that may be erroneous in this as I have done in the other. From Queen Charlotte Sound to Cape Cambel and as far to the SW as the Latitude 43° will be found to be pretty accurate, between this latitude and 44°20' the coast is very doubtfully discribed, a part of which we hardly if att all saw. From this last mentioned latitude to Cape Saunders we were generally at too great a distance to be particular and the weather at the same time was unfavourable. The coast as it is laid down from Cape Saunders to Cape South and even to Cape West is no doubt in many places very erroneous as we hardly ever were able to keep near the shore and were sometimes blowen off altogether. From the West Cape down to Cape Fare-Well and even to Queen Charlottes Sound will be found in most places to differ not much from the truth.

They little knew that their visit would remain long in the folklore memories of the Maori people. At Mercury Bay they left behind them a little boy called Te Horeta who clung to his memories until he was an old man. He recalled the happenings of his youth when a strange vessel had appeared off the coast, of strangely clad men who looked backwards as they pulled their boat. His memories were vague in parts and shaped by years of tradition but

John Beaglehole studied the traditions deeply and was convinced of the truth of the account. He summarised the main facts of the findings which deserve to be quoted in full:

More than eighty years later, when the first settlers arrived in New Zealand, an ancient chief, Te Horeta, a man of blood in many wars, told them of the great happening of his childhood. The ship had come, it seemed a supernatural thing, and its men supernatural beings, for they pulled their boats with their backs to the shore where they were to land — had they eyes at the backs of their heads? They pointed a stick at a shag, there was thunder and lightening and the shag fell dead; the children were terrified and ran away with the women into the trees. But these tupua, goblins or demons, were kind, and gave food: something like pumice stone but sweet, something else that was fat, perhaps whale blubber or flesh of man, though it was salt and nipped at the throat — ship's bread, or biscuit, salt beef or pork. There was one who collected shells, flowers, tree-blossoms and stones. They invited the boys to go on board ship with the warriors, and little Te Horeta went, and saw the warriors exchange their cloaks for other goods, and saw the one who was clearly the lord, the leader of the tupau. He spoke seldom, but felt the cloaks and handled the weapons, and patted the children's cheeks and gently touched their heads. The boys did not walk about, they were afraid lest they should be bewitched, they sat still and looked: and the great lord gave Te Horeta a nail, and Te Horeta said Ka pai, which is 'very good', and the people laughed. Te Horeta used this nail on his spear, and to make holes in the side boards of canoes; he had it for a god but one day his canoe capsizes and he lost it, and though he dived for it he could not find it. And this lord, the leader, gave Te Horeta's people two handfuls of potatoes, which they planted and tended; they were the first people to have potatoes in this country.

(JOHN WHITE: *Ancient History of the Maori*,
Wellington 1889)

CHAPTER 8

AUSTRALIA

To 11 June, 1770

THE ENDEAVOUR LEFT New Zealand at a latitude of 40 degrees and 30 minutes. Cook intended to run down this latitude until he met the east coast of Van Dieman's Land where Tasman had made his landfall in 1642. The ship made fair progress: on a good sailing day she logged over 100 nautical miles but, on 16 April the wind veered to the south, and squalls and gales drove her northwards from the planned course. The spritsail was worn almost to rags, Cook decided he could dispense with it, and John Ravenhill used the canvas to repair two of the topgallants. The jibsail had split and was in a similar condition so Cook ordered one of the tents to be cut up and used for repairs. Two days later flocks of inquisitive seabirds appeared. They swooped and screamed around the alien ship which had entered their waters and the sailors knew that land could not be far away. The weather continued unsettled throughout the day and into the following night but, as dawn broke on 19 April Zachary Hicks was at the masthead. From just north of the sunrise stretching all the way round to the western horizon the first lieutenant saw land. It was a coast which had never been seen before by European eyes.

Over a century had passed since Tasman's voyage to the south seas. There was no reason to doubt the truth of the story in his journals but the new landfall did not fit the position of the place he called Van Dieman's Land. The heavy swell of the sea implied that no land existed in the direction that Cook expected and, if there was no land to the south, then this meant it could not be Van Dieman's Land that they had sighted. The sextant showed that the southerly winds had driven the *Endeavour* about 3 degrees north of Tasman's landfall. Cook therefore expected to find a coastline running north–south instead of east–west.

He suspected that there existed a strait between this landfall and Van Dieman's Land, and that they had stumbled upon the coast of New Holland, but this hypothesis implied that New Holland was a very large island, almost of continental proportions. Was the land before them the east coast of New Holland? Was it an entirely new country? Was it the fabled *Terra Australis Incognita* which they had sailed so far to find, or was it after all just another small Pacific island? The projected route of the *Endeavour* was to sail northwards towards the equator. This meant that to prove the existence of a strait would involve a change of plan and would undoubtedly take a great deal of time. There was obviously much to be discovered in these uncharted waters and amongst the many questions to be answered was whether or not the new land stretched all the way from this latitude to that of New Guinea.

As if to welcome the *Endeavour* the wind raised three waterspouts snaking upwards from the sea. Two of them died away quickly but the third remained in play for a good fifteen minutes. Joseph Banks was fascinated by this apparition:

> It was a column which appeard to be about the thickness of a mast or a midling tree, and reachd down from a smoak colourd cloud about two thirds of the way to the surface of the sea ... When it was at its greatest distance from the water the pipe itself was perfectly transparent and much resembled a tube of glass or a column of water, if such a thing could be supposd to be suspended in the air; it very frequently contracted and dilated; it very seldom remained in a perpendicular direction but generaly inclind either one way or the other in a curve as a light body acted upon

*by the wind is observd to do. During the whole time that it lasted smaler
ones seemd to attempt to form in its neighbourhood; at last one did about
as thick as a rope close by it and became longer than the old one which at
that instant was in its shortest state; upon this they joined together in an
instant and gradually contracting into the Cloud disapeard.*

Cook's journal concentrated on the nature of the land, which he
saw as low and fertile, and on the practicalities of latitude and
longitude:

*At noon we were in the Lat of 37° 50' and Long of 219° 29' W, the
extremes of land extending from NW to ENE, a remarkable point bore
N 20° E at distant 4 leagues. This point rises to a round hillick, very
much like the Ram Head going into Plymouth Sound on which account I
called it by the same name. Lat 37° 29', Longitude 210° 22' W. The
variation by an azimuth taken this morning was 8° 7' east. What we
have as yet seen of this land appears rather low and not very hilly, the
face of the Country green and woody but the seashore is all a white sand.*

The southernmost headland was called Point Hicks after the lieutenant who first sighted it (it seems unfortunate that this name
did not survive, the first settlers called it Cape Everard). The
Endeavour turned eastwards along the coast and it soon became
apparent that it was not a small island but part of a large land-
mass which they had discovered. Cook was shown to be
premature in assuming that it was low country and, as the
weather cleared and visibility improved, a mountain with humps
on it like a dromedary became visible near the shore – it was
named after the animal it resembled. It also became apparent that
if this was the east coast of New Holland, then it was quite unlike
the barren accounts of the western shores which adventurers like
Dampier and the Dutch sailors before him had brought back with
them.

The sailors gazed with awe and interest as each headland was rounded and grand new vistas opened up before them. There followed once more the novelty of naming the new capes and headlands never seen by western man. Cape Upright consisted of nearly perpendicular cliffs, Pigeon House resembled its name, Cape St George was sighted on St George's day, Long Nose and Red Point were named from their shape and colour. The country was obviously populated, smoke could be seen by day and in the darkness of the night the red glow of fire flickered in the woodlands. Before long the natives themselves were seen at a safe distance running down to the beaches and spearing fish in the rockpools.

After less than a day's sail it became evident that the general direction of the coastline had changed from west to north. The *Endeavour* sailed on, searching for a suitable place to land. The coastline alternated between rocky promontories and sandy beaches where white surf broke high and incessantly. A landing must be made as soon as possible, but sheltered bays and deep, safe anchorages with fresh-water supplies were not easy to find, and after seven days no suitable spot had been sighted. It was therefore decided that an attempt would be made to land on one of the surf-washed beaches. The ship stood a safe 2 miles offshore and the pinnace was made ready for the attempted landing but, as soon as it was lowered into the water the boat began to leak so rapidly that it had to be hoisted back on deck for repairs. The yawl was prepared instead: this was a smaller boat just large enough to carry four rowers and three passengers. A party of natives with a canoe waited onshore but, when the yawl approached the beach, the surf was breaking so high at every point that, with seven people in the boat, it soon became clear that a landing was too risky to contemplate. (This first attempt to land on Australian soil was made at a beach between Bulli and Bellambi Point.)

At daylight on the following morning, 29 April, a sheltered bay was spotted which looked a promising spot in which to cast anchor. Robert Molyneux was sent ahead to take soundings. On his return he reported in favour of a deep anchorage. The *Endeavour* was guided into the bay and by the afternoon she was safely anchored in 6 fathoms of water.

The landing party once again approached the shore. The pinnace had been repaired and this time the party occupied three boats and was thirty or forty strong. In the leading boat with the captain were Banks, Solander, Tupia, Cook's wife's cousin, young Isaac Smith, and a number of seamen. At both ends of the beach were small clusters of native huts and opposite the ship stood a group of aboriginal men, women and children. The boats steered purposefully towards the natives in the hope of making contact and discovering more about them, but the Aborigines didn't trust the newcomers and made off into the woods as soon as the boats came close. Their rights were defended, however, by two threatening stalwarts with frizzled hair and bushy beards, lean and raw boned, their bodies daubed with a white pigment – they remained behind to oppose the landing party. The two warriors shook their lances menacingly and shouted words which neither Tupia nor anybody else could understand. Cook fired his musket to frighten them off but this only caused them to run back to where they kept a small store of throwing darts. One man took up a stone and threw it. Cook fired a second time and some of the small shot actually struck one of the men in the leg – this again seemed to have little effect other than to cause him to run back about 100 yards to a hut and to return with a round wooden shield to defend himself.

The boats arrived at a rock which served as a landing stage. The captain made to step ashore but then he suddenly realised the historic significance of the occasion. 'Isaac,' he said with a generous gesture to his eighteen-year-old relative, 'You shall land first.' It was a gesture which Isaac Smith never forgot: he became the first European to set foot on the new continent and it was a story which he often enjoyed repeating in his old age. But there was little time to savour the moment. The natives had deduced that the slow and clumsy invaders could not catch them on their own territory and one of them threw a missile by means of a throwing stick from a safe distance. Sydney Parkinson claimed that the missile fell between his feet: it looked like a lance or a long dart. Cook fired a third shot and this caused the Aborigines to retreat slowly into the woods with some of the landing party in pursuit. Excessive use of firearms in the presence of the natives was uncharacteristic of Cook. He was possibly unnerved after some of his experiences in New Zealand, but he was still very anxious to make friendly contact with the natives.

The small huts, which were seen during the approach to the shore, were inspected and were found to be made from tree bark. Four or five children were discovered inside – they had been abandoned by their owners and were given strings of beads to play with.

The next concern was to find fresh water. This was the factor that would determine whether or not the ship would stay long enough to explore the territory. Brackish water was obtained by digging down in the sand to the water table. Purer water was found when a small stream was discovered, but the trickle was too small to fill the water casks easily.

We found here some fresh water which came trickling down and stood in pools among the rocks; but this was so troublesome to come at I sent a party of men ashore in the morning to the place where we first landed to dig holes in the sand by which means and a small stream they found fresh water sufficiency to water the ship. The strings of beads etc we had left with the children last night were found laying in the hut this morning, probably the natives were afraid to take them away. After breakfast we sent some empty casks ashore and a party of men to cut wood and I myself went in the Pinnace to sound and explore the bay, in the doing of which I saw several of the natives but they all fled at my approach. I landed in two places one of which the people had just left, as there were small fires and fresh muscles broiling upon them – here likewise lay vast heaps of the largest oyster shells I ever saw.

There was much to do. Minor repairs and maintenance had to be done on the ship, the land before them had to be mapped and charted, the log had to be updated, reports and journals filled in and some contact must be made with the elusive natives. The marines organised the defence of the shore party. The sailors continued with the job of re-watering. John Satterly and his mate Edward Terral busied themselves with inspecting the state of the ship's outside timbers. John Ravenhill and his assistant sailmakers spread out the worn canvasses for repairs. A good haul of fish was netted on the north side of the bay. Lieutenant Gore went off in one of the boats to dredge for oysters. Charles Green took the sun's altitude; he calculated the latitude at 34 degrees then applied himself to the more difficult task of finding the longitude. Banks and Solander predictably began to collect specimens and seldom can any botanist have been as content as these avid collectors with a whole new continent before them. So many plants were collected that care was needed to preserve them all and one of the ship's sails was spread out on the beach and covered with 200 quires of drying paper which the botanists used to preserve their specimens. Banks found that by exposing them to the sun for a day and turning them regularly they were kept in good condition for preservation. The artist and draughtsmen busily recorded the specimens and the scenes before them.

A party of natives approached inquisitively to within 100 yards of the encampment. Zachariah Hicks tried to parley and trade with them by offering beads, nails and other presents but they seemed to have no interest in these useless trinkets. John Gore came within 20 yards of another group but he too was unable to parley with them. William Monkhouse met the same group and feigned a sham retreat in the hope that they would follow him: the natives hovered around suspiciously but would not come close enough to make contact. One of the midshipmen met with an old man accompanied by a woman and two small children. He was able to come close enough to speak and to offer them a parrot he had shot, but they recoiled from the dead bird in fear and horror – they seemed afraid and would not utter a word to the white man.

The *Endeavour* remained in the bay for a week. The union flag was flown every day and an inscription was cut on one of the trees showing the date of the visit and the name of the ship. Soon it was time to move on again. At daybreak on 5 May a light wind blew from the north-west, the ship weighed anchor and inched her way out to the open sea. The departure was tinged with a note of sadness when one of the seamen died. He was Forby Sutherland who had been suffering from tuberculosis since before the passage around Cape Horn. He was buried near the watering place at the encampment, half the world away from his home in the Orkney Islands, and Cook thought it fit to name the south point of the bay after him. On the last day the yawl returned with a catch of stingrays which weighed in at 4 hundredweight and on this account the captain thought to call the place Sting Ray Harbour. He thought again, pondering that perhaps the euphoric botanists engrossed in their great store of new specimens were more characteristic of the place. How about calling it Botanist's Bay? He changed his mind again: 'The great quantity of New Plants &c Mr Banks & Dr Solander collected in this place occasioned my giving it the name of Botany Bay. It is situated in the Latitude of 34° 0' S. Longitude 208° 37' W.

The *Endeavour* headed north-north-east along the coast, and after only 3 leagues another bay or harbour was spotted which also appeared to be a safe anchorage – it was named Port Jackson. 'The land we sailed past during the whole afternoon appeard broken and likely for harbours,' observed Banks. The sailors looked straight down the opening at Port Jackson but the ship did not stop to investigate and Sydney Harbour, one of the finest natural harbours in the Southern Hemisphere, remained undiscovered.

For two days the wind came from the north and the ship made

no progress. On the evening of 9 May, offshore from Cape Three Points, the sun came out strongly from behind a cloud and Sydney Parkinson described a bright rainbow complete with secondary bow. 'Two of the most beautiful rainbows my eyes ever beheld: The colours were strong clear and lively; those of the inner one were so bright as to reflect its shadow (Reflection) on the water. They formed a complete semicircle; and the space between them was much darker than the rest of the sky.'

The wind veered to the south and in the next twenty-four hours the ship covered 2 degrees of latitude. The country seemed in character to Botany Bay, but as they sailed northwards the coast became progressively more dangerous and breakers were frequently seen several leagues offshore, an indication that shallow water and shoals existed beneath. One cape was named Point Danger and an inland peak named Mount Warning as a guide to future navigators. The *Endeavour* sailed on at a safe distance from the land, but near enough to continue the charting of the coast with a high degree of accuracy. The next headland was named Cape Moreton after the president of the Royal Society: it was in fact an island but the ship was too far away to discern this fact. A fine bay and a river estuary were visible behind the cape. The captain climbed to the masthead where he could just make out a low plateau of land behind the bay.

The heavy swell from the south-east continued for two or three days, until the ship arrived at the end of a long island with a sandy cape at the northernmost point. There appeared to be shoals ahead and a boat was therefore sent on to take soundings. The ship cleared the end of a long spit and entered smoother waters. The spit was christened Break Sea Spit. The ship's boat continued to take soundings in a smooth sea which was so clear that Joseph Banks claimed he could still see the bottom even at a depth of 20 fathoms. The bay was named Hervey Bay after John Hervey, a naval officer who later became the third Earl of Bristol.

On 24 May the *Endeavour* crossed into the tropics and a

headland which was judged to be at the exact latitude was named Cape Capricorn. Two senior naval officers, Augustus Keppel and Charles Townsend, were commemorated by place names. It was obvious that the ship was sailing sluggishly and her bottom was covered with the weeds and barnacles that flourished in the warm waters of the tropics. A safe estuary was needed with a high rise and fall of the tide, a place where the ship could be safely grounded and hauled over for her underside to be careened. All the inlets they investigated had much the same problem, the soundings showed more shoal water and very variable depth: it was not going to be easy to find the place they wanted. On one occasion the depth registered a good 14 fathoms with the ship close hauled to eastwards. The next cast of the line showed only 3½ fathoms with the ship heading straight for shallow water. There was no time to reef the sails. An anchor was kept at the ready for such emergencies and it was hurriedly dropped over the stern so that the ship was brought to an abrupt halt with all her sails billowing. Valuable time was wasted at one inlet where Cook and Molyneux found a place suitable to lay the ship ashore but the only fresh water to be found was in an insect-ridden stagnant pool. It was named Thirsty Sound.

In spite of the dangers from the shoal water Cook held close to the coastline. He discovered a passage between an island and the mainland; it was named Whitsunday Passage because that was the day on which it was discovered. One island was named Magnetic Island because it appeared to effect the compass readings. This was not the first time the ship's master had noticed fluctuations of the needle along this newly discovered coastline: the variation had been encountered near Cape Dromedary when Joseph Banks had shown some interest in the problem:

The master in conversation today made a remark on the variation of the Needle which struck me much, as to me it was new and appeard to throw much light on the Theory of that Phaenomenon. The variation is here

very small, he says: he has three times crossed the line of no variation and
at all times as well as this he has observed the Needle to be very unsteady,
moving very easily and scarce at all fixing: this he shewed me: he also told
me that in several places he has been in, the land had a remarkable effect on
the variation, as in the place we were now in: at 1 or 2 leagues from the
shore the variation was 2 degrees less than at 8 Lgs distant.

There are several possible explanations for the compass variation: metallic objects in the ship were a common cause of error and the fact the needle did not easily fix implies a large angle of dip in the Earth's magnetic field.

During the search for a suitable place to careen the ship a more urgent problem arose: it was a serious breach of naval discipline involving Richard Orton, the captain's clerk. Orton was not a man without fault; he was sometimes a careless and self-willed copyist and he evidently suffered from the common sailor's fault of drinking too much alcohol – but as far as was known he was popular with the crew and had not made any enemies on board ship. It therefore came as a shock to the captain when he found his clerk in his bunk with all the clothes cut from his back and much worse – the poor copyist was covered with blood and his ears had been cut and mutilated.

The captain was furious. He discovered that James Magra, a midshipman from New York, had once or twice before cut off the clothes from Orton's back in a drunken frolic – and it therefore seemed obvious that Magra was the guilty party. The midshipman strongly denied the charge and there was something in his denial that made Cook feel that Magra might be telling the truth. This created a real dilemma, for who was the culprit if it was not James Magra? The most amazing thing about the affair is that anybody could manage to do such a thing un-noticed in the confined space of a vessel like the *Endeavour*. But somebody was responsible. It was the captain's duty to find and punish that person. Cook tried to be scrupulously fair in all his dealings – but he was unsure about his accusation of Magra and this left him in a difficult and vulnerable position.

With respect to Mr Orton he is not a man without his faults, yet from all enquiry I could make, it evidently appear'd to me that so far from deserving such a treatment he had not designedly injured any person in the Ship, so that I do and shall always look on him as an enjure'd man. Some reason might however be given why this misfortune came upon him in which he himself was in some measure to blame, but as this is only conjector and would tend to fix it up[on] some people in the Ship whome I would fain believe would hardly be guilty of such an act, I shall say nothing about it unless I shall hereafter discover the Offenders which I shall take every method in my power to do, for I look upon such proceedings as highly dangerous in such Voyages as this and the greatest insult that could be offer'd to my authority in this ship, as I have been made against any Person in the Ship.

The *Endeavour* was a Royal Navy ship and all the crew were in theory professional sailors. In practice many had been recruited against their will by press-gang methods, but all were experienced sailors and well used to the cramped conditions below decks. There must have been far more bickering and quarrelling amongst the officers and crew than the journals record, but Cook knew that strong discipline was essential if the men were to tolerate each other for so long in the confined quarters of the lower decks.

The time taken to send the pinnace ahead, the time to make the depth soundings and the time to take bearings for the charts all contrived to make slow progress for the *Endeavour*. But this was almost an ideal situation for the naturalists. In sharp contrast to New Zealand they now had plenty of opportunity to explore the coast and to make the occasional trip inland when the ship was waiting at anchor. Much of the land was covered by trees of which the gum tree or Eucalyptus, so much loved by the Koala, appeared the most common. Some trees resembled the pine and others reminded them of the American Live Oak. One species bore a small fruit the size of a crab apple – it was found to be edible but tasted like a damson and contained a very large stone which made it less palatable. Several varieties of palm were discovered. The coastal marshes, covered by the sea at high tide, were invariably covered by mangroves. Often there existed little or no undergrowth to impede the passage through the trees.

The first inland expedition was undertaken at Botany Bay where the party armed themselves with ten muskets as defence against the natives. This precaution proved to be either quite unnecessary or perhaps an excellent deterrent for in the whole day they saw only one Aborigine and he took flight as soon as he saw them – the only shots fired were to satisfy Banks's insatiable hunting appetite. Most of the terrain around Botany Bay was covered by swampy ground or a light sandy soil. No large animals were seen but there was plenty of evidence that they existed: a kangaroo and a wild dingo had left their droppings behind them. A small animal was spotted which was instrumental in causing Banks's greyhound to meet with a painful accident:

> We saw one quadruped about the size of a rabbit. My greyhound just got sight of him and instantly lam[e]d himself against a stump which lay concealed in the long grass; we saw also the dung of a large animal that had fed on the grass which much resembles that of a Stag; also the footsteps of an animal clawed like a dog or wolf and as large as the latter; and of a small animal whose feet were like that of a polecat or weesel. The trees over our heads abounded very much with Loryquets and Cocatoos of which we shot several; both these sorts flew in flocks of several scores together.

Land animals were initially thought to be scarce, but this was partly due to the ease with which they could hide themselves in the bush. One of the seamen described a creature which was so black and ugly that he thought the devil himself had arrived to carry him off. He described it as 'about as large and much like a one gallon cagg, as black as the devil and had two horns on its head, it went slowly but I dard not touch it'. He also mentioned that this satanic creature had wings – a description which seems to fit the fruit-bat or Australian Flying Fox.

A large, slender, mouse-coloured animal was sighted, quite unlike anything seen in Europe or any other continent. It bounded along balanced by a long tail and jumping like a hare. 'We observed much to our surprize that instead of Going on all fours the animal went upon two legs, making vast bounds just as a Jerbua (Jerboa: a small African rodent which jumps on its two hind feet) does,' wrote the amazed Banks on first witnessing this form of locomotion. 'The head neck and shoulders of this animal was very small in proportion to the other parts,' said Cook. 'The tail was nearly as long as the body, thick next the rump and taper-ing towards the end … its progression is by hoping or jumping 7 or 8 feet at each hop upon its hind legs only, for in this it makes no use of the fore, which seem to be only design'd for scratching in the ground &c.' They were amazed to find that the animal could easily outpace the greyhound, but it must be admitted that the long grass, which the bounding creature easily leapt over, was a great hindrance to the dog. The aboriginal name for it was a 'Kanguru' – a name which the scientist easily adapted to their own language.

There existed plenty of other species. There were bats, lizards, snakes, scorpions, insects too numerous to classify, and at least one sighting of a crocodile. The sea was everywhere clear and well stocked with fish: they found dog-fish, rock-fish, mullets, bream and a great variety for which the sailors had their own names: leather-jackets, five-fingers, sting-rays and whip-rays. The shoreline supported cockles, mussels, crabs, rock-oysters and mangrove oysters, pearl oysters and the large delicious mud-oysters. To his great joy Banks discovered a small fish the size of a minnow which seemed equally at home on land or water. The creature had two strong breast fins which enabled it to leap like a frog along the mudbanks. The naturalists watched with delight as it leapt nimbly and confidently from stone to stone above the water. It was the first sighting of an Australian mudskipper.

The reef was the habitat of the great green-backed turtle. Banks and Solander did not have sufficient time or resources to investigate the teeming and colourful marine life which inhabited the coral reef, but they noted sea snakes and beautifully coloured fish including a garfish which leapt right out of the water and into their boat. Seabirds included the familiar herons, boobies, gulls, curlews and pelicans. Some of the landbirds, the bustards, eagles, hawks and crows, resembled their English cousins but others, like the white and brown cockatoo, the beautiful brightly coloured parrots and loriqueets, belonged to a warmer, sub-tropical climate. Sydney Parkinson, with an artist's eye for colour and detail, described some of the tropical birds and proves himself to have an excellent knowledge of natural history:

Two sorts of beautiful perroquets; a very uncommon hawk, pied black and white ... the iris or its eyes very broad, of a rich scarlet colour inclining to orange, the beak was black, the cera dirty grey yellow, the feet were of a gold or deep buff colour like king's yellow ... ; large black cocatoos, with scarlet and orange coloured feathers on their tails, and some white spots between the beak and the ear, as well as one on each wing; the goat-sucker, or churn owl; merops, or bee-eaters; large bats; a small bird with wattles of a deep orange red; a bird like a Tetrao, having wattles of a fine ultramarine colour, and whose beak and legs were black; an owl, having the iris of its eye a gold colour, the pupil of them dark blue; a large black and white gull, with a bright yellow beak, on the gibbous part of which was a spot of scarlet – the corner of its mouth, and irides of the eyes, were of bright scarlet colour, the legs and feet a greenish yellow: a blackbird of oyster-cracker genus, with a bright red beak, except towards the point, where it was yellow; the iris of its eyes

bright scarlet, the irides of them bright orange; the feet and legs of a
ale-red colour; a large olive coloured bird of the loxia genus having the
iris of its eyes of a gall-stone colour, and the pupils of them black; a
black and white shag, the iris of whose eyes was of a fine dark green
colour, the pupils black, the skin which surrounds the eye was of a
verditer-green colour, the beak a pale grey, on each side of which was a
bare yellow spot, the feet were black ...

On the shoals and sandbanks lived a species of pelican larger than a swan and which stood nearly 5 feet tall. There was a species of bustard as large as a turkey and which looked like a good table bird – Banks decided to shoot one and find out. 'It turned out an excellent bird, by far the best we all agreed that we have eat since we left England & as it weighd 15 pounds our Dinner was not only good but plentyfull.' The fare was pronounced so good that it was agreed to call the place Bustard Bay.

At one stopping place the naturalist discovered a nest of green ants. He watched with interest how they could build a nest by bending down leaves which were larger than a man's hand and many times their own size and weight. The ants scurried and climbed one upon the other to reach the leaf, some pulling it into place and others secreting a glue to hold it in position. The naturalist accidentally caught the branch on which they built their nest. 'Thousands would immediately threw themselves down, many of which falling upon us made us sensible of their stings and revengefull dispositions, especially if as was often the case they got posession of our necks and hair.' At another landing place Banks founds a colony of small black ants which bored out the branches and twigs of the trees to make their nest. He broke off a healthy looking branch only to find that it was little more than a hollow piece of bark swarming with ants on the inside. In the mangrove swamp he succumbed to another insect trap when he discovered a large colony of small stinging caterpillars 'green and beset with man hairs: these sat upon the leaves rangd side by side of each other like soldiers drawn up, 20 or 30 perhaps upon one leaf; if these watchful militia were touched but ever so gently they did not fail to make the person offending them sensible of their anger, every hair in them stinging much as nettles do but with a more acute tho' less lasting smart.' He disturbed a swarm of butterflies so huge that when they took to the air the sky was covered with fluttering wings and vivid colours. 'The air was for the space of 3 or 4 acres crowded with them to a wonderful degree: the eye could not be turned in any direction without seeing milions and yet every branch and twig was almost covered with those that sat still.' He picked a chrysalis from the leaves of a gum tree: it was so bright that it resembled burnished silver and he took it back to the ship for observation. The next day there emerged a beautiful butterfly with wings tinged in black velvet that blended into a shade of deep blue; it was under-marked with many light brimstone spots. New species of flora and fauna were guaranteed at every landing.

Everybody, scientist and seaman alike, was interested in the elusive natives. The Aborigines were straight bodied and of middle stature, their skins a dark chocolate colour. Their hair was dark, mostly lank and cropped short, sometimes naturally curled but not like the short woolly hair of the African. The men had short black beards and although they had no razors they singed their growth to keep them short. They often had a bone 3 or 4 inches long piercing their nose – so distinctive that the sailors called it a sprit sail yard. They mutilated their ears so that they could wear earrings. Sometimes they wore a sort of shell breast-plate and they frequently painted their bodies and faces with a white pigment according to the taste of the individual.

On the few occasions when close contact was made the natives seemed to keep their womenfolk well away from the newcomers, but this did not prevent the men from observing the women through telescopes and eyeglasses whenever the opportunity arose. To the European taste the aboriginal female came closer to the Maori than the Tahitian girls, but the Aborigines were not devoid of vanity and they wore ornaments over their nakedness. They hung shell necklaces around their necks and they fashioned bracelets for their wrists. They had hoops of hair wound tightly round their upper arms – sometimes the hoops were girdled around their bodies.

At one point in the voyage Banks and Cook were able to make much more personal contact. A canoe containing four Aborigines approached the longboat to within the range of a musket shot. The natives shouted and pointed, chattering loudly amongst themselves. By degrees they were coaxed nearer and nearer until at last they came right alongside the longboat. They were given cloth, nails and paper which they accepted but without enthusiasm – then a small fish was thrown into the canoe by accident.

'They expressed the greatest joy imaginable,' said Banks. 'And instantly putting off from the ship made signs that they would bring over their comrades.' The natives returned as they had promised but with spears raised threateningly above their heads. Tupia successfully persuaded them to lay down their weapons and to come forward without them. Some kind of trade was struck: the natives brought fish with them and were accompanied by others of their kin including a boy and a young woman. 'These last two stay'd on the point of sand on the other side of the River about 200 yards from us,' wrote Cook. 'We could see very clearly with our glasses that the woman was as naked as ever she was born, even those parts which I allways before now thought nature would have taught a woman to conceal were uncover'd.' 'The woman did not copy our mother Eve even in the fig leaf,' confirmed Joseph Banks and he tells the same story for the male of the species:

> They were all of them clean limn'd, active and nimble. Cloaths they had none, not the least rag, those parts which nature willingly conceals being exposed to view compleatly uncovered; yet when they stood still they would

often or almost always with their hand or something they held in it hide
them in some measure at least, seemingly doing that as if by instinct.

Weapons were primitive but very effective and they were used
with great skill. The missiles which were thrown at Cook and his
party at Botany Bay were propelled by a thin wooden stick about
3 feet long which looked rather like the blade of a cutlass. With
this weapon they had been seen to hit an animal or even a bird at a
distance of 40 or 50 yards. The darts themselves were made from
bone and had four points: sometimes the points were barbed but
they were not poisoned as Joseph Banks had originally feared.
Wooden harpoons were used for fishing. They sometimes carried
small oval wooden shields, like the one produced at Botany Bay –
but these were seldom used. Their weapons seemed to be primarily developed for hunting and not for warfare. Boomerangs were
seen but their function was not fully recognised by the English
and the absence of the bow and arrow as a hunting device seemed
to escape comment.

In spite of their white paint and sometimes ferocious appearance Cook concluded that they were a timorous and inoffensive
race. They lived entirely by hunting and fishing, and were a
nomadic race with no permanent settlements nor any sign of
farming or cultivation anywhere. They did build huts, but these
were very small and were used for shelter in the wet season and
perhaps for raising young children. They were a Stone Age people
with primitive working tools and with no knowledge of metal.
Their technology was very simple, but they were able to make
boats or canoes by stripping the bark from a tree and simply
drawing and tying the ends together – this made a waterproof
boat of very shallow draught so that they could hunt for shellfish
from the shallows of the mud banks by the river estuaries.
Some canoes were more sophisticated and were fashioned from a
hollowed-out log: at least one canoe was seen with outriggers and
carrying four people. The Aborigines often put out to sea in their

primitive and flimsy boats and there were obvious signs of human habitation on islands many miles from the mainland.

Unlike Tahiti, New Holland was so vast that it was difficult for an organised social hierarchy to evolve. The natives clearly had plenty of contact with each other and a high degree of uniformity, with a common language along the whole of the east coast, but the continent was too large and the people too backward to maintain a stable civilisation at any level higher than the one that existed. Very little real contact was made with the Aborigines. This was not through lack of trying: they were interested in the newcomers but very suspicious of them and disappeared into the bush at the slightest provocation. The widely held belief that the Aborigines completely ignored the *Endeavour* comes from remarks in Banks's journal and was certainly witnessed on several occasions. The degree of contact was much less than in New Zealand and could hardly have been a greater contrast than the arrival in Tahiti when the natives clambered all over the ship and explored every part of it. But the lack of interest cannot be taken too literally: the Aborigines supported as wide a range of individuals as any other race, and to counterbalance the disinterest story there are instances of natives following the ship and the ship's boats with all the excitement and curiosity to be expected from any race of primitive people. Their language, as far as it was possible to tell, had a few words in common with that of Tahiti but it was too far removed for Tupia to be able to converse with them. Eventually some small progress was made towards understanding the speech and a short vocabulary was compiled which consisted mainly of nouns. Parts of the body are described, the names of some animals and familiar objects, and a few family relationships. It was obvious that they had a highly developed language but contact between the cultures was too basic for adjectives and adverbs to be communicated.

The Australian Aborigines raised all kind of questions for the anthropologist. They seemed to have little in common with the

Maoris or other Polynesian peoples but this was something which was easy to accept by the current theories of the times. The fact that there did exist much in common between the races was of interest only to future generations concerned with investigating the origin of species. In the early encounters the Aborigines showed interest in the nails, beads and mirrors which they were offered but they quickly seemed to tire of them. Was this because they already had all they required for their simple way of life or was it simply that the only things of value to them were the very basics of food and possibly clothing? The question was debated in the great cabin of the *Endeavour*. The islanders of Tahiti lived in a world which was far superior to the foggy damp streets of an English sea port yet they had no literature or technology to compare with Europe. Did these things matter and were the south sea islanders actually closer to the ideal life than London society with its clubs, social circle and coffee houses on the Strand? Thus the notion of the primitive savage was raised again and when the findings of the expedition became known it was a question which stimulated the minds of the philosophers at home.

In the sunny evenings the great cabin was a hive of activity. The captain with his officers, compasses and dividers in hand, preparing charts and views of the new coastline. Banks and Solander cataloguing and preserving their specimens with the help of the wet rags, tins and preserving paper. Sydney Parkinson had developed so quick and accurate a hand that he made ninety-four excellent sketches in the space of two weeks. The seamen were always busy about the ship. Pickersgill and Clerk took lunar observations and laboriously used the Nautical Almanac to find the longitude. At night time the ship would sometimes lie at anchor but if a bright moon was in the sky then the *Endeavour* sailed quietly onwards with a lookout at the masthead and a man at the lead. The now familiar southern constellations rose from the eastern ocean, wheeled slowly overhead and set behind the hills to the west.

The method used to chart the coast was by means of 'ship stations'. The ship would sail about 2 miles offshore and anchor at a good vantage point. Bearings would be taken of all the visible capes, headlands and other features and sketches were made from the ship. Latitude and longitude were measured, and then the ship sailed to the next station. The log line was used to determine the distance travelled by dead reckoning and the lead line to determine depth. The latter had to be corrected to give the depth at low tide: this was difficult to measure unless the ship could anchor for a complete cycle of the tide. If the ship sailed overnight then at least one coastal feature must still be visible the next morning to provide a datum for the next station. Azimuth bearings could be taken with the ship's compass but Cook preferred to use the sextant because it gave him much more accurate angles and it could also measure vertical angles to estimate the heights of the hills. Putting together the angles and the sketches to make a chart required great skill. Several of the officers were capable of creating the charts but none approached Cook for accuracy and clarity.

As the ship worked northwards the coast seemed to become progressively more dangerous. Cook and Molyneux were even more anxious to find a place to stop and careen the ship. The surveyors and the naturalists alike still wanted to hug the shore as close as possible, but this meant keeping a man on the lead every yard of the way as large stretches of shoal water were becoming more and more frequent. Small islands and hidden reefs also became more numerous, and breaking water was spotted far out to sea. Cook was aware that reefs of coral existed in places beneath the breakers but the water was generally very clear and the reefs could be spotted at a distance by a man at the mast. He had very little idea of the extent of the coral reefs and he knew nothing of the Great Barrier Reef.

When the *Endeavour* heaved to for the night captain gave all the necessary orders before retiring. He would then tell the night-watch to call him if anything untoward happened during the night. He undressed and went to sleep, usually sleeping soundly through the night. On the evening of 11 June the ship was making good progress under double-reefed topsails with a fair wind. There was a full moon and Cook decided it was safe to sail through the night. He retired as usual with instructions to call him if necessary. The *Endeavour* sailed on with only the creaking of hemp and timber, the lapping of the water against her sides, and the sighing of the wind in her sails to disturb the peace of the warm tropical night. The silence was occasionally broken by the man at the lead calling the depth of water in fathoms. Seven, eight, fourteen, he called a depth of seventeen fathoms.

The leadsman swung the lead again to make another throw but the cast was never made. There was an alarming loud splintering noise and the *Endeavour* was brought to a sudden jarring halt. The swell of the sea caused a sickening sound of broken timbers from somewhere below the waterline. The pale moonlight showed broken planking floating around the ship. The ship was stuck fast on a hidden reef. Coral as sharp as a razor had torn a great hole in her side. The Pacific Ocean was pouring into the hold. The *Endeavour* was sinking.

CHAPTER 9

TRIBULATIONS

To 18 September, 1770

THE SITUATION was very alarming. The sharp coral rocks could be heard grinding and splintering against the bottom of the ship every time she moved in the swell: the sheathing boards had already been scoured away from the hull and the false keel was breaking away. The tide was on the ebb and if the ship became stranded on the rocks then she was in danger of breaking up under her own weight. It was too dark to see how far it was to the mainland but for three or four hours the ship had made rapid progress on a course angled away from land and with a good following wind. The boats would carry less than half of the ship's complement. If the *Endeavour* sank then half of the ship's complement would perish with her. There were no islands near by. If they took to the boats then any who did manage to get ashore could expect a worse and more prolonged death than those who remained with the ship.

The captain was on deck immediately in his nightshirt shouting orders and trying to assess the extent of the damage. He exhorted everyone to keep cool and sent Robert Molyneux out in one of the boats to take soundings all around and to inspect the damage. He ordered the pumps to be manned and prepared to lower the anchors and to put the boats out into the water.

The master confirmed that the *Endeavour* had struck against a coral reef and he reported shoal water all round the ship. The depth was 3 or 4 fathoms at the stern but only as many feet near the bows. By the time all the boats had been lowered the tide had ebbed so much that it was impossible to re-float the ship before the next high water. The stricken vessel settled on the reef and heeled over to one side. The swell of the sea rocked her back and forth causing a horrific grating noise under the starboard bow which was most noticeable in the forward storerooms. The water level was rising in the hold and the pumps were manned in shifts to try to contain it, even the aristocratic Joseph Banks took his turn at the pump handles with the men. Only three out of the four pumps functioned properly: nobody yet knew if they would be adequate to keep the water level down.

All through the night the pumps cranked away laboriously at their work. When daylight arrived the tide had fallen by about 2 feet and was still falling. The land could be seen at a distance of about 8 leagues. The anchors were secured to the bottom and held in readiness for an attempt to haul off the ship when the tide rose again. Cook gave orders to lighten the ship and the ballast was thrown over the side. The six guns on deck were thrown overboard complete with their carriages: they were marked by buoys in the faint hope that they might be recovered later. (It was almost 200 years later, in February 1969, that the guns were finally recovered.) Decayed stores, casks, hoops and oil jars which lay in the way of the ballast were thrown overboard with it. The crisis moulded the crew into an efficient working unit, every man on board not only pulling his weight to the utmost but also remaining calm and hopeful.

'All this time the Seamen worked with surprising chearfulness and alacrity,' said Banks. 'No grumbling or growling was to be heard throughout the ship, no not even an oath (though the ship in general was as well furnished with them as most in his majesties service).' Then the tide began to rise slowly. It was a frightening and nail-biting time as the sea rocked the ship more violently against the coral. The increased pressure from the higher water made the leak much worse and it became harder for the pumps to cope with the ingress of water. The task of saving the ship began to look hopeless and beyond their resources – Joseph Banks thought all was lost. He became so depressed that he gave up all hope and began to pack his belongings into one of the boats.

By noon the tide had reached and passed its highest point. The *Endeavour* heaved and moved a little to try to right herself but, in spite of the fact that 40 tons had been thrown overboard, there was not enough water to re-float her. Cook was faced with a great dilemma for he knew that if he did manage to get the ship back into deep water again he could find that the pumps were inadequate to cope with the increased pressure on the hull. He also knew that if the weather changed for the worse then the sea would simply smash the ship against the coral and would finish her off very quickly. The sailors talked much amongst themselves and assured their fellows that the night tides were always higher than the day tides. This was mere folklore – it was the relative positions of the sun and moon which determined the height of the tide – but it was a straw to clutch at and offered a plausible explanation of why the ship did not re-float. The night tide was the last remaining hope, but it was obvious that the *Endeavour* was very badly damaged. If the weather stayed calm and the night tide rose a foot higher than the day, then the best they could hope for was to re-float the ship, run her aground somehow on the mainland, and build another vessel from her damaged timbers. The pumps continued their monotonous clanking throughout the day and into the evening. There were no sea shanties or muttered oaths, only hard breathing and grim determination. High tide was not until about ten o'clock at night.

The dreadful time now approachd and the anziety in every bodys countenance was visible enough: the capstan and Windlace were mannd and they began to heave: fear of death now stard us in the face; hopes we had none but of being able to keep the ship afloat till we could run her ashore

*on some part where out of her materials we might build a vessel large
enough to carry us to the East Indies.*

As high tide approached the ship righted herself but at the same
time the leak began to gain on the pumps. It was an alarming
reminder of what could happen if the ship was re-floated in deep
water. But there was no other way to save the ship. Cook resolved
that it was better to try and fail than to abandon the ship on the
reef: he decided to heave the ship off if it was humanly possible.
The anchor ropes were taut with one of the large bow anchors
right astern and the other on the starboard quarter. The men
heaved and sweated at capstan and windlass with the white gleam
of the moonlight illuminating their strained faces. The boats
were also out, each with a full complement of seamen pulling
hard at the oars. The creak of the suction pumps and the panting
of the pumpers continued over the breaking noise of the sea and
the horrific grinding of the coral on the hull. At about ten o'clock
there was a small movement. The capstan gave a clank and turned
a little. It gave heart to the men and they strained harder at ropes,
oars and windlass. She moved again. The sailors took up the slack
on the taut ropes. Then the capstan was turning slowly and the
ship was afloat on the tide. The men made one last effort and a few
minutes later the *Endeavour* was off the reef and back into deep
water. It was a marvellous moment.

The problems were not over by a long way. One of the anchor
cables became entangled with the coral and it had to be cut away
and the anchor was abandoned. The carpenter yelled out that the
leak had gained on the pumps and the water in the hold had risen
to an unprecedented level of 4 feet. At this news the weary
pumpers redoubled their efforts and the beat of the pumps
increased accordingly. Luckily it was a false alarm: Satterley had
measured the water level from a different datum to that of the
man who took the previous reading. There was a great sense of
relief when the error was realised. The pumps were just capable

of holding the leak and with the extra effort they had actually gained on it. All the men were weary from twenty-four hours of manning the pumps, the wind was in the wrong direction, the weather looked bound to worsen very soon, and it would take days to get the ship near the land. They had no idea how long it would take to find a suitable place to repair the ship, but the calm still miraculously held and there was now a glimmer of hope that the ship could be saved.

It was the experience of the young Jonathan Monkhouse which now came to the rescue. Monkhouse had once been in a similar situation when he served on a merchant ship bound for London from Virginia. The merchantman had successfully crossed the Atlantic with a leak very similar to the one in the *Endeavour* – it had been stopped by a process known as fothering. The practice of fothering a ship involves stopping a leak by using a sail covered with wool and oakum. It was a tricky operation because the sail had to be taken right under the ship to cover the place where it was holed and worked into the right position to stop the hole. The *Endeavour*'s lower studding sail was taken on deck and prepared by sewing into it tufts of oakum and wool: each tuft was about the size of a fist and arranged in rows a few inches apart. Ideally sheep and horse dung would be thrown over the sail but as the *Endeavour* did not run to these commodities the ship's goat and the grey-hound gladly supplied a substitute. The fothering sail then had to be worked around and under the ship near the starboard fore chains where the hull was damaged. The theory was that the pressure of the water entering the leak would cause the oakum to flow into the hole and plug it.

The seamen waited impatiently for the fothering – they were having difficulty keeping the water level down. By the afternoon the sail had been worked into its place and was secured by ropes at the four corners. The pumps then easily gained on the leak and within the space of an hour the water level was nearly down to zero. The effect on morale was amazing. The men were 'in an instant raised from almost despondency to the greatest hopes'. It was clear that the urgent pressure had been eased. The ship could now be sailed almost normally and it remained to find a suitable place to make repairs. The tension of the previous two days was over. Joseph Banks was amazed and impressed by the way the men had worked to save the ship; it did not bear out the pessimistic predictions of some of his well-informed acquaintances at home:

> During the whole of this distress I must say for the credit of our people that I believe every man exerted his utmost for the preservation of the ship, contrary to what I have universaly heard to be the behaviour of sea men who have commonly as soon as a ship is in a desperate situation began to plunder and reuse all commands. This was no doubt owing to the cool and steady conduct of the officers, who during the whole time never gave an order which did not shew them to be perfectly composd and unmovd by the circumstances howsoever dreadfull they might appear.

Captain Cook was equally generous in his praise for his crew. 'In justice to the Ship's Company I must say that no men ever behaved better than they have done on this occasion,' he wrote in his journal. 'Animated by the behaviour of every gentleman on board, every man seem'd to have a just sence of the danger we were in and exerted himself to the very utmost.' This was high praise from the sparing pen of James Cook and his praise for Jonathan Monkhouse was also unsparing. The whole was a great team effort, the crew had shown an excellent team spirit and every man on board deserved credit for his part in the crisis. Cook scribbled a marginal note in his journal – 'This day I restor'd Magra to his duty as I did not find him guilty of the crimes laid to his charge.' Magra too had pulled his weight and convinced the captain of his innocence.

The next day the *Endeavour* hobbled slowly along the coast picking her way through the shoal water with a boat ahead of her taking soundings all the time. The master and one of the mates took the second and third boats ahead of the ship to examine every possible cove as a suitable place to lay the ship for repairs. It was slow work and Molyneux returned at sunset with the depressing news that the harbour he had found was too shallow to take the ship. The wind began to blow fresher and a gale was brewing up. The men reflected on their good fortune that the weather had held fine for them during the past two days. Cook anchored for the night and an hour later the mate returned from a more distant cove about 2 leagues to leeward with the news that he had found the ideal spot to lay the ship.

In the morning Cook went ahead to examine the place himself. There was a river estuary with a steep sandy beach and with a tidal rise of about 8 feet. The main problem was the entrance to the cove which was very narrow, but he judged that the ship could be guided in with care. A more immediate problem was the weather which had deteriorated significantly so that it was not possible to get the ship safely through the entrance to the cove until the wind and sea became more settled. The exertions and the strain of the past days were beginning to tell on the whole crew: worst effected were Charles Green whose health had deteriorated badly and Tupia, the usually effervescent Tahitian, who was suffering from swollen gums and other symptoms of scurvy.

Cook removed the topgallant yards and took in the jib boom and spritsail yard to lighten the forward part of the ship above the place where the leak lay. As soon as the weather moderated he made an attempt to get into the estuary. The entrance had been carefully sounded and he knew the depth of water, but the passage was narrow and at one point the ship grounded and stuck on a shoal. The seamen heaved her off without too much effort but then she stuck again a second time and remained fast and immoveable. The captain remained calm, he had a favourable wind and the state of the tide was carefully calculated to help the operation. He lightened the ship again by ordering the fore topmast booms to be lowered over the side, and instructed the men to construct a raft out of them. The *Endeavour* edged off again and the sailors hauled at the cables and hawsers to pull her towards a steep beach on the south side of the river. The tide rose slowly and the *Endeavour* was warped up the beach with a creaking of hemp from capstan and windlass. The tide ebbed out and at last the ship was grounded. The anchor cables and hawsers were taken ashore, and the ship was hauled over to one side to enable the carpenters to get at the leak. The carpenters built a landing stage from ship to shore, stores were unloaded and the tents were erected in anticipation of a few weeks' stay.

The river estuary was a most welcome haven after the exertions of the previous week. The carpenters were able to get at the timbers and to do their repair work, and soon the rest of the company could also go about their business. Cook described the large hole in the ship's side, which had very nearly been the end of all of them:

> ... *the rocks had made their way thro' four planks quite to and even into the timbers and wound'd three more. The manner these planks were damaged or cut out as I may say is hardly credible, scarce splinter was to be seen but the whole was cut away as if it had been done by the hands of man with a blunt edge tool. Fortunately for us the timbers in this place were very close, other ways it would have been impossible to have saved the ship and even as it was it appear'd very extraordinary that she made no more water than she did. A large piece of coral rock was sticking in one hole and several pieces of the fothering, small stones, sand &c had made its way in and lodged between the timbers which had stoped the water from forcing its way in in large quantities. Part of the sheathing was gone from under the larboard bow, part of the false keel was gone and the remainder in such a shattered condition that we should be much better off, was it gone also; her fore foot and some part of her Main keel was also damaged but not materialy, what damage she may have received abaft we could not see but believe not much as the Ship makes but little water while the tide keeps below the leak forward.*

The ship's bows were raised well up on the beach but the stern part of the *Endeavour* was still under a minimum of about 8 feet of water. Cook sent three men down to examine the underside and they all came back with the same story. The sheathing had been stripped off from around the mainmast and one of the planks was damaged. It was virtually impossible to repair the damage without proper facilities. The sheathing gave protection against the Teredo worm and the damaged plank would let in some water. Cook knew that it was only a question of time before the worm ate right through the planking, but there was little alternative – if it lasted long enough to get the ship to the East Indies then that would be sufficient. The pumps should be capable of coping with the leak from the damaged plank.

Banks and Solander were very happy to disappear into the country to botanise. A kangaroo had been sighted leaping through the long grass and Banks was determined to add it to his collection. The fishing was good and a few edible vegetables were found. The fresh food quickly cured Tupia of his scurvy and the astronomer recovered sufficiently to observe the moons of Jupiter and apply himself to finding the longitude. He observed the time of emersion of Jupiter's first satellite and this enabled him to calculate the time at Greenwich and compare it with the local time to give a longitude of 214° 42' 30" West. Cook and Green always measured the longitude to the west even though the angles were more than 180 degrees – this was presumably because the *Endeavour* was sailing westwards around the world. A fortnight later Green repeated the measurements and the new figure differed by about 8 minutes from the previous one. The measurements were still very accurate with a mean which was only 4 minutes of arc away from the true position, and this represented the optimum for the Jupiter method.

Repairs to the fore planking were soon completed. The height of the tide was less than it had been on the day of their arrival and Cook began to worry about how he was going to re-float the ship.

Casks were lashed to the bows and thirty-eight empty barrels were lashed to the ship's bottom in the hope that their buoyancy would float her off on the next tide. The attempt was not successful and Cook knew he would have to wait for a higher tide before he could get his ship back to sea.

It was 1 July and the ship's company was very anxious to put to sea again, but many obstacles still lay ahead of them. One problem was the wind which blew consistently from the wrong direction; another was to find a safe passage through the reefs – this was bound to be difficult as the view from the top of a nearby hill showed shoal water as far as the horizon. Cook sent the master out in the pinnace to try to find a passage through the shoals. On his first attempt Molyneux claimed to have found a gap in the reef about 5 leagues distant and with clear sea beyond but Cook was not convinced and sent him off again to investigate further. Cook's instinct was right and a few days later the master returned despondently from a distance of 7 leagues with the news that he had found an outer reef with no way through it. The only consolation was that he returned with a giant turtle to help with the provisioning problem.

Catching the turtles became a new sport: they could be caught only after a chase in one of the ship's boats. The turtles were fast swimmers and with their strong fins they could easily outpace the boats in the water, but they were slow and clumsy animals when crawling over the coral rocks. They lived on the reefs about 5 leagues out to sea and catching them was therefore a time-consuming method of obtaining fresh meat but by one means or another about twelve turtles were caught and brought back to the ship. Cook had managed to re-float the ship in the river, and the turtles were laid out on the deck. At this time Banks and Solander had successfully befriended some of the local Aborigines and in spite of their usual fear and reticence a party of about ten of the natives arrived at the ship. It seemed that they were attracted by the turtles and, although Cook and others tried to interest them in beads and trinkets, all they seemed to care for was the food supply. One Aborigine then tried to steal a turtle by dragging it over a boat and into his canoe. He made two or three attempts but was resisted by the sailors who could little spare to lose such a quantity of hard-won fresh meat. At this the natives took offence and one of them ran to the shore where the shipwrights had a fire burning under a kettle of pitch. He took a brand from the fire and in very little time he had set fire to all the dry grass and stubble around the camp-site.

The British had never before experienced an Australian bush fire and they were greatly alarmed at the speed with which the dry grass took hold. The whole of the stubble, which had grown to 5 feet high in places, was soon burning and crackling furiously. Luckily the wind carried the fire away from the camp and its belongings, but it was a close call for the expedition. If the incident had happened only a few days earlier then the consequences would have been extremely serious because all the gunpowder, which was at that time spread out to dry, would have gone up in smoke and taken many of the stores with it.

The wind continued from the south-east all through July. There were still many more miles to cover to get to the East Indies, supplies of many essential items were running low, and everybody was impatient to put back to sea. The ship was loaded and ballasted and only wanted a fair wind. One night she drifted ashore during the ebb tide and lay with the rudder dangerously fouling the bottom; the tiller was forced hard against some trestles built over the tiller platform and it was obvious that either the tiller or the platform was going to break under the strain. Luckily it was the platform and not the tiller which broke. Still the wind blew from the wrong quarter. Soon it was August and Cook became desperate to put out to sea even though he had still not found a suitable passage through the shoals and reefs.

On 3 August the weather was moderate and he decided to try to warp the ship out of the estuary. At one point the *Endeavour* backed up on to the sand and grounded on the north side of the river, but the men warped her clear again and by evening they had almost hauled the ship out into the open sea. The tide ebbed out and a fresh breeze from the sea put a stop to their efforts for the night. The next day Cook laid out a coasting anchor with a long cable outside the river bar. The sea was still breaking dangerously but the sailors successfully warped the ship over the bar and at last she was using her sails to tack out to sea. As they left the river bank which had been their home for many difficult weeks, Cook decided to call the river after the ship and it became known as the Endeavour River. Cook wrote up a detailed account of the tides and the watering places with a description of the country round about and a valuable chart for the use of future mariners. He also included some notes of the wildlife – the enthusiasm of his gentlemen adventurers was beginning to rub off on him.

The ship now progressed with the utmost care. The pinnace went ahead taking the depth every few yards. A man was stationed at the masthead to look for any sign of coral under the water and an anchor was held at the ready to halt the ship if she drifted in the wrong direction. Things went well until the ship cleared the Turtle Reef but then the wind blew fresh from the wrong quarter and she was forced to ride at anchor for a full day. She remained at anchor all night with the sea tugging remorselessly at her and the anchor slowly dragging along the bottom. At daylight the ship had drifted a full league and the crew found themselves moving towards a dangerous reef. Cook put out a second anchor to try to hold the ship, but the tide and current were too strong and even the two anchors were not sufficient to prevent the steady drift towards the coral rock. Banks summarised the situation as he saw it:

Our prospect was now more melancholy than ever: the shoal was plainly to be seen and the ship still driving gently towards it, a sea running at the same time which would make it impossible ever to get off if we should be unfortunate enough to get on. Yards and Topmasts were therefore got down and everything done which could be thought of to make the ship snug, without any effect: she still drove and the shoal we dreaded came nearer and nearer to us.

The sheet anchor was prepared as a last resort. But during the preparation one of the other anchors grappled something on the sea-bed and held the ship fast to give a breathing space. Cook surveyed the treacherous reefs in every direction: he described the situation as '… dangerous to the highest degree in so much that I was quite at a loss which way to steer when the weather would permit us to get under sail'. He climbed to the masthead and viewed the outer reef but there was no sign of any gap through which to take the ship. Molyneux, who had sounded and explored the area in the pinnace, was all for tacking laboriously back to the south, but retracing their steps against the wind would take so long that Cook insisted on sailing on. A small island with a high hill lay about 5 leagues ahead of the ship. Cook took a boat out to the island and climbed the hill. There he gazed at the grand view of the greens and blues of the Pacific breaking white on the coral of the Great Barrier Reef. At one point there seemed to be a narrow gap in the breakers, it was a slim chance but he sent a boat ahead to take soundings. The boat could not get into the opening because of a great swell on the sea, but the mate came back and reported a depth of at least 15 fathoms of water near the gap.

The pinnace went ahead of the ship through the gap in the reef, a wise but unnecessary precaution. The *Endeavour* slipped easily through and at last she was out again in the open sea. 'Satisfaction was clearly painted on every man's face.' The relief of an open sea with no ground within 100 fathoms was something which only those who had been through the stress and danger could appreciate. The ship was leaking badly and taking 9 inches of water every hour, but the pumps were quite capable of handling this quantity.

The relief, however, was very short lived. For a day the ship made good progress and she stood well off the Great Barrier Reef at night, but in the morning she had drifted dangerously near the sharp coral and the real dangers of navigating these treacherous waters became even more apparent. In common with every other sailing ship, the *Endeavour* was totally reliant on the vagaries of wind and current to make headway. If there was no wind the ship had either to run with the tide and current or to put out an anchor and hope to get a grip on the ocean floor to hold her position until the wind got up. If the depth of the ocean was such that the anchor could not find the bottom then in a dead calm the ship was almost entirely at the mercy of the tide and current. The only alternative was to put out the ship's boats and haul her with the oars – a very laborious task used as a last resort.

The *Endeavour* now found herself in a flat calm. The tide was taking her very rapidly towards the reef where ferocious breaking water was clearly visible at a distance of less than a mile. The barrier reef was a new experience for European sailors: at this point it rose vertically out of the sea and could be seen as a sheer vertical wall of coral rock at low tide. At high tide the sea poured over this wall at a depth of 7 or 8 feet with what was described as 'a most terrifying surf breaking mountain high'. The *Endeavour* was being swept out of control towards the inferno of water and sharp coral – the only way to check the progress of the ship was to launch the boats and to heave on the oars. There was no question of using an anchor: no less than three lines had been joined together for the depth-sounding lead but the line was still not long enough to find the bottom. The pinnace was under repair with one of her planks stripped off, and the longboat was lashed tightly down on deck under all sorts of other deck clutter so that it would take hours to get it lowered over the side. The yawl was so small that it would accommodate only a few rowers. Those who thought the Endeavour Reef was the most dangerous and frightening part of the voyage were very soon to be proved wrong.

Cook's account of 16 August described the dangers well enough, but his professional pride was at stake and his account is aware of this. Banks's journal for the same day makes no secret of the imminent danger they faced. In an eye-witness account he never pauses for breath as he described how it felt to be a single breaker and a breath of wind away from life's end and staring into the watery valley of the shadow of death:

At three O'clock this morn it droppd calm on a sudden which did not at all better our situation: we judgd ourselves not more than 4 or 5 l'gs from the reef, maybe much less, and the swell of the sea which drove right upon it carried the ship towards it fast. We tried the lead often in hopes of finding ground that we might anchor but in vain; before 5 the roaring of the surf was plainly heard and as day broke the vast foaming billows which were plainly enough to be seen scarce a mile from us and towards which we found the ship carried by the waves surprizing fast, so that by 6 o'Clock we were within a Cables length of them, driving on fast as ever and still no ground within a 100 fathm of line. Every method had been taken since we first saw our danger to get the boats out in hopes that they might tow us off but it was not yet acomplishd; the Pinnace had a plank strippd off her for repair and the longboat under the Booms was lashd and fastned so well from our supposd security that she was not yet got out. Two large Oars or sweeps were got out at the stern posts to pull the ship's head round the other way in hopes that might delay till the boats were out. All this while we were approaching and came I believe before this could be effected within 40 yards of the breaker; the same sea that washed the side of the ship rode in a breaker enourmously high the very next time it did rise, so between us and it was only a dismal valley the breadth of one wave; even now the depth was still hove 3 or 4 lines fastned together but no ground could be felt with above 150 fathm. Now was our case truly desperate, no man I believe but who gave himself intirely over, a speedy death was all we had to hope for and that from the vastness of the Breakers which must quickly dash the ship all to pieces was scarce to be doubted. Other hopes we had none: the boats were in the ship and must be *dashed in pieces with her and the nearest dry land was 8 to 10 leagues distant. We did not however cease our endeavours to get out the long boat which was by this time almost accomplishd. At this critical juncture, at this I must say terrible moment, when all assistance semd too little to save even our miserable lives, a small air of wind sprang up, so small that at any other time in a calm we should not have observd it. We plainly saw that it instantly checked our progress; every sail was therefore put in a proper direction to catch it and we just observd the ship to move in a slaunting direction off from the breakers. This at least gave us time and redoubling our efforts we at last got the long boat out and manning her sent her ahead. The ship still moved a little off but in less than 10 minutes our little Breeze died away into as flat a calm as ever. Now was our anxiety again renewed: innumerable small pieces of paper &c were thrown over the ships side to find whither the boats really moved her ahead or not and so little did she move that it remaind almost every other time a matter of dispute. Our little friendly Breeze now visited us again and lasted about as long as before, thrusting us possibly 100 yards farther from the breakers: we were still however in the very jaws of destruction. A small opening had been seen in the reef about a furlong from us, its breadth was scarce the length of the ship, into this however it was resolved to push her if posible. Within was surf, therefore we might save our lives: the doubt was only whether we could get the ship so far: our little breeze however a third time visited us and almost pushd us almost there. The fear of Death is Bitter: the prospect we now had before us of saving our lives tho at the expence of every thing we had, made my heart set much lighter on its throne, and I suppose there were none but what felt the same sensations. At length we arrived off the mouth of the wishd for opening and found to our surprize what had with the little breeze been the real cause of our Escape, a thing that we had not before dreamt of. The tide of flood it was that had hurried us so unaccountably fast towards the reef, in the near neighbourhood of which we arrivd just at high water, consequently its ceasing to drive us any further gave us the opportunity we had of getting off. Now however the tide of Ebb made strong and gushd out of little opening like a mill stream, so that it was impossible to get in; of this stream however we took the advantage as much as possible and it carried us out near a quarter of a mile from the reef. We well knew that we were to take all the advantage possible of the Ebb so continued towing with all our might and with all our boats, the Pinnace now being repaired, till we had gott an offing of 1- or 2 miles. By this time the tide began to run and our suspence began again: as we had gained so little while the ebb was in our favour we had some reason to imagine that the flood would hurry us back upon the reef in spite of our utmost endeavours. It was still as calm as ever so no likely hood of any wind today; indeed had wind sprung up we could only have searched for another opening, for we were so embayed by the reef that with the general trade wind it was impossible to get out. Another opening was however seen ahead and the 1st Lieutenant went away in the small boat to examine it. In the mean time we struggled hard with the flood, sometime gaining a little then holding our own way and at others loosing a little, so that our situation was almost as bad as ever, as the flood had not yet come to its strength. At 2 however the Lieutenant arrivd with the news that the opening was very narrow: in it was a good anchorage and a passage quite free from the shoals. The ships head was immediatley put towards it and with the tide she towed fast so that by three we enterd and were hurried in by a stream almost like a mill race, which kept us from even a fear of the sides tho it was not above G of a mile in breadth. By four we came to an anchor happy once more to encounter those shoals which but two days before we thought ourselves supreamly happy to have escaped from. How little do men know for what is for their real advantage: two days [ago] our utmost wishes were crowned by getting without the reef and today we were made again happy by getting within it.*

'The narrowest escape we ever had and had it not been for the immeadiate help of Providence we must Inevatbly have Perishd,' said Pickersgill. Cook remained outwardly calm but his first draft shows that he too had been moved by thoughts of impending death. For once he allowed his emotions to enter into his journal, and although he characteristically modified his entry when the official copy was made to his superiors, his original thoughts survive in the draft copy. 'It pleased GOD at this very juncture to send us a light air of wind' were his words to describe the perilous escape. It was very rare for Cook to call on his maker. The gap in the reef was named 'Providential Channel'. It prompted him to philosophise on the life of an explorer. It is typical of James Cook that he apologises at the end of the passage for giving us a rare glimpse of how his mind worked, a thing which we would love to read more about in his detailed but dutiful and unemotional journals.

Was it not for the pleasure which Naturly results to a man from his being the first discoverer even was it nothing more than Sand or Shoals this kind of service would be unsupportable especially in far distant parts like this, Short of Provisions & almost every other necessary. People will hardly admit of an excuse for a man leaving a coast unexplored he has once discov'd, if dangers are his excuse he is then charged with Timerousness & want of Perseverance, & at once pronounced the most unfit man in the world to be employ'd as a discoverer, if on the other hand he boldly encounters all the dangers and Obstacles he meets with & is unfortunate enough not to succed he is charged with Temerity & Perhaps want of Conduct the former of the Aspersions I am confident can never be laid to my Charge, & if I am fortunate to surmount all the Dangers we meet with the latter will never be brot in question, altho' I must own that I have engaged more among the Islands & shoals upon this coast than perhaps in Prudence I ought to have done with a single Ship, & every other thing considered but if I had not I should not have been able to give any better account of the one half of it, than if I had never seen it, at best I should not have been able to say wether it was Main land or Islands & as to its produce, that we should have been totally ignorant of as being inseparable with the other & in this case it would have been far more satisfaction to me never to have discov'd it, but it is time I should have done with this Subject wch at best is but disagreeable & which I was lead into on reflecting on our late Danger.

It was of paramount importance to Cook that he should bring back with him a description of the lands, maps and charts of the coastline. He now decided that as long as a passage existed it was far safer to stay within the reef and to sail as close to land as the depth of water would allow. It would be slow progress but there was a current flowing northwards which implied that somewhere to the north there must be an open sea outside the shoals. There was little time for the botanists to land, but there was plenty of time to study the reefs themselves and the naturalists were very taken with the amazing colours and variety of the lifeforms which they discovered. Sydney Parkinson wrote:

> *The reefs were covered with a numberless variety of beautiful corallines of all colours and figures, having here and there interstices of very white sand. These made a pleasing appearance under water, which was smooth on the inside of the reef, while it broke all along the outside, and may be aptly compared to a grove of shrubs growing under water. Numbers of beautiful coloured fishes make their residence amongst the rocks, and may be caught by hand on the high part of the reef at low water. There are also crabs, molusca of various sorts, and a great variety of curious shell-fish, which adhere to the old dead coral that forms the reef.*

After a few days the ship arrived safely at a cape which appeared to be the northernmost end of the land; Cook called it Cape York in honour of the Duke of York. Beyond Cape York the land fell away to the south. Northwards were islands and what appeared to be a strait. Cook wanted to sail further around the coast but the poor condition of the ship and the lack of supplies ruled out this possibility. He resolved to leave the land astern and sail through the straits which he now felt sure were those discovered by Torres long before him.

One thing remained to be done before leaving the coast of New Holland. The country had to be annexed and claimed in the name of the king. At Cape York Cook found a small island where he landed in one of the boats and hoisted the English colours and formally took possession of the whole continent from a latitude 38 degrees south to the place where he now stood. Ahead was an open stretch of water. It was the long-sought passage between New Holland and New Guinea, the passage which was implied by the account of Torres, written so long ago that nobody could be quite sure that the account could be trusted. This was a great moment of the voyage, for if the passage had not existed then the *Endeavour* would have had many more leagues to sail to reach civilisation again, and it is very doubtful if she would have survived. Cook gave the country he had charted the name of New South Wales. It bore very little resemblance to the ancient Celtic land of Wales, homeland of the master's mate Francis Wilkinson and able-bodied seaman Thomas Jones, but there already existed a New England and a New Britain and it was therefore a reasonable choice of name. But why South Wales, why not simply New Wales? Why did Cook decide to spurn North Wales? These questions will doubtless be debated in Australia and in Wales for many years to come. Whatever the reason the name did not become that of the whole country but it was one which was destined to survive as a substantial part of it.

Captain Cook and his party, standing on the barren peak of Possession Island, fired three musket shots. The shots were answered by three volleys from the ship, sounding crisp and clear across the water. The men knew that the signal was a good omen, it meant that at last a clear passage had been found for the ship. Three hoarse but heartfelt cheers followed from the men on the ship: it signified the double achievement of their great discovery and of the passage home.

August was nearly at an end, the *Endeavour* cleared the last of the shoals and islands, she left the great new land behind her and hauled northwards towards the coast of New Guinea. There was a false alarm which looked like another dangerous reef but which proved to be no more than a harmless brown weed growing on the surface of the sea. The ship entered the waters near New Guinea and a landing was made in the hope of obtaining coconuts and plantains to eat. The natives were unfriendly and appeared shouting and throwing fire sticks which burned so fiercely that the English thought they must have muskets and gunpowder. It was decided that there was no time to study the people and the ship sailed onwards – much of the glamour of discovery had faded and there was another problem below decks. Banks gave it a very modern name:

> *The greatest part of them are now pretty far gone with the longing for home which the Physicians have gone so far as to esteem a disease under the name of Nostalgia; indeed I can hardly find anybody in the ship clear of its effects but the Captn Dr Solander and myself, indeed we three have pretty constant employment for our minds which I believe to be the best if not the only remedy for it.*

The *Endeavour* sailed through the Arafura Sea passing the islands of Aru and Tanibar and were soon to sight the coastline of Timor. There was still plenty of interest for the naturalists, but rather less for the astronomers until they arrived offshore from Timor. At ten o'clock one evening a very faint curtain of reddish light was seen in the night sky, a display of the Aurora Australis, a rare sight indeed at only 10 degrees from the equator. The lights covered an area up to about 20 degrees above the horizon and spanning 8 to 10 points of the compass.

The next day the ship was off the western end of the island of Timor with the smaller island of Rotte and a narrow strait to the north and west. More natives were spotted onshore; some were carrying steel knives of European construction and design. The next day another shoal of coral was sighted and the *Endeavour* was offshore from the island of Java. They saw more natives and also a sighting of a familiar large animal which they had almost forgotten existed – a horse. On the horse sat a rider wearing a blue coat and a white waistcoat with a large lace-trimmed hat. He was the first white man they had seen since the departure from Rio on the other side of the world nearly two years earlier.

CHAPTER 10

HOMEWARD BOUND

To 13 July, 1771

THE ISLAND OF SUVA was one of the furthest outposts of the Dutch East Indies. Natives came out to the ship in their boats to trade fruit and coconuts, and they indicated that the main village and trading centre was in a bay on the lee side of the island. The *Endeavour* hoisted her English colours at the top of the foremast and when they arrived at the village they were greeted by a three-gun salute and the Dutch flag was raised onshore. The local rajah was only too pleased to supply the ship with buffalo, hogs and poultry, but it seemed he was answerable to the Dutch authorities through the factor, a conniving politician who wined and dined the officers with a view to extracting a bribe of some kind from them before the necessary fresh meat could be supplied. Luckily, with Java and the port of Batavia only a few days' sail to the west, Cook was able to ignore the complications of bribery and internal politics. He obtained sufficient supplies to cover his immediate needs and set sail again as soon as possible.

For ten uneventful days the ship headed further west, standing well offshore from the island of Java. Tupia, who had been bred on a diet of fresh vegetables, was suffering the effects of scurvy again and Charles Green was finally feeling the stress of the long voyage. When the ship left England there was no Nautical Almanac published for the year 1770 and the lack of the current almanac made it more difficult to calculate the longitudes. A following current helped the ship on its way but, by the time they reached Java Head, the dead reckoning was out by as much as 4 degrees. The *Endeavour* carried maps and charts of this part of the world but they were far from accurate and, when the ship arrived at the entrance to the Strait of Sunda, there was some doubt about her position. The strait was the passage to Batavia. It led between the islands of Java and Sumatra. 'Many of our sails are now so bad that they will hardly stand the least puff of wind,' wrote Cook. The main topsail was split from top to bottom. It was not only the sails and rigging which were worn out: little did the captain know that at one point the planking beneath the ship was eaten away by the worms to within a small fraction of an inch. A Dutch vessel came by, the ships exchanged greetings and gossip. One piece of news was of great interest to the veterans of the *Dolphin* for they heard that the *Swallow*, their companion vessel which they had last seen in the Straits of Magellan, had called at Batavia about two years previously and had therefore survived the journey across the Pacific. Soon the ship emerged from the Strait of Sunda and rounded Bantam Point. There followed four difficult days of sailing into contrary wind and current but on 11 October the *Endeavour* at last entered Batavia Road. Cook sent his first lieutenant ashore to apologise to the governor for not saluting: most of his guns lay at the bottom of the Pacific at Endeavour Reef.

A score of ships were at anchor in the harbour: most were Dutch vessels but there was one English merchantman, the *Harcourt*, and two other vessels from English ports in the eastern seas. One of the Dutch vessels sent a boat to communicate with the *Endeavour*. The Dutch sailors were a sickly looking white-faced crew, and the *Endeavour*'s men were in excellent health and now in high spirits at the thought of a few days on land. They ragged their fellow seamen good naturedly and jeered at their pale faces. Had the sailors known the true reason they would not have made so light of it – they had entered into one of the deadliest and most unhealthy ports in the world.

'I had forgot to mention that upon our arrival here I had not one man upon the Sick list, Lieut Hicks, Mr Green and Tupia were the only people that had any complaints Occasion'd by a long continuance at sea,' wrote Cook. Health apart, he had no choice but to remain for a time at Batavia. It was the only place in the east where repairs to the ship could be carried out and the *Endeavour* was in much too poor a condition to sail any further without a major overhaul and repairs to her keel. He knew that the Dutch looked with suspicion at any exploration in what they considered to be their own waters, and he therefore collected together diaries and journals of the voyage and instructed his men not to gossip to the Dutch about where they had been and the discoveries they had made.

Batavia was founded by the Dutch in the early years of the seventeenth century as a centre for their trade with the East Indies. In the eighteenth century it had become a large and cosmopolitan sea port with a castle, an impressive town hall, and several large churches of different denominations. The main inhabitants were the Dutch, but there were also Germans, Danes, Swedes and Hungarians in great numbers, plus a few English, French and Italians. The south side of the town was shanty built and was occupied by large numbers of Chinese.

Batavia had been planned in the manner of a handsome Dutch town with tree-lined canals to carry local traffic by water. One problem was that Batavia was in the tropics and not at the temperate latitude of Amsterdam. Later in the century an earthquake blocked off all the supply streams and running water – the result was that the canals became stagnant pools where mosquitoes bred and multiplied in their billions. It is perhaps surprising that the Dutch, who were well known at home as very clean and house-proud, persevered with Batavia as a base throughout the eighteenth century for it quickly acquired a reputation as a cesspool of malaria and all kinds of dangerous tropical diseases.

All this must have been well known to Cook and his officers, but the men arrived in excellent health and the calculated risk was one which had to be taken. Banks's journal describes well the main reasons why Batavia was a death trap: he claimed that the shade of the trees which lined the canals did not cool the air but rather added to the oppressive tropical heat:

> Instead of cooling the air they contribute not a little to heat it, especially the stagnating ones of which sort are by far the greatest number, by reflecting back the fierce rays of the sun; in the dry season they stink most intolerably, and in the wet many of them overflow their banks, filling the lower stories of the houses near them with water. Add to this that when they clean them, which is pretty often as some are not more than 3 or 4 feet deep, the black mud taken out is suffered to lie upon their banks, that is in the middle of the street, till it has acquired a sufficient hardness to be conveniently laden into boats; this mud stinks most intolerably, as indeed it must, being chiefly formd from human ordure of which (as there is not a necessary house in the whole town) the Canals every morning receive their regular quota, and the more filthy recrements of housekeeping, which the uncommon police of the countrey suffers every body to throw into them. Add to this that the running ones, which are in some measure free from the former inconveniences, have every now and then a dead horse stranded in the shallow parts of them, a nuisance which I was inform'd no particular person was apointed to remove – which account I am inclind to believe, as I remember a Dead Buffaloe laying in one of the principal streets of a thoroughfare for more than a week, which was at last carried away by a flood.

There were minor language problems. This was a blessing in disguise for it meant that it was more difficult for the crew to communicate with the Dutch about where they had been and what discoveries they had made on the voyage. It must have been difficult for the sailors not to brag and gossip with their fellow seamen about their recent experiences, where they had been and the things they had seen. Sailors were everywhere very skilled at overcoming the language barriers, but the barrier was a great help in Batavia.

The Dutch insisted on a good price for their services to repair the ship. Cook wanted his crew to do the work but the regulations would not permit the Dutch to allow this irregularity. It was going to cost, but the cost would be no more than the Navy could easily afford and when the work was underway Cook was impressed by the efficiency and standards of the Dutch ship-wrights. Beneath the waterline, where Satterly the carpenter had not been able to see, almost all the false keel was found to be gone, the main keel was damaged severely and much of the protective sheathing had been lost. The mariners and the shipwrights were amazed that they had managed to sail so far in such a dangerous and decrepit condition. Two planks were within an eighth of an inch of being cut right through by the coral, and the worms had eaten their way into all the timbers.

There was the job of purchasing new stores for the next part of the journey. There were reports to be written and there was paperwork to attend to. There was the business of catching up with the world news since the ship had departed from Europe more than two years ago. There was news too of Bougainville's voyage two years previously and more about French activities in the Pacific Ocean. Ships were leaving Batavia at regular intervals for Europe and Cook was anxious to send a message to the Admiralty with news of his voyage. He entrusted a precious package with a copy of his journal to a Dutch vessel called the *Krönenburg* which left Batavia on 23 October:

> *I send here a Copy of my journal containing the proceeding Copy which I judge will be sufficient for the present to Illustrate said Journal. In this journal I have with undisguised truth and without gloss inserted the whole transactions of the voyage and made such remarks and have given such description of things as I thought was necessary in the best manner*

I was Capable off. Altho' the discoveries made in this voyage are not great, yet I flatter myself they are such as may merit the attention of their Lordships, and altho' I have faild in discovering the so talk'd of Southern Continent (which perhaps do not exist) and which I my self had much at heart, yet I am confident that no part of the failure of such discovery can be laid to my Charge.

How could any man possibly claim that the discoveries of the voyage were not great? Cook still deeply regretted that he had not found the great southern continent. His report goes on to commend the efforts of the whole crew who 'have gone through the fatigues and dangers of the whole voyage with that cheerfulness and alertness that will always do honour to British seamen, and I have the satisfaction to say that I have not lost one man by sickness during the whole Voyage'. Sickness to Cook meant the dreaded scurvy. Death from consumption, epilepsy, drunkenness and psychological depression were not included in his definition of the word:

Had we been so fortunate not to have run ashore much more would have been done in the latter part of the voyage than what was, but, as it is I presume that this voyage will be thought as great and as compleat if not more so than any Voyage before made in the South Seas on the same account.

This was much closer to the truth than his modest claim that the discoveries were not great, but Cook still decided it was too boastful. He changed part of the draft to the more modest wording: 'I presume this Voyage will be found as Compleat as any before made to the South Seas, on the same account.' He acknowledged generously the contribution of the botanists: 'Valuable discoverys made by Mr Banks & Dr Solander in Natural History and other things useful to the learn'd world cannot fail of contributing much to the Success of the Voyage.' At Batavia Banks and Solander, ever ready to add new knowledge to that concerning the world's flora and fauna, wanted to set off into the country to collect specimens, but their activities were seriously curtailed when Daniel Solander contracted the malaria. Joseph Banks set up himself and his party at an hotel and started looking for a suitable house to live in for the duration of the stay.

The Dutch invited Cook and the scientific gentlemen to watch the ceremony of appointing a commodore of the fleet. This was one of the big events of the Batavian calendar which took place every year. The event was advertised as one of the grandest sights which Batavia had to offer, but Cook thought the ceremony to be very poorly conducted and the Fleet to be greatly undermanned.

In the town were sedan chairs and litters for transport and, when the wealthy went abroad, they rode in wheeled carriages accompanied by a large number of servants. The men wore silk waistcoats and velvet jackets with richly laced and embroidered hats; they sometimes wore wigs. The women mostly favoured chintzes, some in the European fashion, some in the Malaysian fashion. The wealthier women seldom walked: they rode in carriages, carved and gilded, with their maidservants riding on the steps outside. The two people who were most thrilled with Batavia were undoubtedly Tupia and his boy Tayeto. On his arrival Tupia was still suffering from the effects of the voyage and the scurvy but as soon as Banks found suitable accommodation and brought him ashore the Tahitian underwent a complete transformation for the better. Banks describes a delightful and amusing scene as the two Tahitians danced through the streets with joy and wonder at the sights which greeted their eyes:

On his [Tupia's] arrival his spirits which had long been very low were instantly raised by the sights which he saw, and his boy Tayeto who had always been perfectly well was almost ready to run mad. Houses, Carriages, streets, in short everything were to him sights which he had often heard described but never well understood, so he lookd upon them all with more than wonder, almost mad with the numberless novelties which diverted his attention from one to the other he danc'd about the streets examining every thing to the best of his abilities. One of Tupia's first observations was the various dresses which he saw worn by different people; on his being told that in this place every different nation wore their own countrey dress He desired to have his, on which South Sea cloth was sent for on board and he cloathed himself according to his taste. We were now able to get food for him similar to that of his own countrey and he grew visibly better every day, so that I doubted not in the least of his perfect recovery as our stay at this place was not likely to be very short.

Tupia and Tayeto were thrilled and amazed at the sight of themselves and their company in a looking glass, another western wonder. We learn from Parkinson that Charles Green took a great interest in the Tahitians and spent a lot of time teaching English to both of them. When Banks was walking in the streets with Tupia a man rushed out of one of the houses to speak with them – the man was convinced that he had seen Tupia before. It seemed that Banks's Tahitian friend was not the first of his people to visit Batavia and the Englishman heard with interest the story of Bougainville's voyage, about how the Frenchman had been at Batavia on his return journey about eighteen months previously with a Tahitian called Ahutoru in his retinue. Even the story of the Frenchman's lady botanist was well known in the Batavian gossip circles.

We warm to and enjoy the description of the two Tahitians as we see the fresh and innocent joy of a primitive people on their first experience of the western world. It is one of the saddest and most terrible ironies of the whole voyage that within a few days the Tahitians both contracted malaria. Joseph Banks arranged a tent for them on one of the wooded islands well away from the town and where the clean sea breezes blew right over them. It was of no avail and within a few days young Tayeto died. Poor Tupia was inconsolable and cried out in vain for his friend. He himself died only a few days later.

Others of the crew were sick and it was unfortunate that one of the worst sufferers and the first to die was William Monkhouse, the ship's surgeon. The astronomer's servant John Reynolds died, followed by three of the sailors. Practically every man on the ship fell sick with malaria; Banks himself was very ill – 'the fits of which were so violent as to deprive me intirely of my senses and leave me so weak as scarcely able to crawl down stairs'. Solander came very close to death's door. At one stage John Ravenhill, the aged sail-maker, appeared to be the only man not suffering from the fever, a fact which Cook found extraordinary because of his generally managing to be drunk every day. The only small consolation was that the Dutch insisted on using their own labour to repair the ship; Cook's men were much too ill to have executed the work themselves.

Christmas Day 1770 was spent in Batavia. It was not a time for celebration: so many of the ship's crew were sick and unfit for their duties that Cook desired only to leave the port as soon as possible – a wish which was executed on the following day. Seven people from the *Endeavour* had died, the deficiency being made up by recruiting more men including John Marra, an Irishman from Cork who was very anxious to join the crew because he was wanted by the Dutch for desertion from one of their own vessels. As Cook was weighing anchor he spoke with a Dutch captain who assured the Englishman that he was lucky to be leaving with more than half his crew still alive. Once in the open sea the fear of malaria grew less. Solander had recovered but he was by no means reassured as he observed with dread that the mosquitoes from the stagnant canals of Batavia were breeding on the very surface of the ship's scuttlebutt.

It took the *Endeavour* eleven hard days to battle through the Strait of Sunda with a weakened crew, and Cook decided to stop at the island called Panaitan or Princes Island to replenish his ship and to prepare for the passage across the Indian Ocean. On 16 January they left the East Indies for the Cape of Good Hope. At this point on the voyage most of the crew had almost recovered from the fever they contracted at Batavia, but where any other captain would have sailed on and across the Indian Ocean, Cook characteristically decided to stop and obtain fresh food and water. Within a few days dysentery was added to the malaria, and as the *Endeavour* limped westwards, more and more of the ship's company fell sick. Cook blamed himself for stopping at Princes Island where he believed the fruit or water must have been infected. The island already had a bad name with English ships for the poor quality of its water, and he put lime into the sacks in the hope that it would purify the water. The *Endeavour*, which had crossed the Atlantic and the Pacific with less illness and with a healthier crew than any other ship before her, and which only a few weeks before had entered Batavia with a healthy and jovial crew, now entered the Indian Ocean as a melancholy floating hospital with more men taken seriously ill on every day of the voyage. There came a point where only eight or nine men were fit enough to manage the ship.

On 24 January John Truslove, a corporal of marines, died. Then followed Banks's secretary, Herman Spöring. Then the artist Sydney Parkinson died, he who had worked so hard and done so much to record the scenes of the voyage. It is worth reflecting on the feelings of Joseph Banks at this juncture – he had lost two black servants, both his artists, his secretary and the two Tahitians – only Dr Solander, two servants and himself remained from his original retinue. John Ravenhill, the ancient sail-maker, died on the same day as Sydney Parkinson – he escaped the malaria but not the dysentery. Next was Charles Green whose health had never been good but whose devotion to his science was such that he had stood on the quarterdeck with his sextant, making measurements when the ship was within yards of being dashed against the Great Barrier Reef. Then died Sam Moody and Francis Haite, two of the carpenter's mates. The next day four more seamen died. The decks were washed and swabbed with vinegar but it was too late for the sufferers. Every day the macabre story continued and more bodies were committed to the deep. John Bootie and John Gathery died, and the next day Samuel Evans. By 5 February the death toll had reached twenty-four and John Monkhouse, the surgeon's brother who had managed the fothering at the Endeavour Reef, joined the roll-call of the dead. John Satterley, the carpenter who had repaired the ship so well at the Endeavour River, also died. Five more seamen died before the end of February; Cook prayed that these would be the last.

The dreadful passage to Capetown ended on 14 March when the *Endeavour* limped into Table Bay. In the bay was anchored a cosmopolitan assortment of vessels – Cook counted eight Dutch, three Danish, four French and one English merchantman called the *Admiral Pocock* who saluted the *Endeavour* handsomely with eleven of her guns. Cook's first priority was to make some arrangements for the sick members of his crew, and this was quickly attended to. He exchanged news with the other captains and discovered that other vessels on their ways from Batavia had suffered from the dysentery as much as he, even though they had not called at Princes Island for fruit and water – this made him suspect that Batavia was the source of the dysentery as well as the malaria. A few days later another English merchantman, the *Holton*, arrived from India having lost thirty to forty men on the passage and having also suffered from the scurvy even though they had been away from England for less than a year.

Cook did not get much in the way of sympathy. The hardened sea captains of the ships at anchor in Table Bay did not consider the loss of over thirty men to be anything out of the ordinary. The atrocious and insanitary conditions of ship-board life were things which had to be accepted as an inevitable consequence of the times. But James Cook was an outstanding exception to this view – unlike the great majority of sea captains he had actually served below decks. He had proved to his own satisfaction that if the captain was meticulous about obtaining fresh food and pure water at every port of call then it was possible to avoid the effects of scurvy and other illnesses. He did not and could not know how to combat the ship-board diseases which had killed off many of his crew. As we have seen, men had been lost because of a steady succession of accidents throughout the voyage; there had been one case of death from consumption and a case of suicide – but the losses in the passage from Batavia to the Cape of Good Hope accounted for many times the number of men lost on the previous part of the voyage. It was a terrible tragedy after such scrupulous care had been taken for over two years with the health and safety of his men.

Had it not been for these tragic circumstances Capetown would have been a most pleasant and sociable interlude. There was good company, gossip and news of England. The Cape was a great trading centre for many nations, and the comings and goings were such that practically every day a new set of sails appeared over the horizon, and the sailors gazed keenly to see if the new arrival was flying the flag of their own country. Men could be re-mustered at the Cape to replace lost crew members. A wooden jetty ran out from the harbour wall where the ships enjoyed the great luxury of filling their casks with piped water from a stopcock. Clean winds swept down from Table Mountain and blew briskly across the bay. The botanists pottered around collecting specimens, but were saddened by the loss of Parkinson and Spöring. The officers were entertained by the just and humane governor Ryk Tulbeagh, the first governor to allow foreign vessels into Capetown. He was a man reputed to be immune to any form of bribery and had performed his duties impeccably for twenty years. There was also welcome female company and Banks pays a great compliment to the ladies of Capetown:

In general they are handsome with clear skins and high Complexions and when married (no reflextions upon my country women) are the best housekeepers imaginable and great childbearers; had I been inclined for a wife I think this is the place of all others I have seen where I could have best suited myself.

There was news of the astronomers Mason and Dixon who observed the transit of Venus at Capetown in 1761. There were vineyards, orchards and kitchen gardens. There was a menagerie with African animals: long-necked ostriches, antelopes, striped zebras and cassowaries. The energetic John Gore found a local guide and climbed to the top of Table Mountain where he claimed to have seen wolves and tigers (probably the aardwolf and the leopard); he brought back plants in flower to give to the great collectors. All the necessary services were available at the Cape with plenty of provisions to be had at very reasonable prices. 'I had eat ashore some of as good and fat beef as ever I eat in my life,' claimed Cook and he purchased a whole ox for his crew. It turned out to be leaner and thinner than the first one he had tasted but it was still a great delicacy after the diet of the previous two years. He gives a description of Table Mountain with its head in the clouds which almost verges on the poetic, an unusual achievement for the down-to-earth explorer:

In the PM I observ'd a dark dence haze like a fog bank in the SE Horizon and white clowds began to gather over the Table Mountain, certain signs of an approaching gale from the same quarter, which about 4 oClock began to blow with great Voyance and continued more or less so the remainder of these 24 hours, the Table mountain Cap'd with white Clowds all the time, the weather dry and clear.

Cook was critical of the land around the Cape which appeared barren and unwooded to his seaman's eye. Nobody had the time or the means to travel inland and meet the Africans in their own environment, but Banks picked up and repeated an atrociously bigoted traveller's tale about the Hottentots which was not only insulting to their intelligence but bespoke a ridiculous pre-Darwinian dogma about their place on the evolutionary tree:

> There remains nothing now but to say a word or two concerning the Hot-tentots so frequently spoken of by travelers, by whoom they are generaly represented as the outcast of the human species, a race whose intellectual faculties are so little superior to those of Beasts that some have been inclind to suppose them more nearly related to Baboons than Men.

The ship remained at Capetown for just over a month and put to sea again on 16 April. The deceased sailors were replaced by ten new hands signed on at the Cape and most of the remaining sick, with two notable exceptions, had by this time recovered their health. Robert Molyneux, the ship's master and the man who had done more than anybody except Cook to guide the *Endeavour* through the treacherous reefs of the Australian coast, died as they sailed out of Table Bay. 'A young man of good parts,' said the Captain. 'But unfortunately given himself up to extravecancy and intemperance which brought on disorders that put per[i]od to his life.' Cook was never slow to criticise the sailors for their drinking habits so his comment may well be unfair. The other man who was critically ill was Zachary Hicks, Cook's first lieu-tenant and the first man to sight the east coast of Australia.

Cook's log still showed the longitude measured west of Green-wich and creeping closer to the full circle of 360 degrees. On the 29 April it changed from over 359 to under 1 degree. If the Green-wich meridian was taken as the starting point then on this day the *Endeavour* had sailed around the world and Cook recorded the fact in his journal. For some reason, probably connected with his illness, Joseph Banks was two days out in his reckoning of the days – the circumnavigation accounted for one of them but he was at a loss to explain the other and we are left wondering why he never discovered the error during the stay at Capetown. The next day at dawn the island of St Helena was seen about 6 leagues to the north and, as the ship approached, the seamen sighted so many masts that Cook feared that a war must have broken out. Anchored in the roads were HMS *Portland*, a sloop called the *Swallow* and a fleet of twelve Indiamen preparing to sail to England. Cook's fears of war were unfounded but he discovered that the English had in fact fallen out with Spain over the Falkland Islands.

A few days later the *Endeavour* was able to sail in company with the merchant fleet, a welcome and sociable development after the long lonely voyage of the past years. The convoy set off out into the Atlantic to pick up the trade winds and beat northwards towards Europe, but Cook knew that if the weather deteriorated his sails and rigging would not allow his ship to keep up with the rest of the fleet. He entrusted the ship's log and the precious officer's journals to Captain Elliot of HMS *Portland* and took the opportunity to call over the surgeon from the *Portland* to examine Zachary Hicks. The first lieutenant was so ill with consumption that his life was despaired of. The surgeon could do nothing to help.

The weather was hot and sultry. On 15 May there occurred another rare astronomical event, an eclipse of the sun. Such a spectacle was not one to be missed, but using it to measure the exact latitude and longitude of a small patch of ocean was of no use to navigation at all. Cook observed, without his friend Charles Green, 'Meerly for the sake of observing'. Later in the same day one of the fore mainsails was deemed to be completely worn out and the topsail was brought down to the main yard to replace it.

On 26 May there was yet another sad little ceremony on deck. Zachary Hicks died. The man who first sighted the Australian mainland was committed to the deep, never to tell his story to his friends and relatives at home. Thankfully Hicks was the last life to be lost on the voyage unless we count Banks's faithful grey-hound bitch, the famous kangaroo chaser, which let out a loud shriek one night and then fell into a deep silent sleep. In the morning Banks found his 'lady bitch' lying cold and lifeless on a stool in his cabin where she usually spent the night.

Cook had to fit a new backstay to the main topmast, the old one had broken several times. There were still several weeks of sailing to reach home waters and day by day the *Endeavour* fell a little further behind the rest of the fleet. For a few days, when the weather deteriorated, the fleet was out of sight but, when the visibility improved, the sails could be seen ahead of them on the horizon. The weather backstays broke again on the main topmast and the ship's carpenter reported that the mast was sprung in the cap. Two of the topgallants split and flapped uselessly in the wind. 'Our rigging and sails are now so bad that some thing or another is giving way every day,' said Cook. There followed another delay while the carpenter effected what repairs he could manage. The convoy was still just in sight, below the horizon on the weather quarter, but by the next morning the *Endeavour* was all on her own again, and not one of the merchant fleet could be seen.

The *Endeavour* struggled gamely onwards and the latitude increased a little each day. They passed a Dutch galliot and exchanged news with an American brig from Boston. In the morning of 7 July the ship was crossing the Bay of Biscay and approaching nearer to home waters. A brig appeared, coming towards them flying English colours, and they were hailed in north-country accents. The vessel was a Liverpool slaver only a few days out from the Mersey. Later the same day came another brig outward bound from London and three days out from the Scilly Isles. The explorers then discovered that their ship had been given up for lost. For the first time they heard the news of themselves as printed in *Bingley's Journal*, a gossip medium published the previous September, which told its readers the *Endeavour* had been sunk by the Spanish:

It is surmised, that one ground of the present preparations for war, is some secret intelligence received by the Ministry, that the Endeavour man of war, which was sent into the South Sea with the astronomers, to make observations, and afterwards to go into a new track to make discoveries, has been sunk, with all her people, by order of a jealous Court, who has committed other hostilities against the Southern hemisphere.

Mr. Banks, and the famous Dr. Solander, were on board the above vessel, and are feared to have shared the common fate with the rest of the ship's company.

The *Endeavour* had not even reached Batavia when this rumour was published, but Cook reasoned that his wife should by this time have received news via the *Krönenburg* which had sailed from the Cape of Good Hope five months ago. News of their arrival at Batavia had reached London as early as January by way of the last arrivals from the Indies, but no further details had reached the public before May when a new spate of newspaper articles appeared. It was perhaps not surprising to hear that the false account in *Bingley's Journal* was still believed by the crew of a London vessel.

Three days later when Young Nick was on his perch at the masthead there was a cry not dissimilar to the one he uttered half the world away when the ship was offshore from New Zealand. This time it was not a new land which Young Nick had sighted, it was a very old and familiar coastline. Every heart stirred as the cape just showing over the horizon was identified as the Lizard. The next day the sailors passed Plymouth Hoe and the familiar landmarks of the Devon coast and when the next day dawned they were offshore from Dorset. In spite of the state of her sails and rigging the *Endeavour* raced along the South Coast in fine style: 'Winds at SW a fresh gage with which we Run briskly up the Channell,' observed the captain. 'At ½ past 3 PM pass'd the Bill of Portland and at 7 Peverell point. At 6 AM pass'd Beachy head at the distance of 4 or 5 Miles, at 10 Dungenness at the distance of

2 Miles and at Noon we were abreast of Dover.'

The *Endeavour* brought back dossiers full of drawings and sketches of the South Pacific. She brought observations of the transit of Venus across the face of the Sun, observations of a transit of Mercury, and dozens of readings which helped to determine the latitude and longitude of many little-known and hitherto unknown parts of the surface of the Earth. There were coastal views, logs and journal, and sailing directions. Her hold was packed with natural history specimens of all kinds, enough to keep the Royal Society busy categorising and cataloguing for generations. She brought back maps and charts of distant and fertile new lands on the far side of the globe: lands which were destined to be colonised by the British and to become part of a worldwide empire on which the sun never set.

The story may be apocryphal, but it is said that as the weather-beaten North Sea collier passed the roads at Portsmouth the great three-decker ships of the line hove to and saluted her with their 32 pounders as she passed by. Cook's report from Batavia had arrived at the Admiralty about two months earlier. The expected arrival and the discoveries of the voyage had been reported in all the newspapers. Their families and loved ones knew that the *Endeavour* was homeward bound. The whole nation knew of their exploits. The whole nation waited to salute them.

Had there ever been a voyage of discovery, before or after the *Endeavour*, which brought together so many aspects of the sciences and the arts? It is difficult to find any subject which the voyage did not touch upon. There were the mathematics and astronomy, navigation, anthropology, botany, natural history, geography, geology, draughtsmanship, art, cartography, medical science, military science, nutrition, linguistics, psychology and many others – not to mention the management and organisational skills required to provision the ship and keep the crew in good health and spirits for three years on the far side of the globe.

Together they had sailed round the world in their wooden-walled ship, powered only by the sails of canvas and ropes of hemp. Together they had sailed the world at the mercy of the elements of air and water, wind and wave, by their own exertions of human sweat and brawn, on ropes and cables, by agility and skill as the sailors set mainsails, topsails and topgallants to catch the wind. They had navigated their *Endeavour* through coral reefs, river estuaries and harbours, through strange waters where no ship had been before. They had found their position on the great sphere of the Earth by measuring the stars with quadrant and sextant and with only the Nautical Almanac and the battered tables of logarithms and trigonometry to help them with their calculations. They had gazed at the planet Venus on the face of the Sun and they had tried to measure the size of the Solar System, the Astronomical unit which was even then the key to the stellar distances and the scale of the very Universe itself. They had braved the storms off Cape Horn and sailed against the hurricane off Cape Maria Van Dieman. They had manned the pumps for all they were worth when the Pacific Ocean poured into the hold. They had clutched at the ship's rail and stared together into the jaws of death as the ship was swept towards certain destruction off the Great Barrier Reef. They had seen their colleagues die from malaria and dysentery. They remembered Peter Flower, the servants Richmond and Dorlton, William Greenslade, Alexander Buchan, John Reading, Forby Sutherland, Charles Green, Sydney Parkinson, Herman Spöring, John Ravenhill, John Satterley, the Monkhouse brothers, Robert Molyneux, Zachary Hicks and a dozen other colleagues who were no longer with them. The bodies of their friends were scattered around the globe but they had all played their part in the voyage and they were still in the thoughts and memories of the men who worked their *Endeavour* past the white cliffs and through the straits of Dover.

'Home is the sailor, home from the sea.' What thoughts were in the minds of the sailors as the *Endeavour* anchored at the Downs at Deal and the crew set foot again on English soil? Most thought firstly of their homes and their families, their sea ports or their native villages hidden in the depths of rural England. The less fortunate thought only of a few days' shore leave before signing up for another voyage. Joseph Banks thought of the stir he would make in London society and the impact he might have made if only poor Tupia and Tayeto had survived the malaria. He worried over the fact that he must now account for himself and his actions to Miss Harriet Blosset. Cook's thoughts were divided. He could not relax until he had done his duty and reported to the Admiralty in London. Then he would go to the Mile End Road to see his long-suffering wife Elizabeth and his two young sons James and Nathaniel. Would they recognise their father after his being away nearly three years at sea? Would their father recognise them after so long away from home?

A part of his heart went out to his wife and children. Another part yearned to sail the east coast of England again to visit his native Yorkshire, there to meet and gossip in familiar accents with old friends and those of his youth. But there was another part of his heart which was far, far away. In the uncharted part of the Pacific Ocean there was still a huge area where no ship had ever sailed, and there were many new islands still waiting to be discovered and charted. In spite of everything he had done and said he could not be 100 per cent certain about one important point. He knew that there was still room in that great southern sea for a sizeable undiscovered continent.

Already he was planning another voyage. His thoughts harked back to the memories of the last three years. He thought with nostalgia of the days when new capes and headlands were discovered at every new dawn. He thought of the morning mist with the sun rising steeply out of the Pacific Ocean. He was gazing again from the quarterdeck, the ship leaning to starboard with a full set of sails billowing above and flapping in the breeze. The great Pacific swell broke hard against the weather bow and threw the salt spray white and high across the deck. The seamen scrambled again up the rigging to the yardarms, a man hauled at the lead and called out the depth, a sailor stood at the mast-head and pointed forward to a new and unknown horizon. To an uncharted sea where no ship had sailed before.

I must go down to the seas again, to the lonely sea and the sky,
And all I ask is a tall ship and a star to steer her by,
And the wheel's kick and the wind's song and the white sail's shaking,
And a grey mist on the sea's face and a grey dawn breaking.

JOHN MASEFIELD

FAMILY OF JAMES COOK

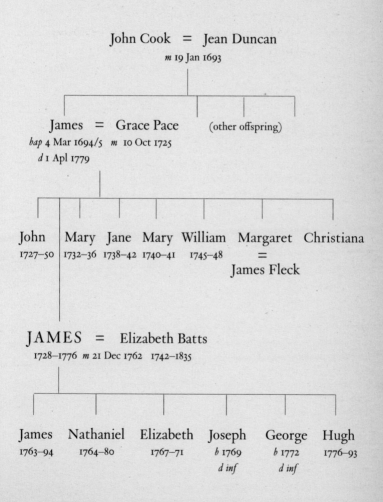

John Cook = Jean Duncan

m 19 Jan 1693

James = Grace Pace   (other offspring)

bap 4 Mar 1694/5   *m* 10 Oct 1725

d 1 Apl 1779

John	Mary	Jane	Mary	William	Margaret	Christiana
1727–50	1732–36	1738–42	1740–41	1745–48	=	
					James Fleck	

JAMES = Elizabeth Batts

1728–1776 *m* 21 Dec 1762   1742–1835

James	Nathaniel	Elizabeth	Joseph	George	Hugh
1763–94	1764–80	1767–71	*b* 1769	*b* 1772	1776–93
			d inf	*d inf*	

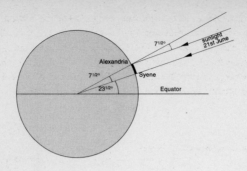

1 Measuring the Earth

Eratosthenes of Alexandria was the first to measure the circumference of the Earth in about 250 BC. He knew that at noon on midsummer's day at Syene the Sun's reflection could be seen at the bottom of a well and the Sun was therefore directly overhead. At noon in Alexandria on the same day the Sun was 7.5 degrees away from the vertical and he deduced that the two places were separated by 7.5 degrees on the surface of the Earth. Eratosthenes measured the distance between Alexandria and Syene, which were almost north-south of each other, and arrived at the very accurate figure of 250,000 *stadia*, or 24,000 miles for the circumference of the Earth.

Later astronomers tried to improve on his figure and Strabo calculated a circumference 180,000 *stadia* (about 18,000 miles). Unfortunately for Columbus he believed the less accurate figure given by Strabo and because of this he expected the westerly route to the Indies to be much shorter.

2 The Astronomical Unit

Kepler's Laws of Planetary Motion and Newton's Law of Gravitation predicted the motions of the planets with great accuracy. If the mean distance from the Earth to the Sun could be calculated then all the planetary distances could be found to the same degree of accuracy; this distance was known as the Astronomical unit. It was a very difficult constant to measure and it needed a fixed point between the Earth and the Sun. In the seventeenth century Edmund Halley claimed that an accurate measure of the Astronomical unit could be made from the transit of Venus and he worked out all the details of the observation. There were two major problems: one was that to obtain better accuracy the observation points of the transit needed to be as far apart as possible (hence the voyage to the Southern Hemisphere). The second problem was that the transit was a very rare event and Halley could not hope to live long enough to observe it himself. (Many readers will know of the similar story of Halley's Comet.)

The observation had to be made from two points on the Earth at a known distance apart. The precise time taken for Venus to cross the Sun's disc had to be measured at each observation point and the ratio of the timings enabled the mathematicians to calculate a value for the parallax of Venus, i.e. the small angle between the two sightings. Knowing this angle, about 40 seconds of arc, the distance to Venus could be found and hence the astronomical unit.

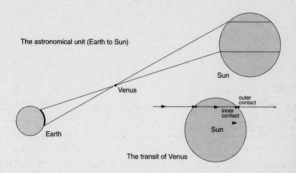

The Earth orbits the Sun in an ellipse rather than a perfect circle, but the variation in the Sun's distance was well known and could easily be allowed for.

Halley worked out that the most accurate way to get the timings was to record the inner and outer contact times of Venus on the Sun's disc, both at entry and exit. The astronomers could then work out the transit time and perform the rest of the calculation. What he did not know was that the disc of Venus did not appear as a sharp circle, it was surrounded by a haze or 'atmosphere' and the astronomers were unable to agree about the time of inner and outer contact with the Sun's disc.

The observation was very unusual in that it was taken in bright sunshine, but the Sun could not be observed with the naked eye. Telescopes were used to project an image on to a screen, much as they are used today to take a photograph, hence the portable observatories which enabled the timings to be made without any danger of blindness from the Sun's rays.

3 Stellar Distances

The Astronomical unit was the key to the stellar distances. Astronomers knew that as the Earth followed its orbit around the Sun they should be able to see the nearer stars move against the background of the distant stars, a phenomenon known as stellar parallax. In the eighteenth century they were unable to detect the parallax and this could mean only two things. Either the Earth was after all at the centre of the Universe, or the stars lay at an incredible distance away. In

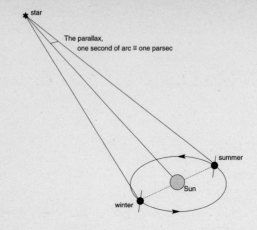

fact the parallax was so small that even for the nearest stars the angle was less than 1 second of arc but, in the nineteenth century when photography first became available, the parallax of all the nearby stars could be measured. The technique was to photograph a star at intervals of six months apart, from opposite ends of the Earth's orbit. The two photographs could be laid over each other, lining up the distant stars, then the tiny change in position of the nearer star could be measured. Knowing the parallax and the Astronomical unit a simple calculation gave the distance of the star. (Stellar distance = Astronomical unit divided by parallax in radians.)

4 Galactic Distances

The galaxies are much too far away to be measured by parallax but their distances can be estimated by looking for Cepheid variable stars in the galaxy. The Cepheids are variable stars and, if their period of brightness can be measured, then their distances can be calculated. The distance to the nearer Cepheids, in our own galaxy, had to be measured using parallax before the brightness/period method could be used.

5 The Edge of the Universe

The distant galaxies are so far away that individual stars cannot be seen. The spectrums of the galaxies show a shift towards the red end of the spectrum and the amount of this red shift gives a measure of the distance of the galaxy. We are now dabbling with the General Theory of Relativity.

Astronomy has come a long way since the voyage of the *Endeavour*. But the Astronomical unit is still a key measurement to the scale of the Universe.

Notes on Sources

Primary Sources

J. C. BEAGLEHOLE (ed.) *The Journals of Captain James Cook on his Voyages of Discovery*, Hakluyt Society Extra Series No XXXIV

J. C. BEAGLEHOLE (ed.) *The Endeavour Journal of Joseph Banks 1768–1771*, Sydney, 1962

SYDNEY PARKINSON *A Journal of a Voyage to the South Seas*, London, 1773

Manuscripts (part published by the Hakluyt Society in vol. XXXIV above):

SHIP'S LOG British Museum Add MS 8959

CHARLES CLERK PRO Adm 51/4548/143–4

JOHN GORE PRO Adm 51/4548/145–6

ZACHARIAH HICKS PRO Adm 51/4546/147–8

ROBERT MOLYNEUX PRO Adm 51/4546/152

WILLIAM MONKHOUSE British Museum Add MS 27889

RICHARD PICKERSGILL PRO Adm 51/4547/140–1

FRANCIS WILKINSON PRO Adm 51/4547/149–50

EDMUND HALLEY 'A method of measuring the solar parallax from the Transit of Venus ...,' *Royal Society Philosophical Transactions* XXIX, 1716
'Observations made, by appointment of the Royal Society, at King George's Island in the South Sea ...,' *Royal Society Philosophical Transactions* LVIII, 1767

JAMES COOK FRS 'The method taken for the preserving the Health of the Crew ... [paper on scurvy],' *Royal Society Philosophical Transactions* LXVI, 1776

Secondary Sources

J. HAWKESWORTH *An account of the Voyages undertaken ... for making discoveries in the Southern Hemisphere*, London, 1773

J. C. BEAGLEHOLE (ed.) *The Life of Captain James Cook*, London, Hakluyt Society, 1974

RÜDUGER JOPPIAN AND BERNARD SMITH (eds) *The Art of Captain Cook's Voyages. Volume One: The Voyage of the Endeavour 1768–1771*, New Haven and London, Yale University Press, in association with the Australian Academy of Humanities, 1985

ANDREW DAVID (ed.) *The Charts & Coastal Views of Captain Cook's Voyages. Volume One: The Voyage of the Endeavour 1768–1771*, London, Hakluyt Society, in association with the Australian Academy of Humanities, 1988

Index